P9-EEA-869

Canadian Churches and Foreign Policy

Edited by Bonnie Greene

James Lorimer & Company, Publishers
Toronto, 1990

To all the children at whose
baptisms I have renewed
my covenant of human solidarity
and to Christa and Annette,
who never let me forget.

Cover photo: Anglican Church of Canada/WM

Canadian Cataloguing in Publication Data

Main entry under title:
Canadian churches and foreign policy
    Includes bibliographical references.
    ISBN 1-55028-287-5 (bound) ISBN 1-55028-285-9 (pbk.)
    1. Christianity and international affairs.
    2. Canada — Foreign relations — 1945-
    I. Greene, Bonnie.

BR570.C35 1990   261.8'7'0971   C90-094009-3   69829

James Lorimer & Company, Publishers
Egerton Ryerson Memorial Building
35 Britain Street
Toronto, Ontario
M5A 1R7

Printed and bound in Canada

6 5 4 3 2 1 90 91 92 93 94 95

CONTENTS

GLOSSARY OF ACRONYMNS

CAF — Canadian Arab Federation

CAWG — Canada-Asia Working Group

CCC — Canadian Council of Churches

CCIA — Commission of the Churches in International Affairs

CEC — Conference of European Churches

CHRP — Churches' Human Rights Programme for Implementation of the Helsinki Final Act

CIDA — Canadian International Development Agency

CJC — Canadian Jewish Congress

CSCE — Conference on Security and Co-operation in Europe

CUSO — Canadian University Service Overseas

EDC — Export Development Corporation

ICCA — Inter-Church Coalition on Africa

ICCCDR — Inter-Church Consultative Committee for Development and Relief

ICCHRLA — Inter-Church Committee for Human Rights in Latin America

ICCR — Inter-Church Committee for Refugees

ICFID — Inter-Church Fund for International Development

IFIs — International Financial Institutions

ILO — International Labour Organization

IMC — International Missionary Council

IMF — International Monetary Fund

MECC — Middle East Council of Churches

NCCC-USA — National Council of Churches of Christ-USA

ODA — Official Development Assistance

SDI — Strategic Defense Initiative

TCCR — Taskforce on the Churches and Corporate Responsibility

UNCHR — United Nations Commission on Human Rights

UNHCR — United Nations High Commission for Refugees

WCC — World Council of Churches

CONTRIBUTORS

Douglas duCharme is a Presbyterian living in Cyprus, where he serves as Canadian Council of Churches liaison staff, working with the Middle East Council of Churches.

Robert Gardiner is an Anglican priest who served as the original director of Ten Days for World Development. He lives in retirement in England.

Bonnie Greene is director of church in society of the United Church of Canada. She is a member of the Human Rights Advisory Group of the World Council of Churches (WCC) and of the Churches' Human Rights Programme for Implementation of the Helsinki Final Act.

Robert O. Matthews is a professor in the Department of Political Science at the University of Toronto.

Kathleen Ptolemy served as the original director of the Inter-Church Committee for Refugees; she currently directs the refugee program of the Anglican Church of Canada.

Renate Pratt served as the original director of the Taskforce on the Churches and Corporate Responsibility. In retirement, she serves with the Canadian branch of the International Defense and Aid Fund for Southern Africa.

Marjorie Ross, a former Presbyterian missionary in Africa, was world affairs staff of the Canadian Council of Churches at the time when the council participated in the foreign policy review. She also chaired Ten Days for World Development. She is currently on the staff of the Taskforce on the Churches and Corporate Responsibility.

Tim Ryan is a priest with the Scarboro Foreign Mission (SFM). He served in Brazil for many years with SFM before returning to Canada, where he served on the Taskforce on the Churches and Corporate Reponsibility and subsequently served as executive director of the Inter-Church Committee for Human Rights in Latin America. He is presently co-director of the Ecumenical Forum, a centre for ecumenical education and missionary formation of the Canadian churches.

Erich Weingartner, a Canadian Lutheran, served as the human rights staff of the Commission of the Churches in International Affairs of the World Council of Churches in Geneva. He is the author of numerous studies prepared by the WCC and by IDOC, the International Documentation Centre in Rome. He presently lives in North Bay, where he works as an author and a consultant on international affairs.

ACKNOWLEDGEMENTS

Those who contributed to this book have worked with hundreds and thousands of people in Canada and in other parts of the world in their pursuit of human rights, economic justice, and peace. Each is part of a group of staff and board members of unique church organizations known as inter-church coalitions: the Inter-Church Committee for Human Rights in Latin America (ICCHRLA); the Canada-Asia Working Group (CAWG); the Taskforce on the Churches and Corporate Responsibility (TCCR); GATT-fly; the Inter-Church Coalition on Africa; the Inter-Church Committee on Refugees (ICCR); and Project Ploughshares.

Some of those who started this work among Canadian churches have retired; others have taken their vision and their commitment into sister organizations. I would like to acknowledge the work of Garth Legge, Everett McNeil, Jack Zimmerman, Don Ray, Eoin MacKay, Clarke MacDonald, Ted Scott, Tom Anthony, Jim Webb, George Cram, John Foster, Frances Arbour, and many, many others.

The Canadian Council of Churches (CCC) has provided steady support to us through its Committee on the Churches and International Affairs, chaired by Professor Robert Matthews of the University of Toronto. That committee provided the organization within which an unwieldy body of opinion could be honed into the ecumenical consensus represented in the CCC's submission to the Special Joint Committee on Canada's International Relations during the most recent foreign policy review. Cranford Pratt and Ernie Regehr were major contributors to that process.

Many of the contributors also received support from Robert Matthews, Cranford Pratt, and their colleagues in the Development Studies Group at the University of Toronto. This group gave non-governmental organizations an opportunity to submit their experience in the foreign policy arena to the critique of those who are professionally trained in the field.

Finally, I acknowledge on behalf of all of the contributors the insight we have received from people in the local ecumenical groups and in congregations of our churches. We who have been privileged to make our living in pursuit of peace and justice stand in awe of the thousands of people across the country who have given their leisure time in order that Canada's foreign policy might indeed be part of the healing of the nations.

Bonnie Greene
November 1989

Introduction

"Then he showed me the river of the water of life, bright as crystal, flowing from the throne of God and from the Lamb through the middle of the street of the city....
"Also, on either side of the river, the tree of life — and the leaves of the tree were for the healing of the nations."
(Revelation 22:1,2)

Whatever else they believe, Christians belong to a faith community that clings to the hope that the tables will yet be turned. Good will triumph over evil. The nations will be healed, as one of the earliest Christians wrote at the end of the book of Revelation, his contribution to the Christian Bible.

The institutional church has hardly lived consistently within that vision. In fact, many times since the Christian church began, it has been utterly indifferent to people's suffering. It has allowed itself to be used to keep people poor and hungry. It has sometimes blessed powerful people as they set out to carry out crimes against humanity. It has organized some of those crimes itself.

On the other side of the ledger are the people who have refused to believe that God is indifferent to people's hunger, homelessness, and fear and who have set out to join God in overcoming human suffering. These are the people who have kept alive in the church the vision of the healing of the nations.

In the past twenty years, members of the major Christian churches in Canada have been so moved by the intense suffering of their colleagues around the world that they ventured into the world of foreign policy in new ways that both surprised and frightened them at times. They decided to throw in their lot with the worldwide movement for human rights, for economic and social justice, and for peace.

They came together as Catholics and Protestants and created a number of modest ecumenical organizations with specialized mandates and staff. These ecumenical coalitions were created to help the churches accomplish the research, analysis, and co-ordination of their work that they needed to act effectively on issues of world hunger, the arms race, apartheid, and many others. Although a few of the earliest groups completed their work and disbanded, the major ones remain. Today they include the Inter-Church Committee on Human Rights in Latin America (ICCHRLA), the Canada-Asia Working Group (CAWG), the Inter-Church Coalition on Africa (ICCAF), the Taskforce on the Churches and Corporate Responsibility (TCCR), Ten Days for World Development, the Ecumenical Coalition for Economic Justice, Project Ploughshares, and the Inter-Church Committee for Refugees (ICCR).

Each organization had a different set of participating churches committed to the work assigned to it, but most included at least the major Christian churches in Canada: Presbyterian, Lutheran, United, Roman Catholic, and Anglican. Some included the Mennonite Central Committee, the Canadian Friends' Service Committee, the Council of Christian Reformed Churches, and a number of smaller denominations. These coalitions became a kind of centre of energy for the churches, around which they gathered from month to month to address a common agenda in a disciplined way and to decide where to go next. Over time they built up a considerable body of practical knowledge of foreign policy issues, as they are experienced by people who have the least to say in the policy formation process. They discovered that with the victims of war, human rights violations, and underdevelopment at their elbows their arguments were lent greater credibility. And they discovered that seeking real change meant moving beyond generalizations to hard debate about the specific policies that might create space for peace and justice to flourish in the world.

An Alternative Vision for Canada's Foreign Policy

The enormity of the change for Canadian churches is perhaps best symbolized by the kind of responses they made to the two foreign policy reviews conducted in Canada in the last four decades. In 1968 the Trudeau government issued a White Paper, *Foreign Policy for Canadians*, a series of small booklets in a slipcase; it was slim by today's standards. The churches' response was equally small. Titled "The Black Paper: An Alternative Policy for Canada Towards Southern Africa," it was a document prepared by an ad hoc group of people with a continuing interest in Africa — the Committee for a Just Canadian Policy Towards Africa. The committee was made up of "churchmen, officials of voluntary organizations, trade unionists, businessmen, academics and returned CUSO volunteers." The paper called for an end to preferential trading relations with South Africa, for an end to the use of public funds to support and promote Canadian investment in South Africa, for a public statement by the government, opposing apartheid, and so on. It was a mere seventeen pages long, and it had no official church endorsation.

When the Mulroney government conducted a second major foreign policy review in the mid-eighties, the resulting Green Paper was called *Competitiveness and Security: Directions for Canada's International Relations*. A special joint committee of Parliament conducted hearings across the country to receive advice from Canadians about the values and objectives to be incorporated in Canadian foreign policy. This time the Canadian churches submitted a document of over a hundred pages, but more than that, the document had been endorsed by the member churches of the Canadian Council of Churches (CCC). It represented the ecumenical common ground on foreign policy — a summary of the ecumenical consensus that had been worked out between churches of diverse background during the intervening years.

The change in the way the churches entered this phase of foreign policy work is also illustrated by the people who participated. Two churchmen were among the four authors of "The Black Paper": Cranford Pratt, a professor of political science at the University of Toronto, who had extensive experience in Africa; and Garth Legge, a former missionary in Africa and the Caribbean, who was general secretary of the Division of World Outreach of the United Church of Canada. These two men also participated in the process that created the Canadian Council of Churches' brief, but now they were part of an enormous ecumenical committee that included heads of churches, laypeople from the universities, staff members of most denominations, and, most of all, activists in movements promoting peace, human rights, and development. This time, churches as official bodies were involved, giving a collective witness to an alternative vision for Canadian foreign policy. While they no longer assumed that their views would or even should automatically be taken for gospel, they believed enough in the alternative vision they had articulated that they felt it must be inserted into the public debate.

When the final report of the Special Joint Committee on Canada's International Relations appeared, it was clear that a new element had emerged in the foreign policy discussion of this country. The list of groups submitting briefs and appearing before the committee included scores of ecumenical committees, individual activists, and even individual congregations. The final report included a photograph of committee members meeting with a group of senior public school students from a Winnipeg church. Whatever the public relations advantage for the committee, for churches the facts were quite clear: young Canadians felt strongly enough about hunger in the Horn of Africa and about the arms race that they were willing to study the issues, decide where they stood, and appear as witnesses before the Special Joint Committmee to present their views.

Given the kind of comments the committee received from Canadians, it seems fitting that the title of its official report was significantly different from that of the government's Green Paper. The title was *Independence and Internationalism*.

An Ethic for the Real World

Between the team of Pratt/Legge et al. and the Sunday school class in Winnipeg something profound had occurred in Canadian churches. In every part of the church, people had begun speaking to questions of social ethics, not only of personal morality. And they had addressed questions of social ethics within the framework of foreign policy issues.

There are many possible explanations for this development. Major events had affected all Canadians: the wrenching debate over the Vietnam War and the American role in Central America had inevitably spilled over the border via our televisions and radios; refugees from countries most of us had never seen had begun to knock on Canadian doors, looking for asylum; the United Nations (UN) had sponsored a conference virtually every year for a decade to draw world attention to issues of truly global proportions; cruise missile testing was announced; Canadian reporters were stationed overseas to a greater degree and regularly brought the news of other worlds to Canadians; the Sahel, Ethiopia, Bhopal, Chernobyl, and many other human disasters changed our perceptions of the world and touched most Canadians in some way.

In addition to these reasons, shared by all Canadians, the churches had still other reasons for becoming involved as institutions in foreign policy issues. Some of the best are explored by the authors of the chapters of this book. They boil down to one theme: Canadian church people have been profoundly changed by their encounters with real people beyond our shores.

Item: A Lutheran pastor from Namibia tells Canadian pastors about the effect of South Africa's occupation of his country on his ministry: he must deliver communion to members of his congregation who are in prison without charge and who've been tortured. Before conducting a funeral, he must borrow a car to retrieve the body of a teenager from his church who was tortured and murdered by South African troops in front of his parents in order to frighten villagers who might yield to requests for food from SWAPO members.

Item: A couple from a Canadian congregation for Taiwanese immigrants travels to Taiwan to get "admissible evidence" on the sale of rural girls to brothels for the sex trade. The evidence they bring back makes them conclude that no twelve-year-old services twenty to thirty customers in a night because she likes sex. She does it because her parents are desperately poor. The couple discovers, however, that, as a pariah state, Taiwan is virtually beyond Canada's reach; so are the little girls.

Item: A Guatemalan visitor with Ten Days for World Development is accused, on his return, of committing an act of terrorism during the time when he was meeting with a United Church congregation in rural Ontario. His name appears on a death list; he is detained. Telegrams and letters from Canadian congregations try to set the record straight. The Guatemalans blink and the man is deported to a neighbouring country. At least he is alive.

Item: Three East German Christian students and two Canadians spend a day after the Vancouver Assembly of the World Council of Churches trying to explain to each other what it means to practise the Christian faith in their countries, poised as they are next to two great powers armed with nuclear weapons. When language finally fails them, they sing "Dona Nobis Pacem" for the last hour of their time together.

Item: A church youth worker from Nicaragua describes the dilemmas he faces, now that young people must go into the army to defend the country against the attacks of the contras. He trained to organize youth retreats, to help people with their life choices and their faith, but he and all his colleagues can only work with young people if they travel with the army units. They have become military chaplains; for the pacifists among them, this is a crisis of conscience.

In these stories and thousands like them, Canadian church people have confronted the real story of the lives of people who share a common faith and sometimes a common vocation within the church. People who were once strangers no longer are; the people they care about have become the people we care about. People we might never have met in the church have arrived at our airports, in search of safety from death squads, war, and other unimaginable nightmares. Their children have become our children's friends, and suddenly our lives are inextricably linked. The once-vague concept of God's human family has taken on the faces of real men, women, and children we know.

It is in the lives and experiences of these people who have become part of us that our fundamental beliefs and values have been challenged. For the Namibian pastor, it is not enough to offer prayers and comfort to the parents of the tortured teenager. Their experience is a fundamental affront to the teaching of Jesus and to the belief of the Christian church that to be part of this faith community is to love God and to love one's neighbour. Somehow the story of people's suffering and their struggle against it could not be covered up. We have felt a profound obligation to help prevent more funerals like the one for the murdered Namibian boy. The ancient words "Thy kingdom come, thy will be done on earth as it is in heaven" have become an affirmation that what is cannot be assumed to be all there can be.

Strangers in the World of Foreign Policy

Canadian churches were part of the worldwide movement following the Second World War to create a world order that would address the roots of war and create the conditions for peace. Much of that work went on through the World Council of Churches (WCC) and its strong contribution to the development of some of the United Nations agreements, particularly in the area of human rights. Some of the early leaders of the WCC recognized that the development and use of the atomic bomb had destroyed a fragile moral consensus that had kept the international household in order prior to the Second World War. They recognized that the bomb forced the Christian community to develop a new ethical framework for participating in a changed world; if the community failed to do this, its theological and ethical traditions could be used to justify destroying all of humanity. These leaders also recognized that the church needed to move beyond its own walls to participate in shaping a secular moral consensus that would keep the world from the kind of conflict that would plunge it into nuclear destruction. Agreement among Christians was not enough. The changed conditions in the world required that all people engage in systematically disarming their hearts and their psyches.

From the beginning of the Christian church, members have debated the meaning of Jesus' succinct, if imprecise, directive to his followers to love God and their neighbours. The first followers of Jesus expanded on his concept with some rudimentary guidelines for members of the community:

- Do not inflict evil or harm.
- Prevent evil or harm.
- Remove evil or harm.
- Do or promote good.

The implications of the first and last principles were fairly clear; it was on the thorny question of preventing evil and removing evil that Christian ethics became less straightforward. And once Christianity moved from being an illegal faith of a marginal group, the problem was complicated by the conflict between the Christian church's identity with Jesus and its identity with the state and its interests. The ethical debate within the church was affected in profound ways. Thus, for much of Western history, the church spent a good deal of its time defining the conditions under which it was morally acceptable for the ruler to go to war. Once the nation-states emerged, a great deal of energy was spent defining the morally acceptable ways of conducting war. And during the first part of this century, the debate evolved to include such questions as the morally acceptable treatment of prisoners of war.

The use of nuclear weapons in the Second World War made the ethical consensus worked out through much of Western history largely irrelevant to the changing capacity of some states to wage war of global dimensions. It was clear to the early leaders of the world church that the old Christian ethics could not be used in the new circumstances. Key leaders threw themselves into the effort to establish a new ethical consensus that would address the real dangers of life in an age when one's neighbour may be not only unfriendly, but a threat to everyone on the face of the earth.

When the UN was established, it became for early ecumenical leaders a place to work out the rules of the global household and to agree on appropriate ways to restrain the dangerous bullies who lived there. The UN's Charter and its various covenants, conventions, and declarations came to symbolize a kind of secular ethical consensus to which all member states had agreed in the hearing of their peers and of all ordinary citizens who watched them. For the world church, the challenge was to support churches within each nation in seeking the application of those commitments back home. The challenge was to convince governments and other citizens of the priority of international law over domestic law. Otherwise, commitments given by states in international meetings would be meaningless in moments of heavy confrontation with neighbouring states or with their own citizens.

For Canadian churches, the stories from Namibia, East Germany, Guatemala, Taiwan, and Nicaragua were not only affronts to their Christian values; they were a violation of commitments made to the international community. Governments had broken faith with their own people and with one another in an age where they are well enough equipped with firepower that none of us can feel safe with such betrayal. Like churches in many other countries of the world, Canadian churches began pressing their own government and institutions to live up to the promises made on the world stage.

The people who did this work were not foreign policy specialists. They were church people who examined the real story of what was going on in the world in the light of the values derived from their own commitment to the Christian story and in the light of the only official moral consensus we have in our world — UN standards for human rights, peace, and justice. They presented their conclusions to government, to banks and corporations, to media, and to any Canadian citizen who showed an interest.

Christian Ethics in a Pluralistic Arena

In the Appendices of this book there are excerpts of some of the major briefs put forward to the federal government, proposing ways in which Canada's foreign policy could contribute to the creation of the "good society" on a global scale. They describe steps that Canadians might take in order to pursue a society that is "just, participatory, and sustainable," to use the language of the World Council of Churches. (That language was revised somewhat at the 1983 Vancouver Assembly of the World Council, where the goal of the Christian church became identified as "justice, peace, and integrity of creation," a phrase that recognizes some important changes in Protestant thought regarding the value of the human and the non-human parts of the creation. That aspect of the world church's work is not reflected in this volume, as international standards on the environment are at such an early stage of development that they have not yet become part of the agenda of the usual foreign policy meetings.) The proposals made in the churches' briefs appear, however, in a language that is seldom heard in the pulpits of the country. The specific faith and ethical traditions of each of the denominations are missing. So are references to the scriptures from which Christians draw the fundamental story that forms their identity and their approach in defining the nature of the "good" and the characteristics of the "good society."

There have been times when a few members of Parliament (MPs) or government officials have looked up from such briefs and remarked, "I'm a member of Church X. I don't see how this relates to my faith." Sometimes that question gets at the issue of personal-versus-social ethics. Other times it indicates that, as a community, we don't often spell out the values we believe we are pursuing in choosing this or that particular path in our relations with other large communities.

When the Canadian churches first began taking the stories of their colleagues in Africa, Asia, and Latin America to the government or to the banks and corporations, they tended to talk primarily in terms of the stories and the values that ought to inform our actions. People could walk away from meetings knowing they had been heard and having a sense that there were some shared values among most, if not all, who had participated. Yet behaviour did not change. Gradually, it became clear that the input from the churches had to become quite precise; it had to include proposals for changed behaviour that would incorporate the values we all said we shared. We all agree that apartheid is evil, that torture must be abolished, that children must not be allowed to starve. The debate quickly becomes, What will we do to contribute to ending apartheid, torture, and starvation, or at least to withhold our support from those who are responsible for them?

The briefs in the Appendices are the product of endless processes of ethical reflection in the churches: hearing the concrete experience of people, testing the truth of claims made by all parties to the issue, deciding what those stories mean and what issues they raise, evaluating the issues in the light of our Christian tradition and values, and making up our minds as to where we believe we must move together in pursuit of justice and peace. In this process, once all of that work has been done, a brief is prepared and presented. Little of the ethical reflection actually appears in the brief. Consequently, the values by which the churches are judging what is going on around them are not always spelled out in the public documents.

This book was drawn together to make more transparent the effort of the Canadian churches to participate in the public debate on ethics and foreign policy. The people who contributed to the book have all participated in this venture of the Canadian churches over the last twenty years. They have participated in the ethical reflection, as well as in the public presentation of the conclusions drawn. Each is a practitioner of applied social ethics and of practical foreign policy.

The contributors, like the church groups they worked with, would be the first to say that they do not want to impose a Christian frame of reference on the country; nor do they believe that only Christian ethics have something to offer to the creation of a just, participatory, and sustainable society. They are engaged and committed people who came to the foreign policy arena because they could not stay out of the discussion, knowing what they knew about the lives of people in much of the world.

Each of the contributors has been asked to share the experiences that formed their particular part of the churches' foreign policy work. In telling those stories, they have drawn a picture of a community of people whose assumptions shaped the conclusions they drew about concrete issues. They assumed, for example,

- that it matters when states give their word and international law is created;
- that obligations to their own citizens and to the citizens of other states flow from these commitments;
- that those who are victimized by their governments or other agents, despite these commitments, have the right to call upon Canada and other states for help;
- that such help should entail supporting the victims and restraining the victimizers;
- that the objective is to create an international household in which autonomous and co-operating states pursue both the enlightened self-interests of their own citizens and those of all citizens throughout the world;
- that there should be a transparency and consistency between Canada's commitment to international agreements and its development of its own foreign policy and practice;
- that the Canadian private sector is responsible to live at least by the spirit of international law and to demonstrate the truth of its claims that its presence in this country or that or its production of a new weapons system ameliorates the situation for human rights and development;
- that Canadians are themselves more secure when Canadian foreign policy makers put their minds to seeking the security of all people, rather than the security of only themselves and their friends in the international household.

It will be clear to readers that some of the proposals the churches put forward have been rendered unnecessary by the course of history. Unfortunately, that is the case for only a tiny number of items. Despite the first dismantling of a nuclear weapon and the achievement of some important security agreements; despite the return to civilian rule in many of the military dictatorships of Latin America; despite the elections in Namibia and Poland; and despite the rapprochement between the Americans and the Soviets, the machinery of war-making, of repression, and of starvation still exists. The euphoria created by the changes of the last few years should give us hope, but should not make us forget that African women still look for cures for the kwashiorkor that is killing their children and people everywhere still go without the resources they need for a good life because their collective pockets are robbed to produce the arms no one can use. It is one thing to chart a path to a just, participatory, and sustainable society. It is one thing to take the first steps. It is quite another to walk the whole way. Those whose work is described in this volume look for many companions along the way.

Organization of the Book

This book groups the key foreign policy preoccupations of the Canadian churches under three major sections.

The first section describes the need to learn to live with enemies and to overcome the division of the nations into a bi-polar world organized around an East-West axis. In this section, Erich Weingartner describes a nearly century-long effort on the part of church leaders in many countries to extricate themselves from their earlier support of national policies bent on destroying humanity. Weingartner builds his account around the activities that went on in the World Council of Churches to create a moral vision and a common action for a just peace. Bonnie Greene gives an account of the Churches' Human Rights Programme for Implementation of the Helsinki Final Act to illustrate the practical ways in which churches tried to pursue real security and human rights. As a project of churches in the socialist East and the capitalist West, it demonstrates the difficulty of living without an eternal enemy. And Douglas duCharme describes the fragile solidarity being built between Canadian churches and the Middle East Council of Churches, a regional council within the World Council of Churches. Its witness for peace in the Middle East is a model of what early world leaders called on churches in each country to do in their collective witness to the reconciliation Christians believe in.

The second section of the book examines two aspects of the social and economic development for which much of the world struggles. Robert Gardiner describes the Canadian churches' early efforts to build a counter-consensus among Canadians, a solid body of support in every part of the country for the social, political, and economic changes that will allow just development to take place in the Third World. Marjorie Ross offers an overview of the movement of Canadian churches from emergency relief efforts to development assistance and eventually to solidarity and support for the work of churches and of other people's movements for change in much of the Third World. She also takes a hard look at whether or not the churches can be supportive to serious change, given some of their traditional biases, particularly with respect to women.

The third section of the book covers the churches' work in human rights and corporate social responsibility. Renate Pratt describes the work of bringing the real situation for black miners in South Africa to the attention of Canadian corporations and banks that were investing in apartheid. She examines the contradictions between a foreign policy officially supportive of international human rights standards and opposed to apartheid and a private sector practice that effectively shored up the apartheid regime. Tim Ryan outlines the work of Canadian churches in seeking protection for the thousands of people in Central and Latin America who have been victims of gross and systematic human rights violations. While Pratt describes the work of laying the evidence of human rights violations out on Bay Street, Ryan describes the process of laying it out before the United Nations in full view of the international community. And Kathleen Ptolemy describes the work that goes on when the victims of human rights violations have found no safe place in their home country and land on Canada's doorstep as refugees seeking asylum.

Finally, the Appendices contain the key sections and recommendations of the major briefs on foreign policy issues presented by the Canadian Council of Churches to the government during the period from 1985 to 1989. An appreciation of the content of all chapters is enhanced by the material in the Appendices. However, readers will find it particularly helpful to read these documents in conjunction with the relevant chapters. Appendix 1, on Canada's international relations, complements chapters 2, 5, 6, and 7; Appendix 2, on Southern Africa, chapter 6; and Appendix 3, on the debt crisis, chapter 6.

Bonnie Greene

I
Learning to Live in a World of Enemies

1 • The World Church and the Search for a Just Peace

Erich Weingartner

Throughout the twentieth century, leaders of the Christian church have struggled to find new ways to overcome the divisions that contribute to conflict. The advent of nuclear weapons convinced them that their traditional theology and ethics could no longer be used to justify political decisions to make war. Furthermore, the world faced such grave dangers that Christians must become engaged in the effort to resist war.

The World Council of Churches (WCC) has been the primary arena in which churches that span ideological, political, cultural, and linguistic divisions have worked out a fragile consensus. Their action for resolving conflict has taken three primary forms: overcoming the divisions among themselves; addressing the ethical questions in international relations in the public arenas of the world; and empowering people to work for the kinds of social changes within countries that prevent war. The churches' early quest for peace has become at the end of the twentieth century a quest for a just peace, one that includes the peoples of North and South, as well as East and West.

Erich Weingartner served for many years with the Commission of the Churches on International Affairs of the World Council of Churches in Geneva. He was one of the organizers of the WCC's Public Hearing on Nuclear Weapons and Disarmament (held in Amsterdam at the end of 1981), which heard from such witnesses as Olof Palme, McGeorge Bundy, A. Arbatov, Alfonso Garcia Robles, Inga Thorson, Edward Schillebeeck, Roger Schillebeeck, Roger Schinn, Randall Forsberg, and many others. Mr. Weingartner is also the author of numerous books on international relations, including Human Rights Is More Than Human Rights *(on the Helsinki Final Act) and* The Security Trap.
— Ed.

An Emerging International Consciousness

The foundations of the world church's search for peace were laid at the turn of the century, long before much of the world's population had any real experience of communities beyond their doorstep.

Provincial and highly nationalistic views of the world were the norm for people who had yet to be brought in touch with one another via radio, television, film, and air travel. Yet an international consciousness was emerging at the turn of the century. In the world church, it was fostered by the expansion of international missionary activity, in Africa and Asia in particular. Although the connection hardly seems logical, it was the ecumenical missionary movement that gave rise in the churches to an international consciousness that lead them to take some responsibility for the disorder of human society and to try to find concrete ways for the Christian churches to contribute to shaping a world order in which a just peace would be the norm. From the missionary movement of the early part of the century arose the modern ecumenical movement embodied in the World Council of Churches, including its work on international affairs.

The ecumenical pioneers who began this movement at the turn of the last century had both practical and theological reasons for believing in the unity of all God's people. One suspects that practical reasons preceded theological ones, as is almost always the case. There was the problem of missionary expansion, for instance. It didn't seem like the most fitting example of Christian witness when denominations quarrelled over territory in their zeal to convert the same "heathens" to the same religion! Today it may appear surprising that the first organized ecumenical thrust came from those sectors of the churches that are considered to be the most conservative. For those with a genuine interest in fulfilling Christ's great commandment, to teach and to baptize all nations, the very fact of Christian division became an overwhelming burden.

It wasn't just a matter of dividing up the mission territory, like imperial powers dividing the spoils among themselves. The experience of witnessing to Christ among non-Christians in non-European cultures had brought new insights into the nature of the Gospel, new challenges to the self-satisfied feelings of cultural superiority that were the curse of European and North American churches.

The effort to co-ordinate church activity in the missionary movement was advanced through a great many global missionary conferences and through a formal structure known as the International Missionary Council (IMC). The purpose was "to unite Christian forces of the world in seeking justice in international and inter-racial relations" (Edinburgh Conference, 1921).

There was still another stream of thought in the world church that contributed to an international consciousness at the turn of the century. Some church leaders of the day simply felt that the division of the Christian church was a scandal that no amount of theology could justify. Pursuing unity among the churches was their contribution to building world peace. Theologians and church leaders began serious discussions and study of those elements of doctrine and church structure that unite Christians.

Out of that effort arose a formal movement in the churches to overcome their divisions by dialogue and study. The Faith and Order Movement began as a series of worldwide conferences of Christian churches, with the first taking place in Lausanne, Switzerland, in 1927. From the late 1920s to today, this work has focused on reducing tension and disunity by looking for the common ground churches share in their beliefs, their practices (baptism and Eucharist, for example), and the organization of their institutional life. Within some countries, church mergers were part of this same movement to overcome the divisions that produce suspicion and tension. (The United Church of Canada, for example, is the result of one of the oldest of such mergers.) On the "left wing" (to use a political designation) of the churches was another ecumenical stream, one that put little faith in the ability of ecclesiastical bureaucracies to overcome their divisive self-interest. The Christian movement of the 1930s that eventually became the Life and Work Movement spent little time discussing doctrine. Its leaders were preoccupied with cultivating Christian social responsibility. They emphasized the need for "the application of Christian principles to international relations and to social, industrial, and economic life."

These early efforts by the churches to overcome provincialism were eventually brought together (along with other work) in the World Council of Churches, thus focusing in one organization the churches' efforts to form an international consciousness that would contribute to the peace of the world, if by the rather indirect method of ending conflict between churches.

There was another, more direct effort at reducing the threat of war, one that lasted throughout the first part of the century. In this case, Christian church people spoke not to themselves, but directly to those with the power to deal with the disorder in the world and to prevent war. At the turn of the century, a group of Christians, many of them laypeople involved in political careers, became keenly disturbed by the inability of national governments to forge foreign policies that could contain the political chaos threatening world peace. They knew that the industrial revolution had changed forever the way that wars would be fought, and that through colonialism the concept of national interest had been radically and dangerously altered. They were also aware of the fact that Christian doctrines regarding political ethics and the conduct of nations were inadequate to the new circumstances.

In 1907, a group of Protestant and Roman Catholic laymen (they were all men), led by a British Quaker and member of Parliament, J. Arthur Baker, made informed representations on behalf of the churches to an international conference on disarmament in The Hague. They failed, however, to stop the First World War.

Immediately after the war, strengthened in their determination, they founded the World Alliance for Promoting International Friendship through the Churches in 1919. The alliance was the first institutional attempt to forge a new awareness that churches have a basic responsibility vis-à-vis governments to offer ethical norms and critiques regarding the conduct of foreign affairs. God could no longer be seen as the guarantor of national interest, and the church as its servant. Churches could no longer be expected to provide unquestioning loyalty to national interests as perceived by governments. Their first loyalty had to be towards the God of the *oikoumene* (a Greek word meaning "the whole inhabited earth"). The friendships created in international ecumenical circles were beginning to have a profound effect on people's perceptions of what constitutes an enemy. The universality of the Christian church was beginning to break through as a powerful symbol of the interdependence of the human community.

This insight was to be severely tested by the rise of militant nationalism in the years leading to the Second World War. Speaking to a meeting in Denmark of the World Alliance for Promoting International Friendship, its youth secretary stated in clear terms for the first time that there is no path to peace by way of security. Behind the quest for security there lies the same mistrust and defensiveness that is the root cause of war.

The young speaker was German. His name was Dietrich Bonhoeffer. A year later, in 1935, he wrote an article entitled "The Confessing Church and the Ecumenical Movement." He challenged the ecumenical movement to give guidance on war, racial hatred, and social exploitation. He asked whether, through the unity among Christians of all nations, war itself could one day be made impossible. He posited that it was not the independent realization of individual aims that was demanded by the Gospel, but a collective obedience to God's justice and peace. For being obedient to such insights, Bonhoeffer paid with his life. He was executed by Hitler shortly before the Second World War ended.

The Church's Role: Advising the State or Empowering People

The Second World War interrupted numerous ecumenical efforts, including the project to bring together the various ecumenical movements into one world council of churches. The leaders of these movements were eager to give authority to their concerns by committing official church institutions to their various aims. The war had shown churches the urgency of concerted action. Analysis of the split in the German churches had been instructive. The majority had followed Hitler with blind faith in a theology that endorsed government dictates, no matter where they led. The courageous "Confessing Church" had espoused a new theology of political maturity that could stand in opposition to those in power. That split led to the inescapable conclusion that churches have a grave responsibility to question traditional theological assumptions about the relationship between church and state.

Within the Roman Catholic Church, the practice of concluding "concordats" (treaties governing the relationship between the Holy See and various governments — fascist ones included) aroused a similar fundamental questioning.

Old habits die hard, however, and the First Assembly of the World Council of Churches in Amsterdam in 1948 had to confront the same problem in a new guise. With the devastation of the major European nations, the war had created a "bi-polar" world. Two new nations were to compete for world supremacy. On the one side, the United States stood as champion of individual freedom, the free market economy, and — by historical necessity — religious tolerance and pluralism. On the other side was the Soviet Union, champion of collective rights, anti-colonial liberation, socialist economy, and — equally by historical necessity — hostility towards all religion. Would it not have been natural for the churches to join the former and oppose the latter? The conflict of those two world visions spilled over into the churches' debate.

A prominent American layperson and active ecumenist attending the WCC's First Assembly tried to enlist the WCC in a worldwide crusade against communism, which he saw as the major threat to freedom, democracy, and religion. His name was John Foster Dulles, later to become the powerful postwar U.S. secretary of state. Dulles might have succeeded in his aims had it not been for a prominent East European professor of theology, an equally active ecumenist by the name of Josef L. Hromadka (father of the late twentieth-century Czech leader of the same name). The Czech theologian, who had taken refuge in the United States for ten years, returning to Prague after the war, challenged this "Western self-righteousness." Hromadka argued that the Western approach disguised the theological link between middle-class thinking and the ideological assumptions of the Cold War.

The churches, Hromadka warned the First Assembly, must not be drawn into this ideological polarization. They must study and confront all political streams in light of the Gospel, and create a universal community and common world ethos capable of bridging political barriers. Was it theologically sound, he asked, to assume that capitalism — which glorifies greed at the expense of the poor and the weak — provided the best environment for Christian witness? Or was not communism — whose aim was the eradication of exploitation and the provision of basic necessities to all — much closer to the essence of Christian ethics?

The churches gathered in that first assembly reached at least a minimum ecumenical consensus that laid the foundation for building a deeper moral consensus, one that would be adequate to the new conditions of the world. They agreed that Christians must ask God to teach them together to say "NO" to all that denies the love of Christ: NO to every system, every program, and every person that treats anyone as an irresponsible thing or a means of profit; NO to those who defend injustice in the name of order; NO to those who sow the seeds of war or describe war as inevitable. The churches also agreed that Christians need to say "YES" to all that conforms to the love of Christ: YES to all who seek justice, to the peacemakers, to all who hope, fight, and suffer for the cause of humanity. Although the full implications were not clear, they had together grounded their work in their religious faith, rather than back one of the competing political approaches to the world.

That churches could reach such a consensus in the climate following the Second World War was in itself remarkable. That the churches reaching it transcended traditional barriers of race, class, culture, and ideology made their work all the more important for the future of the global churches' search for a just peace. Having seen the use to which their own doctrines and institutions could be put, as states waged war with one another, they committed themselves to achieving agreements among themselves on the difficult ethical questions related to building a new world order. In that first assembly, they declared the principles that they believed ought to guide that task. They said flatly that war is contrary to the will of God. Peace can only be achieved if we address the causes of conflict between the world powers. All nations must acknowledge the rule of law and support the development of international institutions such as the United Nations; churches, for their part, must provide a moral foundation on which support for an international system could rest. Human rights and democratic freedoms (largely individual) must be pursued in each country and internationally. And the churches and all Christians must shoulder a grave responsibility in the face of the disorder in world society. Conventional as these principles now seem, they were critical to the growing commitment of churches within individual countries to international law and to resisting war.

Not that these principles were easy for the world church to implement. The heritage of division in Christianity and a chaotic variety of theologies assured that discerning this YES and NO in practice would take a good deal of experimentation. Different sectors within the churches saw different priorities. In the immediate postwar period, the member states of both the newly founded United Nations (UN) and the newly created World Council of Churches were in their majority from the North Atlantic. Western values and problems tended to predominate in all international institutions.

The founding meeting of the WCC's Commission of the Churches on International Affairs (CCIA) had the same characteristics. (The CCIA was at this time jointly sponsored by the WCC and the International Missionary Council.) It was held in Cambridge in 1946, under the chairmanship of John Foster Dulles. Over half of the delegates were from Anglo-Saxon countries, one-third from the United States alone. Only two Eastern Europeans attended, and only one from the "younger churches" of the South, as they were known at the time.

The churches created the CCIA to advise them in their approach to international problems and to serve as a "source of stimulus and knowledge ... as a medium of common counsel and action, and as their organ in formulating the Christian mind on world issues and in bringing that mind effectively to bear upon such issues." The staff appointed to it were to serve the world church as respected non-governmental diplomats, bearing a message from the churches as the nations began to formulate international law through the United Nations.

In the first two decades of their work together, the churches gathered in the WCC wanted to have the CCIA deal with issues of war and peace, the reconstruction of world order in the wake of a devastating war. Another voice emerged within the world church to balance the perspective of Western churches. The International Missionary Council was concerned with efforts to deal with the ills inherited by churches from the colonial period. The weakening of the European powers through the Second World War accounted for the success of many anti-colonial struggles in the postwar period. The emerging "Third World" states on the whole had little sympathy either for missionaries or for their converts, whom they saw as collaborators in an oppressive colonial history. Missionaries were often deported, and local church leaders were arrested or put under enormous pressures.

Protecting the younger churches became a major concern of the fledgling CCIA, and the United Nations was seen as the appropriate instrument to get the job done. This explains in part the feverish activity aimed at including human rights in the Charter of the UN and the CCIA's ground-breaking work on the Universal Declaration of Human Rights, in particular Article 18, dealing with religious liberty.

These activities, applauded by Western governments, were not appreciated by East European Communist states, who abstained from voting on the Human Rights Declaration. Christian efforts on behalf of human rights were also viewed with great suspicion by governments from the Southern Hemisphere. Why did these Christians get so excited about human rights only at the end of colonialism? What had they done to combat the gross violations of colonial exploitation or to aid the decolonization process?

The questions were valid ones. They called for repentance for past mistakes. They launched the churches on a policy of vigilance, which soon resulted in their becoming actively involved in the decolonization process, even though it earned them a reputation for supporting violence and revolution.

By the time the churches gathered at a global level in Uppsala, Sweden, in 1966, the world had changed dramatically, forcing them to face new issues. The civil rights movement in the United States and movements against racism in many parts of the world erupted on the agenda of the world church. The participation of many more churches from the South in the World Council also changed the way in which the path to peace was defined. At that gathering, churches recorded a new consensus that peace and justice are inseparable. The pursuit of human rights and of nation building through economic development emerged on the churches' agenda as the paths to a just peace for all people.

The 1966 gathering of churches in Uppsala also marked a change in the churches' approach to seeking peace. The first twenty years had been marked by the effort to speak to the powerful, to be the "respected non-governmental diplomat." The issues of human rights and development placed on the agenda by the Third World churches required a new approach. The empowerment of people and their movements for social change in each country became the method of the 1970s and 1980s. For example, through the WCC, the churches created the Programme to Combat Racism, which still makes grants to hundreds of groups struggling against racism in their own countries.

The early method of speaking to the powerful was not entirely displaced; in fact, it is still critical in situations where small minority churches and related movements need protection from repressive regimes. Still, churches had been learning, even before the Uppsala gathering, that the method has serious risks and that mistakes in judgement could have long-term negative effects.

Learning Humility from Past Mistakes

For the world church, Korea was a case in point. The United Nations made the first major mistake by allowing itself to become a combatant on one side in the Korean War (1950-53) rather than remaining true to the spirit of its Charter, as an inclusive body capable of playing a mediating role. Almost forty years later, American troops in Korea are still mobilized under the UN flag, although the UN has not the slightest power to command or to remove them. As a result, the UN is totally incapable of dealing with a major crisis situation that continues to threaten regional and world security.

The churches made a similar mistake. When the Korean War broke out, the WCC Central Committee issued a statement stressing that an on-the-spot United Nations commission should identify the aggressor. It supported the UN for authorizing a "police measure" and emphasized the need for action towards a "just settlement by negotiation and conciliation." The Commission of the Churches on International Affairs worked closely with the UN, contributing to the establishment of a "Peace Observation Commission" by the 1950 UN General Assembly. What could not have been foreseen by the CCIA is that there would be only two UN observers, both of them Australians; that they would take a tour of the 38th parallel dividing North and South Korea a few days before the war, guided at all times by South Korean military officers; that the report in which they identified the North Koreans as aggressors, exonerating the South Korean army as being arrayed purely for defence, would then be written up by another UN representative who was a Chinese from the nationalist regime, with links to American intelligence.

The CCIA also helped to initiate a "Plan for Deferred Action on Prisoners of War in Korea," designed to facilitate a truce without forcible detention or repatriation of prisoners. This was meant to deal with a serious obstacle in the armistice negotiations.

When misunderstandings erupted between the South Korean government and the UN High Command, the CCIA director, O. Frederick Nolde (an American), flew to Pusan and Seoul for consultations with church leaders and served as an intermediary between contending parties within the United Nations forces. This venture was formally recognized by the U.S. government as "a factor in creating an atmosphere conducive to peace."

The development and expansion of a church-sponsored program of relief in Korea increased the importance of a close liaison between the WCC and the United Nations' Korean Reconstruction Agency.

What then was the mistake? As Professor Hromadka, a WCC Executive Committee member at the time, would point out repeatedly, it was the WCC's one-sided orientation to Western social and political perspectives. It was the naive assumption, though never openly articulated, that the United States necessarily stood on the side of freedom, democracy, and justice. It was the inability of even progressive ecumenical Christians to remove themselves emotionally and intellectually from their own contexts in order to be open to the concerns, needs, insights, and predicaments of others.

It was likely also the seductive pride that comes with being accepted as a partner by those in positions of power. The result was that the WCC and the CCIA were accused of functioning as a mouthpiece of Western imperialist powers. The result was that the WCC's president from China, T.C. Chao, resigned his position and the Chinese member churches withdrew their participation in the WCC. A decade later, the WCC would have to stand by as a helpless outsider when the Cultural Revolution in China confiscated church properties and put scores of pastors and priests into re-education camps.

The result was also that those Christians who remained in North Korea have had to struggle for their existence not only completely cut off from their sisters and brothers in South Korea, but also isolated from contact with Christians in the rest of the world.

Mistakes cannot be undone. They have to be overcome and lessons learned. The failure of the churches' quest for peace in the Korean situation offered them an important lesson: questions of peace and justice must be dealt with in close consultation with all those immediately affected. The churches must build bridges, not pass judgement or carry out sentences. That kind of experience, coupled with the changing membership of the world church, meant that the call to support people in their efforts for human rights and development found a receptive ear.

Confronting the Fear for Human Survival

The Korean experience also taught churches the extent to which fear frustrates the search for a just peace. It has been the most effective instrument for fuelling the Cold War and the arms race worldwide. To the individual fears that are the remnants of a traumatic past have been added national fears for security and economic stability. And acting as a backdrop to these fears is the global fear for human survival.

The birth of fear for human survival as a whole must surely be credited to the advent of nuclear weapons. The devastation of Hiroshima and Nagasaki ushered in a fear that shattered, or at least questioned radically, many traditional assumptions about politics, foreign affairs, and theology.

Unfortunately, fear is not a good counsellor. The danger of a global conflagration of unprecedented proportions had already been recognized at a 1946 meeting of the Provisional Committee of the WCC, which stated, "Man's triumph in the release of atomic energy threatens his destruction. Unless man's whole outlook is changed, our civilization will perish."

Although the WCC repeated similar assertions time and again during the following four decades, it was only at the Vancouver Assembly in 1983 that the ecumenical body was able to declare "that the production and deployment as well as the use of nuclear weapons are a crime against humanity and that such activities must be condemned on ethical and theological grounds."

Even then, there was no unanimity, and after the Assembly a lively debate reigned over whether the WCC had actually condemned the possession of nuclear weapons or had simply recommended that the churches become involved in "a fundamental examination of their own implicit or explicit support of policies which, implicitly or explicitly, are based on the possession and use of these weapons."

Why this sensitivity? Fear of the enemy obviously still outstrips fear of the means of destruction, that is, the fear of self-annihilation. No sovereign state has yet relinquished its right to a final recourse to war as the extension of politics by other means, and churches on the whole are still reluctant to call for limits on those other means. The fine distinction being made is that although the use of nuclear weapons must be prevented at all cost, there may still be valid reasons for possessing them.

This argument has been put forward forcefully by the Holy See of the Roman Catholic Church, which has repeatedly called for negotiations to reduce nuclear arms, with a view to their eventual elimination. Nevertheless, the Catholic Church has at the same time continued to insist that, considering the imperfect world in which we live, the possession of nuclear weapons for the purpose of deterrence is a necessary evil.

This was the major point of contention for the Vatican regarding the contents of the "Pastoral Letter on War and Peace," issued by the National Conference of Catholic Bishops of the U.S.A. in 1983. The result of a series of what insiders indicated were intense pressures by the Vatican on the U.S. bishops was the inclusion in the Pastoral Letter of "new insights" on the morality of deterrence expressed by Pope John Paul II to the UN Second Special Session on Disarmament (1982): "In current conditions 'deterrence' based on balance, certainly not as an end in itself but as a step on the way toward progressive disarmament, may still be judged morally acceptable." What is even more significant in the Pastoral Letter, however, is its detailed analysis of how the church's traditional "just war" doctrine applies to the prospects of nuclear war. The evident conclusion is that this doctrine could never justify the use of nuclear weapons.

This observation had been made already during the WCC's First Assembly in 1948. In a statement entitled "War Is Contrary to the Will of God," the Assembly concluded that in the light of nuclear and other weapons of indiscriminate destruction, "the tradition of a just war, requiring a just cause and the use of just means, is now challenged. Law may require the sanction of force, but when war breaks out, force is used on a scale which tends to destroy the basis on which law exists."

At the same time, the statement noted a predicament in Christian moral thinking on war, which is obviously still awaiting resolution. Unanimity could not be found, and the statement "frankly acknowledge[s] our deep sense of perplexity in face of these conflicting opinions." The three positions outlined came to be known as the "ecumenical trilemma":

(1) There are those who hold that, even though entering a war may be a Christian's duty in particular circumstances, modern warfare, with its mass destruction, can never be an act of justice.

(2) In the absence of impartial supra-national institutions, there

are those who hold that military action is the ultimate sanction of the rule of law, and that citizens must be distinctly taught that it is their duty to defend the law by force if necessary.

(3) Others, again, refuse military service of all kinds, convinced that an absolute witness against war and for peace is for them the will of God, and they desire that the Church should speak to the same effect.

Hammering Out a Consensus for the South

If there can be no unanimity on so basic a question, is any consensus on a just peace possible? Can the churches or the ecumenical community speak authoritatively to governments on these issues? The history of the World Council of Churches, the Roman Catholic Church, ecumenical organizations, and churches at a national level in many countries indicates that they can — most definitely!

During the last fifty years, the most effective work of the churches on a world scale has been done ecumenically and internationally on concrete conflicts. It has been in the churches' struggle to apply moral and theological principles to the concrete policies of powers and principalities that the greatest ecumenical breakthroughs have occurred.

Service to humanity takes place in the realm of daily life, where right and wrong have to be discerned with fear and trembling, where the principle of justice, as the Oxford World Conference on Church, Community and State declared, is "the relative expression of the commandment of love in any critique of economic, political and social institutions." Today, as in 1923, the slogan "Service Unites, Doctrine Divides" retains its validity.

What churches learned in addition, however, is that service can also test the validity of their doctrines. This challenge to doctrines, hitherto taken for granted, can in turn cause division. The guardians of doctrine, be they clergy or lay, are not easily swayed by practical arguments. One part of the human predicament is that complete unanimity on any issue is humanly impossible. The same moral principles sometimes lead people to opposing conclusions in practice. This is perhaps the most frustrating part of ecumenical thought and action. The churches struggle for unity, yet every division, every misunderstanding, every breakdown in communication thwarts the hope for unity that lies at the root of ecumenism. On the other hand, lack of unity is the raison d'être of ecumenism. Disagreements must never be ignored. They must be scrutinized carefully for the presence of nuggets of wisdom, which hide beneath all serious conflict.

Though the commitment to unity may not require absolute unanimity, it does require a stubborn determination to remain in communion and communication with those whose deepest sensitivities to the Gospel of Christ differ from one's own. That is precisely how the ecumenical movement learned that the search for peace can never be fruitful in the absence of a burning concern for justice.

As the ecumenical family expanded southward, as an increasing number of newly independent churches joined the WCC from newly independent countries, the search for peace became overshadowed by the concern for human liberation. Churches from the poor countries of the Southern Hemisphere were unimpressed by the depth of concern the rich churches of the North had to prevent war in a Europe and North America infested with a self-inflicted epidemic of nuclear weapons.

War for them was not a future danger to be shunned, but a present, everyday reality. Death from famine, disease, economic exploitation, and repression claimed, and continues to claim, the lives of hundreds of millions, even in the absence of military conflict. Those living in a world of surplus and waste had to learn from the impoverished, the wretched of the earth, that redemption requires repentance, that it is the poor whom God prefers to the rich, that it is the meek who shall inherit the earth.

It has proved to be the most difficult lesson for the churches to learn. Certainly, they responded to these calls for justice with a plethora of development programs and charitable organizations. Consciences had been stretched to the breaking point, and money was the salve on wounded self-righteousness.

But it was not charity that was being asked for. It was not the crumbs from the tables of the rich that the poor lusted after. Their hunger was above all for just relationships. "Liberation" was the watchword, and though many turned to Karl Marx for comfort, at least as many turned to the God of justice whose witness they found in the same biblical scriptures used by the rich to justify their quest for supremacy.

For those outside the nuclear clubs of East and West, the peace debate sounded like a luxury. Not only that. It sounded like a desire to stabilize the world as it is, to freeze the present division of power and wealth, to secure existing political and economic institutions. It appeared as though the aim of peace was to rob those who have nothing of their final resort: the opportunity to overthrow those who oppress them, if necessary by violence.

When the Helsinki Final Act on Security and Co-operation in Europe was signed in 1975, countries outside the North Atlantic sphere expressed some alarm. To them, it felt like an agreement among the rich to better their ability to exploit the poor.

Instead of charity, what Christians from the Third World required of their ecumenical friends in countries like Canada was, above all else, solidarity. They wanted to be understood in their aspirations and supported politically in their struggles. They wanted Canadian churches to involve themselves in an active, impassioned debate with their own people and their own government about what Canadian foreign policy was doing for the Third World.

It would be dishonest to suggest that this appeal did not meet with response. The present book is testimony to the churches, organizations, and individuals who threw themselves wholeheartedly into the enterprise and who with the help of God have accomplished miracles on the way. The ecumenical movement worldwide has been at the forefront of efforts aimed at an equitable world order, free from hunger, racism, and exploitation. Some of the most creative initiatives taken up by the United Nations system have their origins in ecumenical programs. But it would be equally misleading to suggest that these activities and involvements have had the backing of an unopposed Christian endorsement. More often than not, ecumenical endeavours for global justice have met with virulent opposition. The most common criticism heard in both church and government circles is that religious institutions "should not meddle with politics." The prevailing attitude continues to be the one initiated by the Roman Emperor Constantine in the fourth century A.D.: Christian faith should be subservient to political power.

The Church and the Unfinished Task

Consensus building can take many years. In the case of the peace-versus-justice debate, it took until the WCC's Sixth Assembly in Vancouver, 1983, to reach a consensus. And yet, in essence, Vancouver's "Statement on Peace and Justice" repeats what had already been said by Dietrich Bonhoeffer fifty years earlier.

For some, the process takes too long and achieves too little. What we have witnessed in the past decade is the "emigration" of many of the churches' most promising young people out of the churches and into secular peace, ecology, and political movements. Still, even the most impatient activist will admit the necessity of obtaining the backing of a constituency in order to be able to accomplish any social goal whatever. The churches have the potential to provide such a constituency, and to provide it at an international level, spanning all geographical and political boundaries.

What is required is not only the political and theological work necessary to forge a moral consensus on the issues of the day, but the transmittal of these insights and conclusions back to the church constituency, in particular its young people.

As timidly as churches often go about this business, it would be hard to find another institution nationally or globally that could compare to the Christian church's breadth and variety of membership, its pluralist and tolerant outlook, or its intellectual and ethical potential.

That is not to say that the church ever completely fulfils this potential. The fact that the benign and banal often triumph does not, however, diminish the importance of the church's role in international affairs. It is, after all, a human and therefore fallible institution. But it is an institution whose purpose for existence is to conform to the truth and will of God. As such, it has an in-built mechanism of reform and renewal, because those who seek to discern the will of God for each age will not allow the church to drift for long in blissful irrelevance.

Without doubt, the churches' international co-operation in pursuing a just peace not only will survive, but will experience a startling revival. The survival of our planet necessitates an effort of global dimensions, and the Christian churches can hardly remain aloof. That is how it was for ecumenical pioneers at the turn of the last century. That is how it will have to be at the turn of the next.

2 • Bridging the East-West Divide: Beyond the Cold War

Bonnie Greene

By the mid-1960s church leaders in Europe had realized that there would never be a just peace as long as the world was divided into East-West camps, each organized to defeat or deter an "eternal enemy." What was needed was a new approach to organizing the human household, one that would go beyond the assumptions of the North Atlantic Treaty Organization (NATO) and the Warsaw Treaty Organization.

For the churches of Eastern and Western Europe, the most hopeful opportunity lay in the Helsinki Final Act of the Conference on Security and Co-operation in Europe (CSCE). They determined to live in the "spirit of Helsinki" and to draw Canadian and American churches into the task of holding the nations of the Helsinki region to their word by pressuring them to implement international agreements on peace and human rights in their own countries. Their project has been a unique experiment in dealing with the concrete sources of conflict that fuelled the arms race during the past four decades.

Bonnie Greene is director of church in society for the United Church of Canada, where she has worked on CSCE issues since the late 1970s. She serves on the central committee of the Churches' Human Rights Programme for Implementation of the Helsinki Final Act, a program of the Conference of European Churches, the National Council of Churches of Christ-USA, and the Canadian Council of Churches.

— Ed.

Aftermath of the Second World War

At the end of the Second World War, the people of Europe found themselves divided in every possible way. The wounds of the war were deep, and a divided Europe seemed to some to be the only way to keep peace between peoples who had been badly wronged and whose collective anger threatened to create still more explosive situations.

For the people of the churches of Europe this was a painful fact of life, but also a denial of their basic belief that "we are all one in God's family." Flesh-and-blood families found that the political divisions of Europe into East and West kept relatives from attending simple events such as weddings, baptisms, and family reunions. Regional meetings of churches were disrupted by borders between Eastern and Western blocs. World communions of churches — such as the reformed and methodist — were also divided into alien camps, not by their own disagreements, but by the decisions of states.

Unfinished business following the war meant that allegiance either to NATO or to the Warsaw Treaty Organization became the de facto unifying thread, binding real human beings into camps in which those on the other side were by definition the enemy. Within some countries of Europe, whole groups of citizens — some racial and ethnic minorities and members of religious communities, among others — were also defined as enemy within their own countries.

Attempts to Build Bridges

In the early 1960s European church leaders began to reject this way of life. They asserted among themselves: "We will not live as enemy to one another any longer. We are one family in God, and we will live in that spirit as a witness to our visible unity in Christ." They set out to gather together people from the churches of all of Europe and the Soviet Union in an effort to help them know each other, at the very least. The theory was that those to whom we are strangers can quickly become the enemy. Therefore, the best way to avoid becoming enemies is to make sure we are not strangers to each other.

Finding a place for a religious group from Eastern and Western Europe to meet in the 1960s was an enormous challenge. The meeting could not be held in countries where it would be impossible to get visas for people from the "enemy" camp. Therefore, the European churches rented a large ship and met in international waters. It was an extraordinary act of faith for them and a visible means of saying that they were determined to emerge from the divisions reinforced by the Cold War.

They met periodically as church representatives to develop their relationship and eventually decided that a similar process might contribute to healing the divisions between the states of Europe. And so, in the mid-1960s, they called on the countries of the region to create an arena for pursuing security by the resolution of conflicts and the rebuilding of trust and normal relations. If NATO and the countries of the Warsaw Pact were occupied with each side's preparedness for defeating the enemy, this new arena must take an alternate path in order that a regime of intimidation could be put aside. Because Canada and the United States had been so intimately involved in the Second World War and in the military alliances that emerged after the war, they were included in this process.

An Alternative Political Process

The Conference on Security and Co-operation in Europe (CSCE) was the result. The motives of many of the key players differed greatly from those of the church leaders. The process has also been plagued by less than noble behaviour. Nevertheless, the CSCE quickly caught the imagination of hundreds of thousands, if not millions, of people who recognized its potential for creating a climate in which they could move into a new way of life for themselves and their neighbours.

Despite ample doses of bad faith and cynicism on the part of governmental representatives, the CSCE process has endured as an intergovernmental "process," a moveable feast of meetings between signatory states to review the commitments that have been made to the rest of the CSCE "family" and to measure progress in implementing agreements. In many ways, the vision of church people has been a "family meeting" for the household of Europe and North America. What they have desperately hoped to do was to bring the residents of this very large household together to resolve their conflicts and write out — in full public view — the rules of the household that would make life bearable for all the siblings.

Like family meetings, the CSCE vision has not always been realized in the process. Some members of the family do not play by the new rules of the household. They continue to act as if other members are enemies, instead of siblings. They refuse to put pen and ink to agreements on which everyone has reached a verbal agreement. They disregard evidence that suggests they have not been keeping their commitments back home in their own countries. And some of them try to act as regional police officers, taking responsibility for everyone's behaviour but their own. New ways of living never come about by direct paths.

Nevertheless, the CSCE process has become a reality and, since the Vienna Review Conference, concluded in February 1989, has begun to make real progress. The Final Act of the original CSCE was signed in Helsinki, Finland, in 1975 by the representatives of thirty-five states: the U.S.S.R., the countries of Eastern and Western

Europe, the United Kingdom, Canada, and the United States (only Albania refused to join). Given the odds against such a large multilateral conference ever accomplishing anything, the most charitable observers have tended to remark that at least states continue to meet, develop a consensus document, set a new agenda of issues to be addressed, and establish a set of working sessions on the way to another major review conference. The consensus to stay with the process has often had to satisfy anxious citizens when their states could not agree on the content of the statements to which they would commit themselves.

Despite its limitations and the limited public support it has received in Canada and the United States, people from the churches of Europe — especially Eastern Europe — have insisted that the CSCE be taken seriously. The Helsinki Final Act, as the first Concluding Document is called, was not a treaty and therefore was not legally binding. Nevertheless, the commitments made in it were viewed by ordinary citizens as having moral and political power. Church leaders viewed the agreements as promises freshly made by states to their own citizens, in the hearing of all neighbouring states. These were promises to be taken in good faith, no matter how cynical others might choose to be about their significance. For Christians from some countries, these commitments meant the difference between being isolated from the rest of the world church and having the opportunity to join others at international conferences. For others, it meant the hope that the climate of war preparedness might dissipate enough to allow ordinary people to travel abroad for family visits.

The Helsinki Final Act was particularly important for people from Eastern Europe, the U.S.S.R., and the neutral/non-aligned states because it was an agreement to which both of the great powers and all their allies had agreed in public. Therefore, ordinary citizens could pursue its implementation without being accused of being under Western influences. Furthermore, it incorporated the basic principles of the United Nations' Charter in a regional security agreement. The principles adopted at a world level in the arena of the UN were thus brought home to a specific region, where their practical application could be written down and agreed to. UN standards thus became a moral benchmark, at the very least, for holding states accountable for their treatment of their own citizens and of other states.

The Helsinki Final Act appealed to churches in the region because it avoided the traditional logjam between Western, Eastern, and Third World concepts of human rights. The first section of the Final Act laid out the basic principles to which signatory states would adhere in seeking security. These principles included statements regarding non-intervention in internal affairs, as well as respect for human rights and fundamental freedoms, including the freedom of thought, conscience, religion, or belief. Security in the CSCE region was inextricably linked to the pursuit of real human rights of all people in the region and of people's economic and social well-being. In the other two sections of the Final Act, even the relationship between the CSCE region and the Third World was addressed. This allowed the church to address the issues of the region in a comprehensive way, including the issues of civil and political rights, as well as social, cultural, and economic rights. The Final Act and the CSCE process offered the churches the possibility of transcending the ideological approach to human rights, peace building, and economic development and of adopting instead an approach that addresses concrete issues in a comprehensive way.

Taking Human Rights Seriously

The intergovernmental CSCE process might well have moved along on its own, without further church involvement after the initial agreement was achieved. The process did not (and still does not) provide for a formal role for non-governmental organizations and individual citizens. However, the debate on human rights in Europe and North America gained such momentum in the churches of the region that they could claim a minimum consensus among themselves that the violation of human rights was one of the most pressing issues facing society. In some Eastern European countries, church members feared that the leaders of the global ecumenical movement would divert all of their energies to human rights in former colonies of the Third World, completely ignoring the real situation in Europe.

At the 1975 Assembly of the World Council of Churches (WCC) in Nairobi, Kenya, this issue burst onto the world church agenda via a challenge from members of the Russian Orthodox Church, who were active in the church renewal movement. They issued an appeal to the Assembly to recognize the violations of human rights in Europe, with particular attention to religious liberty and the situation of religious minorities. The clear message was that international human rights standards needed to be pursued with vigour in all parts of the world. Regional churches needed to be encouraged by the WCC to carry out their responsibilities in their own backyards if the statements of the churches at the global level were to have substance and integrity back home.

The Conference of European Churches (CEC) set about building support for this work among its own member churches, which included all the major Protestant churches of Eastern and Western Europe, the U.S.S.R., and the United Kingdom. By 1979 the churches of Canada and the United States had been drawn in to complete the church network within the CSCE region. Representatives of the three regional councils met in Cartigny, Switzerland, in early 1979 to create a mechanism that would allow them to act together on priority issues within the CSCE framework.

The mechanism was a joint project of the three councils called the Churches' Human Rights Programme for Implementation of the Helsinki Final Act (CHRP). Between them, the three councils could represent or develop relations with virtually all churches within the region, including those that were not members of the World Council of Churches. The three councils hired two staff people to help them build a consensus among themselves on the key contentious issues, on the issues that most required the churches' attention, and on the best ways of working together in "accompanying" the CSCE intergovernmental process.

The early leadership for this venture came from churches in the German Democratic Republic, the Federal Republic of Germany, and Switzerland. Not only were major churches in the Protestant part of Europe deeply committed, but their leaders came from extremely high positions within the churches. Had this not been the case, the project might never have developed into one of the most unusual non-governmental human rights networks in the world.

Confidence Building among Churches

In the first three years of the project, the churches set out to examine the key concepts of the CSCE agreement and to build church consensus across the divide that had been created by many years of forced separation. They decided that their central concept must be "confidence building" and doing away with "enemy images." At first, these terms were explored primarily in theological terms with which many church people were very familiar: forgiveness, reconciliation, truth telling, and transparency. Canadian, British, and American churches tended to be impatient with this approach; they preferred to act together on concrete human matters, having only a little tolerance for discussing the kinds of middle axioms social ethicists might provide. Furthermore, these countries were initially reluctant to discuss anything beyond the impact of their countries' foreign policies on the human rights situation in Third World countries.

Since the churches came to their common table with differences nearly as fundamental as those of the countries within which they found themselves, the task of building confidence between churches and shaping a human rights network in the CSCE region became paramount. Regional consultations took place in North America, northern Europe, southern Europe, and the Danube region, with a CSCE churches' gathering in Bucharest from which a basic "Concluding Document" offered an emerging church perspective, on which future work could be built.

During the early 1980s, both Europe and North America were gripped by a deepening of the Cold War, as well as by a wide public consciousness that the great powers and their military alliances were taking new steps that increased the threat of nuclear war. Further, there was an undermining of the confidence building that had gone on since the Helsinki Final Act was signed. Therefore, the churches of the region needed to make concrete progress on several of the thorniest issues that reinforced the ideological divisions between states. They held two seminars: the first was on the theme "Universal Human Rights and National Sovereignty" and the second on the theme "Peace and Human Rights: Theological Roots and Political Implications of Confidence Building Measures." These seminars helped to establish principles on which churches from different theological and ethical traditions could approach the issues blocking progress on real human rights situations, without falling into ideological traps.

Towards the middle of the decade, the churches of the region also took on the task of developing an agreement on how churches should work on human rights violations in their own situations. Occasionally, possible solutions were raised by example. At one major workshop, the chairperson was forced to leave in mid-meeting to intervene on behalf of people from the independent peace movement in his country who had been arrested. His departure offered a concrete model of human rights work within Eastern Europe to church leaders who had never even considered such a risky action. Eventually, this led to a series of network meetings in which skills in human rights work could be shared between churches. Of course, not every church wanted to be involved in more than a discussion of human rights between churches. For example, when the joint program of the three councils presented information about the violations of the rights of minorities in Romania, certain church representatives flatly denied it and blocked action in Europe. Some churches were far more willing than others to act on what they knew.

In the meantime, the intergovernmental CSCE process had moved along, with review conferences being concluded at Belgrade and Madrid. Although progress on many of the human rights issues of greatest concern to the churches had been minimal, the Concluding Document of the Madrid Review Conference had included a commitment to a major review conference in Vienna, beginning in November 1986, with several preparatory experts' meetings on specific topics between the review conferences. One of the preparatory meetings was the Human Rights Experts' Meeting to be held in Ottawa in the spring of 1986.

The North American location and the focus on human rights gave the churches of the region a chance to test their ability to take their consensus into the intergovernmental arena. The Canadian Council of Churches (CCC) used the occasion to make the Canadian government aware of the consensus and the network that the churches of the CSCE region had managed to develop, despite the obstacles thrown in their path by the collapse of détente and the politicizing of human rights that both the Soviet Union and the United States had indulged in. The CCC's goal was to press Canada as host country to create a climate that would allow progress. An observer team of two church people from the G.D.R. and the F.R.G. came to Ottawa to lobby the country delegations and to introduce them to the churches' concerns in the area.

Based on this first experience, the churches determined to address future human rights meetings with more precision. Prior to an intergovernmental meeting in Bern, Switzerland, on "human contacts" (one of the areas to be examined at the Vienna Review Conference), the churches gathered in Bern for a "shadow conference" on the topics on the official conference agenda over which they had the greatest concern: racial, cultural, and ethnic minorities; religious intolerance; the situation of youth; and the new poor emerging within the region — guest workers, immigrants, refugees, and others. There were extended and heated debates about how to introduce into the CSCE process principles regarding the impact of the CSCE states on the Third World. Although the churches could not agree on how to establish this principle, the presence of so many church people from former colonies in the CSCE states and the arrival of refugees at CSCE borders made it clear that the issue would eventually demand the attention of even the most reluctant states.

The churches' conference in Bern was sponsored by the Swiss Protestant Federation, with co-operation from the Council of European Bishops, which was not at that time included in the preparations of the Holy See for the government meetings. The Swiss churches set up the shadow conference so that official delegations representing the churches of the entire region would receive briefings from governmental experts in CSCE, as well as from church people from the human rights and peace movements. Delegates also spent time in working groups, assessing how well the CSCE states had implemented the agreements they had already made and building consensus on the priority areas for work by both governments and churches.

The churches' Concluding Document became a generic statement for introducing to each of the country delegations at the Bern intergovernmental meeting the consensus achieved by those whom governments defined as "enemies." Churches within each country were able to present it to their government as an expression of one community's desire to find common ground and pursue real human rights throughout the region. The regional and ecumenical character of the statement also reminded some governments that the minority churches presenting the document had colleagues abroad who were looking out for them.

The experience at Bern became the first step in the churches' efforts to "accompany" the Vienna Review Conference. The growing momentum in the churches for human rights work was scarcely matched by momentum in the intergovernmental process. Most observers were convinced that keeping the CSCE going would be a major accomplishment. Nevertheless, the churches determined to stay with the process in the hope of holding ground, if not gaining some new ground, on such issues as religious liberty, minorities, human contacts, and youth.

They decided to send teams of church observers — one from the East and one from the West — to Vienna each month, as long as the conference lasted. They also asked the Austrian churches to establish a liaison body for the churches, which would monitor developments at the conference, introduce the observer teams to government delegations, and develop a profile for the continuing presence of the churches, watching in the wings. When the plan was adopted, no one imagined that the Vienna Review Conference would drag on for just over two years. (The financial implications eventually became a bit daunting, since Eastern churches needed support to deal with their non-convertible currencies.)

As the conference opened, churches of the region approached their governments to press for a particular approach to the issues.

The top priority was overcoming a bloc approach to all debates, which had characterized much of the debate on human rights during the 1980s. The success of churches within each country in reaching their delegations was mixed, depending on the nature of the church's relationship with the government. Some churches of Eastern Europe could go no further than to send an official letter from the ecumenical program; nevertheless, being part of a non-bloc opinion shared by many churches was an important step. Churches in some countries were invited by their governments to put members on the country delegation, a step generally discouraged by other churches. In North America, governments did not seem inclined to take Vienna very seriously. Although they received the churches' comments, the dominant message was: don't expect much — the Soviet Union has yet to move beyond human rights rhetoric to real implementation.

As the international church observers travelled to Vienna each month, they managed to build up a body of knowledge of the proposals that were placed on the table and a network of informed contacts in the government delegations. Although the official meeting was closed to non-governmental organizations, it was possible to make appointments with country delegations and to attend media briefings conducted by some countries. The observers also managed to pick up copies of all the working texts tabled by country delegations. These were collected in Geneva to create a full docket for the churches' use.

By two-thirds of the way through the Vienna Review Conference, the churches felt the need to consolidate their learnings and to prepare a new document that would guide their observer teams in pushing for real progress in the Concluding Document. The documents being debated by governments and the broad participation of observers from throughout the region were critical to the next steps in accompanying Vienna in a serious way.

Observers and key church leaders met, in the summer of 1987, to review all the proposals tabled by countries for possible inclusion in the Concluding Document. Using their knowledge of the real situation these proposals were supposed to address, they were able to select the ones they wished to support. They also developed amendments to strengthen those that were priorities for the churches. Then they circulated the joint recommendation to all member churches to assist them in approaching their own delegations once more. The observers who went to Vienna from this point were thus equipped with a document that offered precise suggestions on wordings for new government commitments, suggestions that emerged out of the real experiences of churches on the ground in each of the countries, as well as from real issues on the intergovernmental agenda.

The Watershed Year of 1989

The churches participating in the CSCE work gathered again in Bern, in the wake of the momentous autumn of 1989, as country after country in Eastern Europe ended one-party rule, as revolution overtook the Ceaucesceau regime, and as a spirit of people's participation in shaping their own societies swept through Eastern Europe. The churches had gathered to prepare once again to accompany the CSCE process in another review of member states' compliance with human rights agreements. The Concluding Document of this shadow conference was both familiar and new. It called on governments to agree to principles that would have been grounds for arrest and detention for some participants only months earlier. For example:

1. People are both the subject and object of the CSCE process. The concept of the "human dimension" refers to the personal experience of women and men seeking peace, co-operation, and human rights in every sphere: political, economic, social, cultural, humanitarian, and so on....

2. The concept of the "human dimension" must challenge us to combine both major threads of our human rights tradition — individual freedom and social justice — in the pursuit of the common good, promotion of just, participatory, and sustainable societies and preservation of the fragile environment for future generations.

The document also called for a kind of social charter for economic development, a priority for European churches in the face of the "free trade" promised by the Single European Act of 1992.

To Westerners accustomed to writing social charters and bold declarations for the common good, the Concluding Document would seem distinctly modest. To Christians from many Eastern European countries, it was a sign of something new. The after-hours conversations told the story. The leader of one delegation had spent time in prison for his convictions, yet now he had been asked to help write the new constitution of his country because of his expertise in international law and protection of minorities. Another participant who had been silenced for over a decade because of his support for human rights and for the Czech human rights group, Charter 77, now found himself among the new leadership of his country, one of the few people whom the citizens trusted to be committed to the common good.

For the first time, people felt free to speak openly of all that their countries had gone through in the struggle to create a space in which men and women could pursue the realization of the human rights — of both the Eastern and Western traditions — that they had been promised. In the German Democratic Republic, for example, the church had been able to keep alive people's longing for a just peace and a healthy environment, even when discussions were illegal in their country. The church had provided a protective umbrella, where people came together to talk about values, peace, and the environment. It had been dangerous and there had been many conflicts with authorities, but it had been essential.

At the churches' shadow conference in 1989, it was possible to speculate that the Conference on Security and Co-operation in Europe was no longer necessary. Possibly they could turn their attention to something more pressing. The people who had lived in the spirit of Helsinki for so many of the coldest years in East-West relations were very clear on the subject. Now more than ever, the CSCE process held promise for a region of the world in which people were willing to live without an eternal enemy and to pursue a household that would meet the needs of all members of the very large family it contained. Co-operation with one another and with the earth defined the only possible path forward.

An Emerging Ethic for a Fragile Earth

All of this work on the part of the churches took place before the new openness within the Soviet Union had fully entered the consciousness of Western nations. Therefore, the Concluding Document that was finally signed at Vienna went further than the churches had dared to hope in addressing questions of religious liberty and in defining human rights issues as more than "human contacts" in a divided Europe. Instead, it named the real concern as the "human dimension" of life in the European household. In the churches' words, this was an orientation to security and economic development, signalling a recognition that people and their environment mattered. For a group of people who had set out nearly thirty years earlier to become neighbours, rather than eternal enemies, the breakthrough was highly significant. What's more, people were delighted at the willingness of the Soviet

Union and others to allow believers to be active members of religious communities and of society, rather than simply individuals who kept their faith in their hearts.

When the churches of the CSCE region first began this work, they were motivated by faith convictions, as well as by the real pain of separation experienced in everyday life. Their belief in the capacity of human beings to take responsibility for the way their societies are ordered and to bring about change where it seems most unlikely was critical to the early stages of this unique project. At bottom, however, they refused to give up their belief that God unites all of humanity in one family of infinite value. The CSCE process created an opportunity for examining the implications of these beliefs for the real lives of people living with the warring ghosts of the past and the potential nuclear nightmare of the future.

During this period, there were important shifts in thinking in several fields that advanced the debate on the possibilities of an ethic appropriate to the nuclear age. This work lent credibility to the churches' pursuit of a way of ordering relations between states that would be based on co-operation between siblings rather than on competitiveness between enemies. It also confirmed the churches' choice of the CSCE process as a practical, if fragile, way of overcoming some of the dynamics of war making in favour of peace building.

In terms of politics and international relations, the population of much of the region was going through a shift in its views of how nations could achieve peace. The oldest and dominant view during the period following the Second World War was that peace could be achieved through force, with which one would intimidate, defeat, or possibly destroy the enemy. A second, less widely held view was that peace could be achieved through development and social justice; adequate social programs within countries, peaceful trade and investment opportunities, co-operative development programs with poor countries, and other such programs were part of this approach. The third approach has not quite jelled but is commonly known as the "green vision": peace can be built for the earth and all its people through a determined effort to live in a co-operative and ecologically sound manner.

The first approach — defeating or destroying the enemy — was the one with which the churches felt the greatest unease. Living with an eternal enemy created a fundamental gap between their profession of faith and their daily life. The second approach offered the possibility of building a new way of life without an eternal enemy. In its most idealistic form, the Helsinki Final Act and the CSCE process offered the best opportunity on the horizon for shifting the approach to the issue of security for the peoples of Europe and North America. The third, or green, approach is just beginning to make an impact on the CSCE process and could, of course, overtake it altogether.

During this same period, a shift in ethics was taking place in North America, in particular. This shift fostered new perspectives on the ethical thinking that churches had brought with them from the era prior to the nuclear age. Up to and including the 1960s, the prevailing approach to moral development was described in terms of hierarchical stages through which human beings advanced on their way to becoming mature moral beings, able to distinguish right and wrong and to make good decisions. It was also commonly thought that the more good individuals a society had, the more that society would realize the objective of becoming the "good society." Well into the 1980s, the shortage of "good individuals" was used as a rationale for preparing to destroy an enemy nation, such as an atheistic state like the Soviet Union.

At the time, the fully developed moral individual tended to be defined in North America as autonomous, self-actualizing, and capable of making independent moral decisions, characteristics that psychologists discovered were exhibited by far more men than women. Research appeared to show that women tended to develop only to the third of six stages of moral development, where their commitments to others tended to create ethical dilemmas for them. Those who made moral decisions in this way were seen as weak. At the time, the problem was seen to be with women — not with the definition of what it takes to create a good society or good people.

During the 1970s and 1980s, feminist researchers began shedding new light on this story. The work of Carol Gilligan was especially important in challenging the classical view of moral development and its use to justify the killing of an enemy or even the destruction of an enemy nation. Gilligan studied boys and girls at play, as well as adults facing key moral decisions later in life. Her interviews with girls indicated that when they ran into conflict during games, they tended to stop the game rather than force an individual to lose in the conflict. The relationship took priority over the individual's desire to win. Girls' games tended to emphasize taking turns and inclusion. The games boys were encouraged to play tended to involve teams or individual opponents, who must be defeated if one side is to succeed at the game.

When Gilligan interviewed adult men and women about the moral decisions they had to make and the grounds on which they made them, she discovered that men tended to be much clearer about what was right and what was wrong. Women, however, found themselves debating the impact of each decision on the multitude of relationships they had. Their decisions were seldom as clear-cut and straightforward as those the men were taking.

At the time, the prevailing wisdom was that men were more fully developed morally than were women. This was the argument used during the 1960s against a woman becoming prime minister of Canada or, God forbid, president of the United States and thus responsible for deciding when the Soviet Union had gone too far and had to be destroyed.

The values fostered in the "ethically mature" male — integrity, self-actualization, survival, competitiveness, growth, and so on — were worthy values related to the worth of the individual. However, Carol Gilligan's work led others to question whether the approach women took to moral decision making might also have something to contribute to the protection of communities, to the protection of the weak, even more, to the development of a "good society" in which it is possible to live without the concept of an enemy to be defeated. The values women tended to realize in their decision making were inseparability of community, mutuality, human solidarity, and solutions that include everyone. At some level, these values suggested, every human being was linked to another part of the human community by an umbilical cord that could not be severed in any final sense without causing the entire human family to bleed to death.

In domestic conflict resolution, this insight has been incorporated in approaches that seek "win-win" solutions or mutually acceptable outcomes for the entire community involved in the issue. In international conflict resolution, the traditional models have relied on a de facto enemy and the assumption that the solution must meet our interests, but not the enemy's. The arms race and the economic burden it has imposed on the entire world are the obvious outcomes of this model.

Work such as this by ethicists and political scientists seeking a new approach to the use of power has fostered the hope of some that human beings can take responsibility for their collective behaviour. Instead of pursuing the triumph of one state over another, they might develop international political processes in which the interests of the "parts" are advanced by pursuing the interests of the "whole." On that basis, our international order would emerge from the interaction of states that are both co-operating and self-determining rather than a homogenized internationalism.

In the light of this kind of thinking, it is not surprising that the CSCE process has taken on such importance for the church people in the region. The ideal it represented had at least turned their collective faces in a new direction, one that was consistent with the desire to live as one human family. However fragile the experiment may be, the churches of the CSCE region have stumbled intuitively into a way of relating to one another that feels more congruent with the values that emerge from their identity as a faith community.

3 • Learning to Live with Enemies: The Churches and the Middle East

Douglas duCharme

If there is a just peace for the Middle East, the Canadian churches would be the last to claim that they know where it lies. Their historic ties to the holy sites in the region, their history of conflict with other faith communities, and their fear of endangering small gains in inter-faith dialogue have rendered them largely silent on one of the most dangerous conflicts of the day.

In recent years, they have taken a small step in search of a just peace in the region through a new partnership with the Middle East Council of Churches (MECC). The MECC represents ancient Christian churches that have always been a minority in the Middle East and that can make their contribution to the region's peace movement through humanitarian work and dialogue aimed at building trust between those who regard one another as enemy. The Canadian churches' relationship to the churches of the Middle East is an example of the kind of solidarity that minority churches worldwide have sought in support of their work for social change that will allow a just peace to be built.

Douglas duCharme is a Presbyterian minister living in Cyprus, where he works with the Middle East Council of Churches as liaison staff of the Canadian Council of Churches. He has served the Canadian churches in numerous areas of work related to foreign policy, in helping to prepare their submission to the foreign policy review conducted by the Mulroney government in 1985, and in lobbying at the UN Commission on Human Rights.

— Ed.

Building Bridges to the Middle East

"If God is dead, as some people now claim, then he died trying to find a just solution to the Arab-Israeli conflict." These words opened an analysis of the Middle East written in 1967, in the aftermath of the Middle East war in June of that year. The phrase was repeated in a small but important book written over ten years later, in 1978, by a group of Canadian academics and church people who were brought together to discuss and report on the prevailing situation in the Middle East. They had taken on this task at the request of the Ecumenical Forum of Canada, a centre for ecumenical education and missionary formation in Toronto. The forum asked the group to consider "what might be the main components of a responsible Christian position regarding the Middle East." According to the study group, the situation in 1978 did not look much better than that reflected by the wry remark written in 1967.

In the early 1990s, after forty years of conflict and five wars, the phrase still evokes something of the frustration felt by people concerned about the Middle East the world over. Yet as intransigent as the Middle East conflict may seem, it has not remained static. The understanding of what a "just" solution might involve has changed as the Iran-Iraq War, the Lebanese conflict, and the Palestinian Intifada have affected people's perceptions of the region. Western understanding of the conflict itself has also changed: the Arab-Israeli conflict, increasingly focused on the Palestinian-Israeli conflict, has come to be seen as but one component of the region's troubles, and not the sole issue at hand.

However, emphasis remains on that troubling phrase "a just solution." Solutions have been proposed, and some parties have tried to impose de facto solutions, but as yet a just solution remains to be found, especially one in a form that could be both acceptable to and implemented by the parties involved. It is this, then, that necessitates and defines reconciliation, or living with the enemy, in the Middle East. The bitter history of the conflicts has favoured confrontation and mutually exclusive interests, with even-handedness having become a victim to this hostile legacy. In view of this, what possible role could exist for the churches, and the Canadian churches in particular, within this volatile climate? If reconciliation is the fabric that must be woven, out of threads of bitterness and distrust, where does the vocation of the churches lie?

Before we take up this question, we must face another in all honesty: By what right do the churches even consider playing the role of reconcilers in the Middle East conflict? This question is often asked, in just such uncompromising terms, by various parties to the conflict and within the churches themselves. The church, after all, carries a heavy burden of guilt for the Holocaust, for the appalling inheritance of centuries of Christian anti-Semitism. The Nazis, while ostensibly working within pagan themes, were able to fan the flames that were kindled in Christian discrimination and prejudice. Who then are the churches now to presume to act as reconcilers in the Arab-Israeli conflict?

Muslims in the Middle East ask a similar question. As the authors of the Ecumenical Forum report note, "It was Christians of the Middle Ages who dismissed the Muslims as worse than pagans and initiated the vicious havoc of the Crusades. The West's tendency to dismiss Arabs produced in this century callous treatment of the remnants of the Turkish empire in the Levant and Palestine, and the unilateral disposition of Middle Eastern territory."[1] In view of this history of prejudice and broken political promises, we must again ask, Who are the churches to step in now as reconcilers?

In fact, the church has much to repent in light of this history. This conviction has finally taken root, and is bearing fruit, not only in the church's relations with groups who have suffered prejudice and persecution at its hands in the past, but also within the self-understanding of the church and within its theology.

What gives the church credibility in the conflicts of the region and the ever-present history that fuels them is the churches of the Middle East, the churches that have been a living presence and witness to the Christian faith in the Middle East since the first century. These churches are not implicated in the Jewish Holocaust, nor can their tradition of Christian theology be interpreted as providing a foundation for anti-Semitism. As Arabs, they are themselves a part of the Semite family of peoples. Neither can they be seen to be part of the legacy of Western imperialism, as they too were victims of the Crusades and of great power political strategies in the region after the two world wars. The Arab churches have lived side by side with their Muslim and Jewish neighbours for centuries, sharing their culture, traditions, and suffering.

Through the Arab churches in the Middle East therefore, and within the ecumenical movement, the Canadian churches, together with other churches around the world, have found a fresh and credible point of entry into the Middle East conflict. Through dialogue with Christians in the Middle East, the Canadian churches have gained reliable and sometimes surprising insights not only into the Middle East conflict, but also into themselves as Christians. Through these churches, Canadian churches have been able to glimpse the Middle East conflict from the inside and to gradually form a credible vision of justice, of peace, and of what it means to work for reconciliation in the region from that intimate perspective.

"The Middle East is not far from Canada," wrote the then general secretary of the Canadian Council of Churches (CCC), the

Rev. Dr. Donald Anderson, in his introduction to the trip report of a CCC-sponsored delegation that travelled to the Middle East in September 1987. He noted that, as a nation of immigrants, Canada has become a new home for hundreds of thousands of people from Middle Eastern countries over past decades and that they, as others, have contributed to the rich fabric of Canadian life. As a consequence, among the sixteen member churches of the CCC there are those whose roots lie in the Middle East and who are also to be found among the member churches of the Middle East Council of Churches (MECC).

Nevertheless, for many years the Canadian churches did not count the Middle East as an area of significant contact or action. Some involvement was present, through Christian-Jewish and Christian-Muslim dialogue, and through MECC-co-ordinated inter-church development and aid programs, particularly in Lebanon and among the Palestinians. However, it took some time before these contacts developed into a wider sensitivity to the conflicts that lay behind the issues raised in dialogue and the visible needs met by inter-church aid. A sense of solidarity was long in taking shape.

The Canadian churches reflected Canadian attitudes in general and Canadian government policy in particular. In his book *Canada and the Birth of Israel: A Study in Canadian Foreign Policy*, David Bercuson argued that Canadian policy towards the crisis in Palestine during the crucial years from 1947 to 1950 was primarily shaped by Canada's commitment to the North Atlantic triangle of Britain, the United States, and Canada, with Canada trying to mediate between the contrasting policies of the United States and Britain to preserve a consensus. Pro-Zionist groups in Canada seem to have had surprisingly little effect on Canadian policy making at that time. In fact, as Bercuson sees it, "The Department of External Affairs and the cabinet determined Canadian external policies; the House of Commons had, and has, almost no impact on the process."[2]

During the conflict leading up to the formation of the state of Israel, these policy makers were largely left to determine their policies undisturbed because the Canadian public, apart from a few pro-Zionist groups like the Canadian Palestine Committee and the United Zionist Council, was generally neutral, not to say apathetic, about the whole situation. A February 1948 Gallup poll showed that 23 per cent of all Canadians supported the Arab cause in the fighting then going on as the British brought their Palestine mandate to an end; only 19 per cent backed the Jews. A solid majority, 58 per cent, had no opinion or were neutral.

Reflecting such sentiments, official Canadian policy advocated doing as little as possible (apart from occasions where the situation proved to be an irritant in U.S.-British relations), since it was assumed that there was little direct Canadian national interest involved in the region. In the words of a senior civil servant at External Affairs in those days, "I would be myself loath to see any strong advocacy by the Canadian government of a particular solution to the Palestine problem.... Palestine will remain, for a long time, a troubled area ... in which it is most unlikely that Canada will have any very direct interest."[3] In fact, Canada did not have an embassy anywhere in the region until 1948, when it opened one in Ankara, Turkey.

Nevertheless, due to its high regard in international diplomatic circles, particularly at the United Nations (UN), Canada found itself playing a significant role in the Middle East during the 1940s and 1950s. People such as Lester B. Pearson, Justice Ivan Rand, and A.G.L. McNaughton played important parts at the UN during the debates on the 1947 UN partition plan for Palestine, on the acceptance into membership of the UN of the newly formed Israeli state, and on the formation of the UN peace-keeping force, put forward by Pearson during the 1956 Suez Crisis when Britain, France, and Israel invaded Egypt.

Since that time, Canadian diplomatic representation has increased in the region (there are now ten embassies covering fifteen countries); trade has grown ($4.5 billion to the Arab world annually); and Canadian troops are serving on three UN peace-keeping forces in the region. However, Canada now exerts almost no influence in the Middle East peace process.

The Canadian churches have reflected this hands-off policy. They have never had mission personnel in the region, nor very strong or regular contact with the Middle East churches themselves. Statements on the region from church synods and councils are rarely to be found, and when they do appear, in response to a major crisis such as the June 1967 Middle East war, they tend to be vague and hesitant. As the Ecumenical Forum group observed, such statements from Catholics and Protestants alike "lack decisive clarity because traditional and emotional attachments to the Arabs and Israelis, to Muslims, Jews and Eastern Christians, have translated the political conflict into one embedded in the conscience of the concerned Christian. It is this internal debate that is reflected in the hesitations and ambiguities of the Churches' official documents."[4]

But that situation has changed. Involvement in the humanitarian work of the Middle East Council of Churches, and visits to the region to view projects that Canadian churches were helping to fund, brought a growing awareness of the urgent issues of justice and peace that lay behind the humanitarian programs. Visits to Canada by members of the MECC staff, including its general secretary, Gabriel Habib, broadened the Canadian churches' understanding of the political and social realities that fed the complex dynamics shaping the region. Such contacts also helped to break through the stereotypes and oversimplifications that have blinded Western churches to events in the region and their impact on individuals and communities. This growing awareness became particularly evident in the aftermath of the Israeli invasion of Lebanon in June 1982.

In an initial response to this new awareness and concern, and in an effort to build bridges of reconciliation within Canada, the Canadian Council of Churches in 1984 tried to initiate a dialogue between the CCC, the Canadian Jewish Congress (CJC), and the Canadian Arab Federation (CAF) on a wide range of issues. Despite long-standing and fruitful contact between the CCC and the CJC, the latter refused to take part in the discussions. The Canadian Arab Federation, lacking any previous contact with the CCC, also expressed some reservations about the proposal, but in the end agreed to participate. The discussions went forward between the CCC and the CAF, lasting some eight months.

The dialogue focused in large part on the report that emerged from the joint MECC/World Council of Churches (WCC) Consultation on Christian Presence and Witness in the Middle East, held in May 1983. The CAF representatives approved the substance of the report, including the three principles that were subsequently adopted at the WCC's Sixth Assembly: the withdrawal of Israeli troops from all territories occupied in 1967; the right of all states, including Israel and the Arab states, to live in peace with secure and recognized boundaries; and the implementation of the rights of the Palestinians to self-determination, including the right to establish a sovereign Palestinian state within historic Palestine. The report, however, did not necessarily represent the policy of the Canadian churches, nor even of the CCC — which raised the issue of the CCC's ability to take a stand on issues raised in the dialogue, including endorsement of the WCC statement. While the CAF was able to take a clear position, the CCC could not take any decision independent of its constituent denominations. This proved frustrating for the CAF representatives.

Points of agreement emerging from the discussions included the need to educate the Canadian church constituency about Middle East-related issues, the racist stereotypes held by many

Canadians regarding Arab people, and the need to maintain constructive working relationships between the CCC and the CAF, both on a formal and, perhaps more importantly, informal basis.

On one point, however, there was no agreement. Whereas the CCC representatives tended to see the Arab-Israeli crisis as a conflict between rival perceptions of legitimate rights, and were hence not anxious to take sides, the CAF representatives pressed their concern over moral principles involved in the issue, primarily Israel's brutal treatment of the Palestinians. The CAF representatives were disappointed that many of the CCC participants, while recognizing that it was undoubtedly the Palestinians who were suffering, were unwilling to take an uncompromising pro-Palestinian position, preferring instead to hold that the key to peace and security lay in the ability of both parties to give up some rigidly held principles.

Meanwhile, developing contacts between the CCC and the MECC led to an invitation from the MECC for a delegation from the Canadian churches to visit the Middle East so that they might see the situation in the region first-hand and contacts between the two communities of churches could be strengthened. The invitation was given personally by the MECC general secretary when he addressed the CCC General Board in October 1986. In his invitation, Gabriel Habib underlined the constructive role that could be played by the Canadian churches in view of the fact that neither Canada, nor its churches, had a history of colonial interference or of adverse missionary activity among the churches and peoples of the Middle East. The opportunity was there to open a constructive partnership with the churches of the Middle East on an equal footing. In accepting the invitation, the CCC general secretary noted that the "pilgrimage" that would be undertaken by the delegation "would not end with the visit," but would "engage our understanding and commitment on a much longer journey."

Even as the delegation began its visit, that long-term commitment to involvement in the Middle East through the MECC began with the appointment of a CCC Middle East liaison. The role of this staffperson would be to work with the MECC in the region for part of each year and with the CCC in Canada for the rest of each year, doing interpretation and building solidarity within and among the Canadian churches, deepening their partnership with the churches in the Middle East.

As a result of these initiatives, the CCC's Middle East Working Group, which had been formed in 1986 to co-ordinate the churches' work in the region, was able to present a draft statement on the

Middle East to the CCC Triennial Assembly in Montreal in May 1988. The draft statement was intended to provide a basis for discussion on the Middle East and the means for bringing about reconciliation in the particular situations of conflict that persist in the region. The draft statement was received for discussion by the churches, setting in place a year-long process of study and evaluation that also included the Canadian Jewish Congress and the Canadian Christian-Jewish Consultation. The statement was revised in light of the comments and remarks received and presented to the CCC General Board in October 1989 for approval as a policy document, a guideline for the churches' ongoing involvement in the Middle East.

In this new phase of their work, the Canadian churches have chosen to work in close partnership with the MECC as their involvement in and commitment to the Middle East have deepened. What has this meant for the nature of that encounter? Six elements deserve to be highlighted in this regard. They show that the impact has been two-way — affecting how Canadian churches have come to view the Middle East as well as how they are challenged in their own life and ministries in Canada.

Presence and Witness

Although Western churches are often blind to this fact, the churches of the Middle East date from the time of Christ and the formation of the first Christian community in Jerusalem. Over the centuries they have faced many difficult challenges, among them the rise of Islam and the Crusades, but they have nevertheless remained a vibrant and witnessing community of faith, which today represents about 10 per cent of the population of the region, numbering some fourteen million people.

The churches of the Middle East are used to being in the minority. They live, in effect, in a pre-Constantinian age, where the church is a qualitative rather than a quantitative influence. They have found creative ways of responding to their powerlessness — as the salt in the stew and the leaven in the loaf of society. However, the conflicts of the past forty years have created a sense of deep insecurity among many people in the region, and many Christians have turned to emigration as the only solution to the situation they face. The churches are coming to represent an increasingly smaller minority.

At the same time, Christians are trying to overcome the impression, even among their Muslim and Jewish neighbours, that the church is not a truly indigenous presence in the region, an impression bred by the traditional contact with churches outside the Middle East, particularly in the West. This problem has been compounded by the activities of many Western fundamentalist groups whose missionary activities are pursued without regard for the church in the region, in a manner which is often divisive, creating suspicion among both Christians and non-Christians. The fact that a number of these groups proclaim themselves to be "Christian Zionists" and unquestioningly support the state of Israel on the basis of a literalist interpretation of selected biblical texts only worsens the situation.

For the Canadian churches, this situation has aroused a concern for the continuing presence of the church in the Middle East as an indigenous part of the religious and ethical fabric of the region. Support for their life and witness through prayer, solidarity, and active involvement has also brought the Canadian churches opportunities for rediscovering their own roots, recovering aspects of their own identity, through an encounter with the spirituality and prophetic witness for justice and peace of these churches in the holy lands where the mission and message of the church began. Mission in this context has become a partnership between the churches in Canada and the Middle East, a relationship that holds the promise of renewal for both.

Unity and Partnership

The Canadian churches have, from the start, approached their involvement in the Middle East ecumenically. None of the churches in Canada have a tradition of activity in the Middle East. As a result, they determined to act together in developing the relationship. This has been a unique experience for the churches, providing a concrete opportunity for ecumenical co-operation on a matter of common concern.

At the same time, the Canadian churches came to see that one of the most essential sources of renewal for the churches in the Middle East was the ecumenical movement in the region, particularly since the formation of the MECC in 1974. The churches of the Middle East recognized that it was there that the first divisions within the church took place, and resolved that they had a particular responsibility to become more united in their vision and practice in order to begin healing those historic divisions. The ecumenical partnership of the Canadian churches with the MECC has therefore been a tangible indication of support for the unity of the churches in the region, as well as a contribution to the ecumenical movement in Canada, where the renewal through unity is also sought.

Diversity and Equality

The ecumenical movement in the Middle East is not only a source of renewal and the basis for a credible witness for the churches in the region; it also provides the framework through which the churches view many of the conflicts that divide the region. It is the conviction of the MECC and its member churches that a just resolution of the two primary conflicts in the Middle East today — Lebanon and Palestine — rests on finding the means to enable the diverse religious and ethnic communities in the region to live within a pluralistic environment, respecting one another's distinctiveness within the context of equality and democratic rights and freedoms. In Lebanon, communities fight for dominance despite the fact that it has long been clear that no one group can succeed in presiding over the others. Meanwhile Israel has determined, on the basis of an interpretation of the tragic history of the Jewish people, that security lies in each community possessing its own exclusive confessional state, running its own affairs in isolation from, and even in disregard of, other communities.

The MECC has come to recognize that it is only by building trust and interdependence between communities that the project of forming just and peaceable societies can succeed in the midst of the diversity of the Middle East. A recent series of MECC policies on Lebanon makes this approach clear:

> The response to the Lebanon conflict is a witness to reconciliation, justice and peace, motivated not by any party politics or ideology, but by Jesus Christ's love for humanity as the basis for equality, freedom and human dignity.... Lebanon represents a privileged and unique ecumenical experience, on both the inter-Christian and inter-religious levels. It reflects an experience of dialogue of life, without which dialogue remains simply speculative, without historical impact or effect. By daring to venture through this experience of dialogue, the MECC maintains hope in the possibility of finding a creative model of conviviality that is viable in respect for the mutual rights and equality of all communities.

This model for resolving of the Middle East's central conflicts is particularly evocative in Canada because of our own experience with building community out of communities. We are familiar with the tensions this creates and the determination necessary to bring such a vision to life. It is therefore understandable that the Canadian churches have been influenced by this vision as they have sought ways of showing solidarity with the people of the

Middle East — Christian, Muslim, and Jew — and of supporting the MECC as it endeavours to sow seeds of reconciliation among communities in the midst of conflict.

Courage and Wisdom

Within the disorienting climate of the Middle East's interrelated conflicts, the churches seek to act in faithfulness, not on behalf of any political platform or ideology, nor as a front against any community or group, but out of an awareness of Jesus Christ's love for humanity as the basis for equality, freedom, and dignity. In this spirit the MECC aims to promote a common and inclusive response by the churches to issues threatening justice and peace.

This has several implications for the MECC's work. This approach addresses issues of human rights and peacemaking with a mixture of courage and wisdom. The MECC must have the courage to take initiative, to not always be in the position of reacting to events as they unfold, of falling into a minority mentality that breeds inaction and isolation among the churches of the region. The churches of the Middle East must try to take positive steps to challenge the patterns of violence and oppression that have been so costly and self-defeating. It takes a certain wisdom and patience to face these challenges, considering that, in their view, the solution is ultimately the result of the action of the Holy Spirit, whose time cannot be questioned. Reconciling courage and wisdom in confronting the forces of death and division in the Middle East has been a crucial lesson for the churches in Canada as they have become active in a region where lines are not easily drawn between victim and oppressor, empowerment and the oppressive exercise of power, where all have suffered but where suffering has all too often brought isolation and exclusiveness rather than solidarity.

Information and Interpretation

This predicament, where victims become oppressors and oppressors victims, where cycles of injustice have been repeated "unto the next generation," has created much confusion in the minds of observers. Rathering than facing the difficult task of presenting the region in all its many facets, observers have been tempted to force it into the stereotypes of good guys and bad guys, white hats and black hats, which just adds further to the confusion.

The MECC has put a priority on its task of responsibly informing and interpreting the history, people, and events in the region, with a view to contributing to the forces of change. This task has also been picked up by the Canadian churches as they seek to explain their concern with the region and its churches to Canadians. Stereotypes and oversimplifications tend to serve one community over another. To take the task of reconciliation seriously, the churches have had to rebuild a responsible and reliable understanding of the events and issues that have shaped the region, while at the same time showing that the picture does not need to be as complex as some groups would like to make it appear to be. People can gain an objective understanding, and that in turn can enable them to see concrete ways of becoming involved in bringing just peace to a region traumatized by war, misunderstanding, and suspicion.

Theology and Scripture

As the home of the three Abrahamic faiths, the Middle East remains charged with the passion of religious conviction, both within and among religious communities. Unfortunately, while one might hope that this would provide an ethical and tolerant framework for resolving disputes and regulating relationships among communities, it has all too often fostered intolerance and absolutism. Religious perspectives are used to support political programs; religious sentiment is used to suppress human conscience. Misuse of religious sentiment can be a potent force in the promotion of injustice and conflict.

The MECC has therefore been determined, where possible, to criticize the misuse of theological and scriptural traditions and sources — misuse that betrays the very foundation of common spiritual heritage that binds the three faiths together. Such criticism is combined with a forceful restatement of themes of tolerance, liberation, freedom, humility, and love — themes all too regularly pushed aside in favour of assertions of power, exclusivity, and divine right. Canadian churches, in their statements and discussions on the region, have also tried to respond to the deeper issues that often fuel antagonism and aggression, which then erupt in confrontation, conflict, and more human suffering. Having seen the cost of the misuse of Christian theology in the past to oppress and destroy, the Canadian churches are determined to bring to the surface such distortions now, lest they breed even worse wars and holocausts in the future.

Canadian author Robertson Davies once said that while Canada wasn't at the heart of the action in the world, it was nevertheless "an excellent seat." Until recently, that remark was certainly apt, in a cynical way, in regared to the involvement of the Canadian churches in the Middle East. But no longer. It is, after all, hard to read about Jerusalem, Bethlehem, Damascus, Tyre, and Sidon in the Bible and then turn on the radio to hear about uprisings, civil wars, and occupations in the Middle East without beginning to put the two together — much as we would like to avoid it.

Reconciliation is costly. This is particularly true in the Middle East, where passions run high and where the Western churches have been confused by guilt and cultural inheritances that have fostered inaction and ignorance. The Middle East has been the orphan of the peace movement for too long. The conflicts have cost the lives of hundreds of thousands of people and have threatened on many occasions to draw the rest of the world into their grip.

The primary image of reconciliation for the Christian church is that of Christ on the Cross. The mystery of his suffering, and the reconciliation and hope it brought, has nurtured Christian community ever since. Having been shaped by the traditions of faith that arose in those lands, Christian churches are co-operating across political borders to take up their responsibility to support the work of shaping a new future for the people who now call those lands home.

II
Promoting Change and Development

4 • Building a Counter-Consensus in Canada

Robert Gardiner

In the early 1970s, Canadian officials used to tell heads of churches that Canada was unable to be more assertive in promoting the global changes that would allow just development in the Third World. The government lacked the mandate for that sort of action. Canadians didn't care about the Third World, and few members of Parliament heard such issues raised in their ridings. Church leaders were not willing to accept that judgement. These were the days, after all, when the misery in the Sahel and the horrors of apartheid filled the television screens of the nation.

The church leaders set out to demonstrate that there was indeed a counter-consensus in Canada, one that favoured justice for the Third World. The project became known as Ten Days for World Development. It is a development education program in which thousands of Canadians work annually at the task of deepening that counter-consensus and of ensuring that MPs hear how much Canadians care about foreign policy as it affects the poorest of the poor.

Robert Gardiner is a retired Anglican priest who now lives in England. As the first co-ordinator of the Ten Days for World Development program, he helped the churches develop a balance of educational resources and Third World visitors to provide support for the public education efforts of local organizers.

— Ed.

The Origins of Ten Days for World Development

People found it hard to believe, at first, that what the churches were up to was consciousness raising about world development, not money raising. The guts of the Ten Days for World Development program, launched in the early seventies, was to proclaim the priority of justice over charity. The churches of Canada were second to none in their commitment to charity. The people of Canada had always responded compassionately and generously to disaster and distress, often through the charitable organizations of the churches. But the churches had enough experience with relief efforts both domestically and internationally to know that charity was not enough.

Because of their worldwide missionary contacts, the churches had always been channels for overseas relief efforts. These led logically to development programs, nurturing and funding a wide variety of Third World self-help projects in agriculture, housing, medicine, and small industry. In the sixties, church "relief" agencies were amending their names to "relief and development" agencies. By the early seventies, these agencies were co-operating ecumenically through ad hoc gatherings of what went by the mouthful of the Inter-Church Consultative Committee for Development and Relief (ICCCDR).

Ten Days for World Development was the brainchild of ICCCDR. Something dramatic needed to be done to make Canadians more conscious of world development issues and to convert them to an awareness of the importance of justice over charity. Why not have the top brass of the five mainstream churches go on a high-profile junket to selected cities in Canada? Surely the arrival in a city on the same plane and proclaiming the same message at rallies, on TV, on radio, and at meetings with government, business and labour of the Anglican primate, the president of the Canadian Conference of Catholic Bishops, and three Protestant church moderators ought to convince people that the churches had buried their differences and were united in the urgent cause of Third World development. The Canadian International Development Agency (CIDA) was sufficiently intrigued by the idea that to get it off the ground it chipped in money to match that of the churches. Staff was hired. An educational packet was widely distributed. Two films were produced for showing on CBC TV for the occasion. A joint policy statement entitled "Development Demands Justice" was prepared. Cities in which some inter-church development education was already occurring were selected and alerted to make their most appropriate use of the leaders' visit. Early in 1973, Ten Days for World Development was launched.

The "Ten Days" themselves referred to a period from a Friday to one week from the following Monday, during the weeks after Christmas and before Lent, for which resources were provided to encourage development education events in as many Canadian communities as possible. The expectation, of course, was that such a once-a-year concentrated effort would stimulate year-round activities on behalf of the people of the Third World. This has proven to be so.

The leaders' tour was a resounding success. In Vancouver, they made TV and radio open-line appearances and addressed a large gathering of business and government people. A stopover media interview occurred at the Calgary airport. In addition to public and media appearances in Edmonton, a brief was presented to Premier Peter Lougheed and his cabinet that resulted in provincial matching of contributions to Third World causes and financial support for development education efforts within Alberta. There was also an exchange with trade union leaders. Media and public appearances were repeated in London and Toronto. In Ottawa, the leaders appeared as witnesses before the All-Party Parliamentary Committee on International Affairs. Members of Parliament (MPs) claimed that their constituents never raised Third World development matters ("not a sexy issue," they declared). It was a reality that would take time to correct. They also didn't seem to comprehend that the churches were as much, if not more, concerned with trade and structural issues as with aid. This too would take time. A detailed expansion of the "Development Demands Justice" policy statement was presented as a brief to the federal cabinet. Quebec City was the site of a large media-covered gathering at a church in the "Quartier des Pauvres" and of the presentation of the justice brief to Premier Robert Bourassa and his cabinet. Halifax made good use of the leaders in a series of public and media events.

There were a couple of ironic qualifications to the success of the tour. There were some CBC television interviewers who asked such silly questions as "How much do you expect to raise in this campaign, Bishop?" It would take a few more years to crack this mind-set. In fairness, it must be said that many interviewers did their homework with the advance publicity packets and conducted thoughtful, in-depth interviews. There was also the problem that many people were so awed by the sight of the top leaders of the mainstream churches in agreement on the same platform that their message was obscured. Again, it would take time to establish that the churches were at one on international justice issues.

How do you follow such an act? You don't. You keep plugging away at citizen awareness of the structural and systemic causes of why the wretched of the earth are getting more wretched and the fat cats, fatter. Ten Days did this by continuing pressure and slow growth throughout the remainder of the seventies and the early eighties. Well-researched and attractive packets were important supports for the local leaders who undertook this effort. After a few years of nationally sponsored tours by Third World figures, volunteers in the regions wanted Third World resource people to work in depth in one region, rather than a few to travel the entire country, hitting only the biggest cities. In time, there would be regional representation on the central planning committee.

In the early days, the themes people tackled were geographic. In 1974 the Sahel drought was creating misery; Angola, Mozambique, and Guinea Bissau were still under Portuguese domination; there were glimmers of hope from Tanzania; and the horrors of apartheid were becoming better known. An informative African packet and a national tour by Bishop Peter Sarpong of Ghana fed the need for the facts.

That issues of international justice and national justice are interrelated was patent but needed spelling out in detail. In 1975 groups worked on the parallels between Canadian and Third World problems: for example, the impact of tourism on Prince Edward Island and on the Caribbean, the threat to cultural autonomy in Quebec and the American media invasion of Latin America. "The Voice of the Third World," Dom Helder Camera, bishop of Recife, Brazil, inspired and stimulated audiences in several Canadian cities. When he spoke to a capacity audience at the St. Lawrence Centre, he received exhaustive front-page coverage in the *Toronto Star* the next day. He enthralled audiences, young and old, church and secular, in Ottawa and Montreal. When he understood the facts about Canadian provincial disparity, he insisted upon going to St. John's, Newfoundland. A true apostle of peace and justice was in our midst.

When the United Nations (UN) began promoting the New International Economic Order through the UN Conference on Trade and Development (UNCTAD), the churches ran up against the problem of popularizing a complex and abstract concept. The solution was one that helped shape the churches' preference for the concrete experience of people in the Third World as well as serious analysis. The resource team that year was made up of two people: Marion Gallis, an UNCTAD economist, and Subir Biswas, a Calcutta pavement worker. Against all odds, their trans-Canada tour worked.

Ten Days' Decision to Focus on Specific Issues

By the late 1970s the commitment to development education had taken root and committees had formed in many cities and towns across the country. People were caught up in the momentum; development issues were better understood, and increasing numbers of volunteers and participants were looking forward to each year's educational materials and resource persons. The time had come for people to work with an issue for more than one year. The churches decided that three full years would be spent on the food issue. These were three years of disciplined study during which local leaders were able to build on the previous year's work, to learn from their mistakes, and to make steady progress as volunteers in the development education field. The food issue captured the imagination and sympathy of thousands of Canadians, in part because it created an "optic," understandable to virtually everyone, as an entry point for studying international economic issues. The information packets explicated the reality and dimensions of malnutrition and scarcity throughout the world. The role of women in Third World food production was underscored. The exploitation of Third World families by the dumping and high-pressure promotion of infant formulas by companies such as Nestlé was exposed. Francis Moore Lappé of *Diet for a Small Planet* fame came to Canada to explain the wastefulness and injustice of eating off the top of the food chain. Susan George, author of *How the Other Half Dies*, outlined how the operations of international agri-business promoted hunger, malnutrition, and death. Gonzolo Aroyo of the University of Paris shared his research into the economy of world agriculture. Many people wanted Ten Days to stay with the food issue. But the planners of the program, which now included grassroots volunteers, saw that its mandate was the broad theme of international justice and chose to push on to other issues, knowing that many other organizations would keep up the pressure on the food issue.

The Issue of Work in the Third World

Over the three years of the focus on food, people had identified hunger as a symptom of some people having too little money in their pockets to survive (rather than the world lacking the resources to feed the population, as some claimed in those days). Therefore, a logical progression from the food issue was the issue of work. The next couple of years were devoted to it. There was not the enthusiastic response to the work issue that there had been to the food issue. This was no doubt because this theme lacked the substantial theoretical analysis that lay behind the food issue. There was also the timidity of middle-class church and community volunteers in approaching and harnessing efforts with local trade unions. However, the reality of the new international division of labour by which Third World countries were no longer just suppliers of raw materials but assemblers and manufacturers of goods was elucidated. Individual life stories helped to put flesh on this rather abstract and distant trend. You only had to see the long queues of emaciated 'teen-age girls waiting in Columbo, Sri Lanka, for buses into the free trade zone to realize that here is the new proletariat!

From Theory to Action

At a World Council of Churches (WCC) meeting in Geneva in the mid-seventies, development educators remarked that the Canadian churches produced some of the best development education print materials in the world but that they completely lacked any follow-through action component! By the early eighties, the hundreds of people involved in leading local groups of Ten Days committees were making plans to correct this deficiency. A strong action program was initiated. The focus was at first geographic, concerning Central America, particularly Nicaragua. In addition to its ongoing provision of educational materials and Third World resource persons to the regions, action packets and leaflets giving background and advice for lobbying efforts with Ottawa and MPs were widely used. It was delightful to receive a complaint from people at External Affairs that the department had been so inundated with letters from across the country that they had to hire additional staff to handle the load. How did we expect External Affairs to get on with its important work if its staff had to deal with so much mail from the Canadian public? How ironic in view of the parliamentary criticism at the launch of Ten Days that the churches were not doing enough to stimulate concern among Canadians for Third World issues! The churches had set out to build a consensus in favour of justice for the Third World. They had discovered that many Canadians, in fact, shared a passion for such justice. What it took was a bit of effort to create public moments when that counter-consensus could coalesce and people could make their views known in their local communities and with public officials.

After nearly eighteen years of life, Ten Days has evolved from being a program in which the top brass of churches try to stir up interest in development to being a movement of people across the country engaged in development education for the long haul. Some 250 local committees now plan the program that is most suited to the communities they work in. Those committees — made up almost entirely of people working in their leisure hours — meet in regional and subregional networks, circulate reports on their successes and failures, and send representatives to an annual national consultation to set objectives for the next year's work. At this end of the project, it is obvious that the church leaders who toured the country back in the early 1970s were really catalysts for bringing people together around a subject they care about passionately — whatever the claims of people in Ottawa.

Probably the entire program would have died if the movement had not taken over the original project. By the mid-eighties, no one expected a Third World visitor and a bishop to capture national media attention anymore. Once or twice is the limit for that sort of coverage. Trying to do development education via media headlines was not enough. The local committees became the carriers of the vision and provided the momentum for a different perspective to enter their local schools, media, and churches.

In the hands of local committees, the action component has put a different spin on the churches' conventional methods of raising foreign policy issues with government. Instead of in a letter signed by heads of churches to the secretary of state for external affairs and to opposition critics, the issues began to be raised in meetings between committed and informed citizens and their own MPs. Those same MPs have served on panels in local public meetings on subjects such as the Canadian link to the Third World debt crisis or the ways in which Canada's development assistance programs could be changed to make them more supportive of real development. Citizen diplomacy of this sort is important, according to a group of MPs who were surveyed in 1985. A Progressive Conservative wrote: "Your support in urging the Canadian government to pursue an enlightened and progressive policy toward our Latin American neighbours is greatly appreciated. Together we *will* make a difference." Another MP wrote that he appreciated the local educational opportunities in his riding and the effort to influence government policy.

Back in the early seventies, Canadian church leaders stepped out together to try to drum up a bit of support for Third World development issues. What they found were thousands of Canadians passionately committed to justice for the peoples of the Third World. What they were looking for was a bit of effort to create public moments when that counter-consensus could coalesce and people could stand up and be counted in their local communities and with public officials. No church leader could have asked for more.

5 • Setting the Table for All God's People: Canadian Churches and Development

Marjorie Ross

Canadian missionaries formed a kind of underground contact with people in much of the Third World, long before that term had entered the vocabulary. Their efforts drew churches into programs of emergency relief for people in the countries where they worked. But, by the end of the 1950s, it had become clear that development assistance was more important than emergency relief. By the 1970s, those early missionary contacts had fostered something else altogether: a sense of solidarity with people engaged in movements for change in newly independent nations.

Canadian churches have had to struggle with their own biases in funding development and solidarity projects overseas. They have also had to engage the members of their congregations in advocating the political and economic changes that would allow us to welcome everyone to God's table. In the process they have had to question their own capacity to promote change, particularly when the people being welcomed to the table are women.

Marjorie Ross has served as a missionary in Africa and has represented the Canadian churches in many regional consultations on development and human rights, including a major conference on women and development in Nairobi. She was World Affairs staff of the Canadian Council of Churches in the mid-1980s, where she was responsible for co-ordinating the churches' foreign policy review and their work on official development assistance. She is currently on the staff of the Taskforce on the Churches and Corporate Responsibility, where she has guided the churches' debates on Third World debt.

— Ed.

Introduction

Canadian churches have had first-hand experience in developing countries for one hundred and fifty years. For more than half that time, it was the letters home and the speaking tours of Canadian missionaries "returned from foreign lands" that gave Canadian communities their only direct contact with Africa, Asia, South America, and the Pacific Islands....

Our churches are still closely involved, through the invitation of independent national churches, in the lives and struggles of ordinary people in Africa, Asia, and Latin America. We see the effect, for good or ill, of Canadian aid programs in those countries. We know personally the tragic stories of refugees in Southeast Asia, of urban slum-dwellers in Latin America, of poverty-stricken rural women in Africa. We know the aspirations of the people of the least developed countries. We are friends and colleagues of the leaders of churches in South Africa and human rights organizations in Central America who are working to bring justice to their people, often at the risk of their lives. Our learnings from these men and women, our church partners around the world, have formed the basis of our recommendations for Canadian government policy.[1]

These paragraphs are contained in the foreword to a major brief prepared by the Canadian Council of Churches (CCC) for submission to a parliamentary review of Canada's foreign policy in 1985. They were quoted several months later in a World Council of Churches (WCC) publication, a gratifying recognition for the brief's authors, since Canadian churches often feel overlooked in Geneva.

From the perspective of almost four years since that time, there is probably not much in these paragraphs that we would change. In fact, the last sentence is more significant than it seemed to us at the time. It is true: we *have* learned from our partners and from our shared experiences over the past two decades. What we have learned — about mission, about partnership and solidarity, about development and how change takes place, about evil entrenched in systems — is the subject of this chapter.

The Churches and Development: Structural Change and Solidarity in the Struggle

When those most closely involved in the development work of the churches today are asked to define what it is all about, they usually use two phrases: "working for structural change" and "being in solidarity in the struggle." We may not realize that behind these two phrases lie twenty-five years of changing perceptions. It is helpful in understanding the unresolved issues facing churches today to know the distance we have travelled and some of the landmarks along the way.

From Famine Relief to Structural Change

In the past, Canadian churches related to the developing world in two ways: as "sending" or missionary churches and as providers of relief for victims of wars and disasters. The first role underwent a transformation approximately twenty-five years ago, with the transfer of power and control from Canadian mission boards to newly independent local churches. At about the same time as the colonial powers were divesting themselves of their possessions, the missionary churches of the First World were relinquishing control of their carefully nurtured dependencies. The churches moved out of the missionary era and entered a much more complex period of mission partnerships and development activity.

For the churches with historical mission programs, the first stage in this development activity — emergency aid — evolved naturally, for an important dimension of "foreign work" had always been the relief of famine and assistance in the material aspects of life. Countless bales of clothing had been sent overseas to the victims of wars and disasters, and special collections for the hungry millions of China and India were a familiar part of Canadian church life.

Famine relief in those parts of the world that were Canadian "mission fields" consumed part of overseas mission budgets, but in the years following the Second World War the needs of a war-devastated world necessitated numerous special appeals. Each of the churches established its own agency (to a greater or lesser extent separate from their main fund-raising structures) to handle the funds raised by these appeals. The Anglican primate, having made special appeals in each of the previous five years, established the Primate's World Relief Fund in 1959; the Presbyterians appointed the Committee on Inter-Church Aid, Refugee and World Service, named after the World Council of Churches' (WCC) aid agency; and the United Church formed the Committee on Overseas Relief and Inter-Church Aid.

Two other Canadian churches — the Lutherans and the Mennonites — had a shorter history in this country and so lacked the history of overseas mission involvement. However, their members, largely composed of recently arrived immigrants, were also strong supporters of refugee and relief organizations. Each had a denominational organization — Canadian Lutheran World Relief and the Mennonite Central Committee (Canada).

It was from these relief organizations that the present church development agencies have evolved, and all of them continue to carry the responsibility for channelling emergency funds overseas. The Roman Catholic agency, the Canadian Catholic Organization for Development and Peace, was created later, and although it too has a relief function, its primary purpose has always been development, not aid.

Meanwhile, international church relief organizations had come into being and provided channels through which the small Canadian churches could direct their emergency assistance, a practice that continues to this day. (It is ironic that the six churches that now make joint grants through the Inter-Church Fund for International Development [ICFID] continue to work denominationally through four international networks: CARITAS [Development and Peace]; Commission on Inter-Church Aid, Refugee and World Service — CICARWS [Primate's Fund, Presbyterians, United Church]; Lutheran World Relief [Canadian Lutheran World Relief]; and Mennonite Central Committee [Mennonite Central Committee (Canada)]. The three churches that work through CICARWS meet together in the Development and Service Committee of the Canadian Council of Churches. Thus, the fragmented international scene intrudes in a rather confusing fashion into Canadian ecumenicity.)

So, by the late 1950s, some Canadian churches were consciously moving into a new era of "mission partnership," and all had developed structures through which relief could be sent to the "less fortunate people overseas." A shift of focus had taken place: with the recovery of Europe almost complete and with China closed to the West, the new countries of Africa and Asia were seen as in most need of help.

It was at this point that there was a shift in thinking about Third World aid, from a "relief" mentality to a "development assistance" approach. A slogan used at this time (and which still strikes those who hear it for the first time as profound) was "Give a man a fish, and you feed him for a day; teach him how to fish and you have fed him for a lifetime." The advance from relief to development is neatly captured; so is the paternalistic belief that people in the Third World go hungry because they lack the technology we in more developed countries have acquired. Canadians came to understand that relief, although always necessary in emergencies, was not the long-term answer to poverty. The answer for the early 1960s was economic development. This was an easy transition for most people to make: it fitted neatly into the pride North Americans felt in their prosperity and "know-how." It also appealed to the generosity of spirit of many good-hearted folk who wished to share some of their good fortune with the rest of the world, and saw this as a more practical way to help than by endless handouts. Exactly the same approach was — and is —

taken towards the marginalized in Canada. Conventional wisdom says that training programs are better than welfare.

The churches received a significant impetus towards development from the example of their government. Canada had been asked by Britain and the United States "to share the burden of assistance to the newly independent countries of Asia and Africa."[2] Canadian churches reflected their government's newfound interest in Third World development and redirected some of the energy and resources that had supported the missionary movement into small-scale economic development overseas.

In this new era of independence, it was assumed that the tasks of evangelism and nurture of the community of believers could (by and large) be left in the hands of the local church. A major role of the former "sending church" was to back up the efforts of its partner with technical assistance as it worked to improve the quality of life for its community. For this task, Canadian churches sent new kinds of missionaries — agriculturalists and water engineers.

While the transition from relief to development assistance was accomplished very smoothly, another change, considerably more radical, was soon to follow. As Canadian churches participated in these 1960s development projects, something happened that changed their outlook on the world. A whole new crop of ideas took root, whose seeds may have blown in on the 1960s winds of change, but more likely were the result of the experiences of some (not all) of the young Christians they sent out as "new style" missionaries.

Many of the young Canadian missionaries went out with some of the same motivations as their contemporaries, the Canadian University Service Overseas (CUSO) and Peace Corps volunteers whose programs were launched at the same time. They also went with some diffidence, fully conscious of the mistakes of the past, but willing to learn from the people with whom they were to share their technical knowledge. As it turned out, many of them learned far more than they were able to teach.

Like their secular colleagues, they returned, if not radicalized, at least having had their world view profoundly changed. Many had become convinced that the development programs in which they had worked could never come close to addressing the problems of underdevelopment or to righting global injustices. From the perspectives of the African bush or Latin American barrios, these injustices, only dimly perceived before, were glaringly obvious.

They had found that the slogan about teaching people to fish had severe limitations. What good did it do a people to know how to fish (assuming they hadn't known before) or to have better boats and nets as gifts from Canadian Christians if their traditional fishing grounds were polluted by the waste of a factory or a mine owned by a foreign corporation? What use was better equipment if their government, a corrupt dictatorship, leased their beach to a foreign-owned tourist hotel and declared it off-limits to fishing boats? What use was the equipment if foreign-owned trawlers with mile-wide nets stripped their fishing grounds bare?

In each case, there would be those who argued (often including the country's government) that "development" meant that these people should abandon fishing and subsistence farming to become workers in the mines and factories and tourist hotels. More objective observers of these situations saw that the people were being forced out of comparatively self-reliant situations in which they were at least able to feed themselves into dependency as employees of companies in which the decisions were made in other countries. Their situation was incomparably worse than, for example, a Canadian employee in a U.S. branch plant, since they had no protection in law and their government was controlled by a wealthy upper class whose economic interest coincided with that of these same foreign companies.

Certainly it had been helpful in a small way to assist them to obtain better boats, but any real or lasting improvement in their lives would have to come as the result of profound political and economic changes. Some, like land reform and the achievement of truly democratic government, could only come about internally, through the actions of the people themselves. Others involved changes in international laws and in the trading relations between rich and poor countries, which would require the co-operation of the whole world community.

The goal was still the same: to enable people to meet their basic needs. But the way to reach that goal had become far longer and more difficult. For these young Canadians, development had ceased to mean small-scale projects like digging wells; it had come to mean change in the economic and political structures.

Moreover, the corollary to this realization was that it was no longer adequate to give people wells or tools or boats. What was needed was support for them as they struggled to achieve the rights that in justice were theirs. The history of the Primate's Fund describes this change.

There was a move from a response of simple charity to a deep concern about justice....

"Aid" ... had something to do with the right of peasants and workers to a living wage, access to land and some share of the wealth of their country; development, furthermore, had something to do with the right of people to organize themselves in peaceful efforts to improve their lives, without the fear of arbitrary arrest, torture or assassination. Development was inextricably linked, whether we liked it or not, with social, economic, and political justice.

... Scripturally, [this change of thinking] represented a deeper understanding of Matthew 25 in light of Christ's declaration of his mission (Luke 4:16-19). Not only are we required to give water to the thirsty, clothe the naked and feed the hungry, but we are required to lift the yoke of oppression. We are to go about the work of Christ in bringing about the Kingdom of God. And what is meant by the Kingdom of God? ... whatever else, it certainly means working for the establishment of a "new order," in which "God's will is done on earth."

Closely allied to this was the realization that the task of the Church was not to preserve the *status quo* but to *transform* society in accordance with God's will.[3]

Those who had thought to find in development a secular substitute for mission found that their experiences of poverty and injustice in the Third World brought them back to theology on a more profound and complex level.

During the late 1960s and early 1970s, this awareness of the implications of development spread beyond the ranks of returned volunteers and a few insightful church leaders and gradually became part of church policies. World events taking place at the same time reinforced a wider acceptance of what had seemed at first to be radical concepts. In retrospect, the most important of these events were the struggles in Southern Africa, the civil strife in Central America (the revolution in Nicaragua and the human rights abuses in El Salvador), and the failure of the United Nations (UN) to revise the terms of trade in ways that would benefit the Third World.

Early in this period, in 1967, the Canadian Catholic Organization for Development and Peace (called Development and Peace) was founded as a conscious response to some of the influences just described. (An additional impetus was the contact the Canadian bishops had with their colleagues from the Third World during the four years of Vatican II.)[4]

Very important for all the churches — although it took longer for the Protestants to realize it — was the emergence of liberation theology in Latin America, Christianity as understood by the poor. After a visit to one of the base Christian communities, even the most skeptical of Canadian observers had to concede that the Good News of Jesus Christ not only had taken root in the lives of ordinary men and women, but was leading them to challenge the injustice and oppression that weighs so heavily on them and their neighbours.

Gradually, through the 1970s, the Canadian church development agencies moved to understanding development as structural change. But it is a long road from theory to practice, and it was far simpler to agree on the inadequacy of 1960s-style development than to determine what Canadian churches should do instead. Step by step, sometimes through trial and error, a common program evolved. A few churches moved ahead more quickly in some areas than did others; typically, ecumenical activities were often slightly in advance of what the majority of the churches were doing individually.

At the same time an evolution was taking place in our relations with our Third World friends. Since this had a direct impact on the application of our development theories, we should pause in our discussion of structural change to look at "solidarity" and what it has come to mean.

Solidarity in the Struggle:
Has More Changed Than the Language?

Despite its earlier radical overtones, the word "solidarity" has acquired respectability, even in rather conservative circles, probably because of its use in Poland. It is now in common use in development circles and marks a significant evolution from earlier language.

As we have seen, the first development concept was that we in the North would teach those in the Third World, theoretically "to bring them up to our level." This was rapidly supplanted by a new awareness that no truly valid development can take place unless it is initiated by the people themselves in response to a felt need. We also came to realize that all too often it is not lack of knowledge but lack of justice that keeps people poor and hungry. The next stage was a period where we spoke of "helping our partners in their struggle." This is language that still creeps into the vocabulary, particularly in connection with oppressive situations where human rights are violated to such an extent that staying alive becomes the only possible goal.

More and more, however, our friends in developing countries point out that this way of describing development implies that they are the only ones who must struggle. They ask, "What are the problems you must work to overcome? Are not some of them very similar to our own?" And, in fact, we realize that we have allowed the differences in our economic levels to blind us to the unjust economic structures that operate in Canada as well as in Brazil. The language of "helping" still has about it the old paternalism, which, albeit well-meaning, is the antithesis of our present understanding of partnership.

"Partnership" itself is a loaded word, for this is the term that was introduced to mark the change in the relationship between the "sending" or "mother" churches and their dependent "mission churches." Canadian churches have participated in long and often painful discussions in WCC and Catholic conferences on this subject. What are the implications of partnerships in which one partner from Europe or North America has all the money, while the other from the Third World is scrambling to find projects and programs that will win support?

The most creative contribution to this dilemma in relationships came in two WCC conferences held in 1987, one in Larnaca, Cyprus, and one in El Escorial, Spain. Christians from the South argued eloquently that we must come to know one another as Christians and as human beings before we start talking about sharing money. As a woman from Africa put it, "Let us share the 'who' we are first, before we share 'what' we have.... Christians are called to share the understanding of (each other's) pains before sharing the resources to remove them."[5] This understanding of resource sharing suggests that the word "partnership," with its emphasis on a shared venture, has perhaps some monetary overtones. Many have suggested that "companions" travelling together to a common goal is a better description.

For all these reasons, the current emphasis in development relationships, if it is about helping at all, is about mutual help. Christians from North and South are working side by side in a common task.

Different churches, and many people within those churches, are at different points along the continuum just described, but since one concept evolves from another, there are no very sharp disjunctures.

The Churches and Their Struggles with Structural Change

The problems are much more evident when we return to the question of how the churches cope with the concept of development as promoting structural change. While these problems seem to be related to the issue of our relationships in the Third World, they also reveal the churches' frailties as human organizations.

Very simply stated, working for structural change means taking sides, and it means getting involved with politics, neither of which seems, for many, to be part of Christian charity. Furthermore, it brings us face to face with the reality that here and in the Third World the church is allied with the "haves" rather than with the "have-nots."

Contained in the policies of several of the development agencies are attempts to articulate what is meant by this structural change. The Anglican General Synod, meeting in 1969 (when it may have appeared that the old order was changing altogether too rapidly!), changed the name of the Primate's Fund to include the word "development" and approved a policy that contains the following point: "Society must increase its capacity to incorporate change, even fundamental and radical change without chaos."[6] When the fund's general policy was approved by the Synod in 1973, it seemed that fears of chaos had receded, for this point is worded as follows (emphasis added):

> *Society must increase its capacity to incorporate change, even fundamental and radical change.* More devastating to society than low levels of consumption is flagrant disparity between people; more explosive today is the grossly unequal power of different elements of the population. *The past and the future must be held together in a dynamic way; this means fluid and adaptable institutions, and the right and ability of people to change their institutions.*[7]

The Mission Statement of Presbyterian World Service endorses change by implication: "Development is a process through which individuals, groups, and societies move towards fullness of life as God intended."[8] Its list of criteria for projects that will be funded is more specific. Among other things, a project should work "to increase awareness [in those affected by the project] of systemic deficiencies and [provide] tools and skills to create change."[9]

The question is, how is this support for systemic change to be expressed in projects? The practical problems for the volunteers who regularly screen and approve projects are obvious. It is one thing to agree that many institutions, structures, and systems do not operate to everyone's benefit. The next step is also fairly easy: we can agree that such systems are evil and must be changed. But how will that happen? How do we get there from here? Or, to use the Anglicans' more elegant phrase, how do we hold the past, the present, and the future together in a dynamic way?

To take a practical example, it is a considerable leap from acknowledging that poverty will never be alleviated in Central America without land reform to providing funds for a group of peasants who are actively working towards that end. There are many questions. The peasants' gain will be the landowners' loss; how would we feel if we were in the landowners' shoes? How would homeowners in Canada's major cities feel if house prices were arbitrarily lowered to make shelter available to the poor? What if this group we are funding resorts to violence? All of these questions worry us and slow our hands when it comes to actually funding change.

In the end, it is far simpler for a church development agency to support a water project or a community centre for those peasants than to support them in the organizing and conscious-ness-raising activities that must precede political action. All the more conservative churches, the Canadian Baptist Overseas Mis-sion Board (CBOMB), the Salvation Army, and others fund water projects, community centres, and similar projects exclusively. The temptation to take the easy course is always there, even for the churches that believe that development means radical change.

It is very much to the churches' credit that this temptation is so often resisted. However, the smaller churches, perhaps more conservative, certainly closer to their constituencies, tend to fund the human rights and structural change projects, which are politi-cally sensitive vis-à-vis their contributors and the Canadian Inter-national Development Agency (CIDA), through the Inter-Church Fund for International Development. Their own lists of projects are much less controversial. (It should be noted, however, that Presbyterian World Service has recently given these ICFID grants publicity in its quarterly newsletter.)

The Church's "Partners" in Development and Structural Change

There are many who ask if it is possible in the long run for the institutional church, itself a conservative structure, to fund and promote real change. The question becomes especially pointed if the Canadian institution tries to effect change in a developing country by working through its church partner, another institution, which, if not part of the problem, would certainly rather baptize and bury the faithful than take sides in a political struggle. (It is interesting to speculate how Canadian churches would react if a church agency from Chile, for example, began to fund groups working for radical change in Canada.) The argument tends to focus on the weight that should be given to preserving and enhancing church partnerships as compared with that given to promoting development activities that will produce change.

This last point is at the centre of most of the controversies in church development circles. At the risk of oversimplifying, we can situate the churches in ICFID along a continuum that begins at one end with top priority going to mission partnerships (with development criteria a close second) and continues to the other end where development criteria are clearly most important, and church partnerships, while a welcome adjunct, are by no means essential.

What we are describing here are admittedly only nuances of policy, but these are sufficiently strong to have sparked some heated debates. An indication of the strong feelings involved was the objections by Catholic members of the Debt Study Network, which drafted a working paper on international debt, to the use of the phrase "church partners."[10] Representatives of Development and Peace and members of the Catholic orders urged that this phrase be altered to "partners from churches *and popular groups* in the Third World."

Behind this caution concerning church partners is a reality that Development and Peace has long faced. In many countries its partners are community groups, which may well have a church base and whose members are certainly Christian, but which receive very little support from official church structures. In some instances, the hierarchy is actively opposed to these groups' activities. In these cases, Development and Peace carries out its development activities quite separately from, rather than in partnership with, the official church partner.

Protestant development agencies also work with these groups in Latin America, but do not have the problem of relating to the hierarchy. This problem arises for them, in a slightly less acute form, in India, where the grass-roots Christian groups are far more dynamic than the official Indian church development agency.

Several of the churches have struggled with the dilemma of the long-standing partner who resists tackling the hard issues in its country — the human rights abuses of minorities or the root causes of poverty. A few are considering reducing some partnerships to the level of courtesy visits while diverting funds to other countries. New partners are often chosen on the basis of their attitude towards development; frequently the ecumenical council in a country will prove to have a more open attitude than a single denominational partner — again, not unlike the Canadian situation.

But the question raised above, as to whether the church is by its nature the wrong vehicle to promote change, remains unanswered. Many in development circles (and in ecumenical justice circles in Canada) would say that it is; they would urge that the church launch initiatives out into society, support them with funds to some extent, but let them develop independently. Canadian churches found that, with the more "cutting edge" development projects, they are relating to groups with fairly tenuous official church connections. There will continue to be worried people on project-selection committees who want to be assured that every project has official church sanction. For them, the response may have to be, "Take a chance with giving them a grant, and see what happens. By their fruits you shall know them."

Canadian Participation in the Struggle: Education and Advocacy

Promoting structural change and practising solidarity with our partners come together in the Canada-focused programs of the development agencies: education and advocacy.

Canadian Christians, who see their partners in the Third World struggling with almost overwhelming problems, frequently ask them, "What can we do?" Often their partners request support with financial grants, but they also respond by saying, "Tell your people. Tell them what is happening to us; help them see that because they are part of the worldwide economic system, they are part of the problem. Help them see they can also be part of the solution. You and your people must struggle in your situation, just as we are struggling in ours to bring about change." As we have seen, the churches moved from believing that "the right kind of development" would raise the living standard of the people of developing countries to realizing that projects alone could never achieve that goal unless structural change took place. They soon learned that very few shared this understanding of the realities of development; theirs was a rather lonely vision. Before long, the sharing of this vision (a process perhaps rather patronizingly termed education) became a priority.

Moving from Promotion to Education to Action

Although the importance of education was recognized very early, moving to implement educational programs was not a smooth process for most of the Protestant church agencies. (It has been part of the mandate of Development and Peace from the beginning.) For a number of reasons, the establishment of denominational development education programs lagged behind the ecumenical program — Ten Days for World Development — for a number of years. (Ten Days was started in the early 1970s by the churches of Canada. It is an education program directed towards informing Canadians about development issues in the Third World.)[11]

Probably the major factor was the ambivalence surrounding development education, and the confusion between it and promotion for fund raising. Behind this lies the reality that the impetus that led to the founding of all the Protestant development agencies was the need for a way to raise and disburse funds, first for relief and then also for development. Hard-headed members of the boards and committees directing church agencies were reluctant to scare off donors by promoting a line of education that to some seemed radical and leftist. The donors themselves saw little reason why they should contribute to a process that would transform their own view of the world. As an interim step to denominational development education programs, the staff of church agencies tried to combine fund-raising appeals and development education in the same materials. They found it a virtually impossible task. There seems to be an inherent contradiction in asking for funds for small-scale development projects with one breath, while in the next describing how poverty is rooted in systemic injustice that can only be overcome if the systems are changed. (Later, when development education was established as a separate function of the agencies, a compromise "both/and" rationale was articulated on the basis that until systemic change takes place we have a responsibility to attempt to alleviate some of the worst symptoms of the problem. Alternatively — although this is a difficult concept to convey — it can be argued that those "cutting edge" projects which aim at building awareness and developing organization at the community level are the first steps towards building the popular movements that can press for change.)

The fact is that the charity motivation dies very hard, partly because giving money is a natural and convenient way of responding to others' problems, and partly because this understanding of development is so widely held. The overwhelming majority of Canadians, including Canadian

Christians, still approach issues of development from a perspective of charity; the parable of the sheep and the goats in Matthew 25, and not the justice message in Luke 4, remains a favourite text for development sermons.

The government's official aid agency, the Canadian International Development Agency, does not share the vision that systems must change. The opening sentence of the principles section in the most recent CIDA policy statement, *Sharing Our Future*, borrows from slogans on church development posters twenty years ago: "The purpose of Canada's Third World development efforts is simple, to help the poorest countries and people in the world to help themselves."[12]

The phrase "structural change" is nowhere to be found in CIDA documents — which is not surprising, since Canadians in the international arena think of themselves as peacemakers and honest brokers, not as agents of radical reform.

However, despite the problems inherent in moving towards separately defined development education program, the move did take place. First the Anglicans in 1979 and then during the 1980s the United Church, the Presbyterians, and the Lutherans took on staff to develop networks of committed activists at the parish level. As was noted above, Development and Peace has from the beginning seen development education as a major part of its mandate and has full-time animators across the country.

The fact that Development and Peace has such an extensive development program of its own has given it a particular role to play within Ten Days for World Development. Whereas the Protestant churches rely heavily (sometimes almost exclusively) on Ten Days for both program and resources, Development and Peace provides both of these itself and looks to Ten Days to offer something different. For the first decade, the Ten Days program consisted of only a ten-day period in the winter when joint educational events could take place. By the early 1980s, however, Development and Peace was pressing strongly for Ten Days to move to a "focused education program *leading to action*."

This proposal met with a positive response from the other churches, which had moved into their own programs. They knew that "action" (by which was meant advocacy) made good pedagogical sense. Where development education had been effective, it had destroyed people's illusions that there is an easy solution to the Third World's problems through "good development." This meant that many concerned supporters of the development agencies who had contributed to development out of their guilt at being born into the world's privileged minority were left with no adequate way to respond to Third World problems. People wanted a way, however small, to act on their new awareness of the fundamental problems, in addition to their continued contributions to projects that addressed the symptoms. It seemed to the agencies that it was vital that development education should include an action component. Otherwise, it could become an essentially negative experience for those involved.

Over the past six years, the Ten Days action program has had three themes: Canadian policy in Central America, Canadian overseas development assistance, and the role of the Canadian banks in the international debt crisis. Each of these illustrates an important part of the churches' present development polices.

Ten Days and Central America: A Success Story

The first Ten Days action program took place in January 1983. It was launched with a letter to the then secretary of state for external affairs, Allan MacEachen, that raised five questions concerning Canadian policy in Central America. The initial response from MacEachen bordered on flippancy. This response, together with a critique prepared by experts on Central America from the Inter-Church Committee on Human Rights in Latin America (ICCHRLA) and its related organizations, was sent to Ten Days groups and interested parishes across the country. They were encouraged to write letters to MacEachen and to their own members of Parliament (MPs).

This first program illustrates three features of grass-roots advocacy as developed by the churches. First of all, the local groups were treated as full partners in the church advocacy strategy and were provided with the fruits of the best research on the issue available through the justice coalitions. Form letters that could be copied and sent in were used sparingly, for all the educators agreed that it was by working through the details of a letter themselves that people really made the issue their own. This also reflects the fact that local activists are taken seriously by the churches.

Second, the requirements of the action program required a distillation of the work of several coalitions, and the co-ordination of the policies of five or six participating churches. This work takes place within a committee of Ten Days called the Policy Integration Committee, which is thus far the most effective forum for co-ordinating the policy work of the coalitions yet devised.

In many instances, policies had to be vetted and revised in the churches. Consequently, a pattern developed of representatives on coalition boards taking back proposals for policy, as thrashed out in the Policy Integration Committee, to their churches and "working them through their systems." This meant a process, different for each denomination, of framing the proposal in an appropriate context and taking it to subcommittees and then to major boards, and sometimes to the highest policy-making body in the church. Thus, the need to define several specific recommendations to propose to government forced the churches to focus their own thinking much more sharply than had been their custom.

Third, the action program from the beginning was designed to empower local committees, parishes, and individuals to engage with their own elected representatives and, later, with the local representatives of national banks. Although writing letters to Ottawa or to remote head offices is usually a component of the action, the emphasis has always been on face-to-face meetings with members of Parliament and bank managers to discuss issues of concern.

For many of those involved at the local level, this has been an affirming experience. Although a few Ten Days groups can call on expert advice in local universities, most groups must rely on their own research and the materials supplied to them by churches. Many groups that approached a first meeting with an MP or government committee with some trepidation found that they were far better informed than their elected representative or the government experts. Ten Days staff have played an essential back-up role in helping groups to "de-mystify" the smooth responses they receive on government letterhead, to find the gaps in the government's position, and so shape their own response.

An unlooked-for benefit of the action program has been to offset the cynicism that had existed in the regional Ten Days networks about action that was nationally organized. This program is not seen as "something laid on from head-office" but as a network of like-minded people working together all over the country with helpful back-up provided from Toronto. An important part of the strategy was to have key members of parliamentary committees receive letters not only from their own constituency but also from selected committees in different parts of the country, thus showing the widespread support for the positions put forward.

For those in the national churches and coalitions, this focus on local activity proved from the beginning to have definite strategic value. For many years, delegations to External Affairs had been pressing many of the same points, only to be brushed off and asked if they were speaking for anyone besides themselves. The goal of the first action program on Central America was to convince policy makers in External Affairs that the national churches did indeed have a constituency. Equally important was lobbying enough MPs across the country so that the caucuses of all three parties would realize that this was an issue to be taken seriously.

It is now generally accepted that the Ten Days program in 1983-85 contributed significantly to the change in Canadian policy towards Central America. First Allan MacEachen agreed to a meeting with the churches that had been sought for several years; subsequently he visited Central America and was briefed by non-governmental organizations (NGOs) before he went. The pressure on MPs to respond to questions on the subject, or even to appear on public panels, forced their researchers to comb the parliamentary library for material on the region.

Even if some aspects of government policies still fell short of what the churches wanted, their advocacy had played a part in putting Central America on the country's agenda. Until then, External Affairs' attitude to the region had been typical of its standard approach to an area in which Canada has no strategic interests and which is evidently in the U.S. sphere of influence: a minimalist position consisting of no particular policy unless, if pushed, one in support of the U.S. position. It was therefore a significant achievement to convince the government that although Canada itself might have little to gain one way or the other in Central America, a large number of articulate and committed Canadians felt strongly that their government should play a positive role in favour of peace in the region and the promotion of human rights.

Many have sensed that it is very appropriate that the actions taken by the grass roots reflect in the Canadian context the development principles being advocated overseas. Ten Days is a movement of ordinary people coming together in order to put peaceful pressure on those in positions of responsibility in support of justice and human rights.

Addressing the Government on Canada's Development Policies

In 1985 the churches responded to the invitation of the Mulroney government to participate in the shaping of government foreign policy. A special joint committee of the Senate and House of Commons conducted hearings on the future direction of Canada's international relations, to which the Canadian Council of Churches submitted the brief referred to at the beginning of this chapter. The CCC submitted another brief[13] in 1986 to a second committee (unofficially called the Winegard Committee, after its chairman, William Winegard), which held hearings on the question of Canada's Official Development Assistance (ODA) program.[14]

Again, as with the Central American focus, the churches' advocacy grew from closely co-ordinated ecumenical policies based on the experience of overseas partners. The contributions of many local Ten Days groups ensured that government heard the same message from many quarters.

Building on the experience gained in letter writing in the previous years, a number of grass-roots groups and individuals submitted substantive briefs. Almost one-fifth of the 280 submissions listed in the Winegard Committee's report are from groups or individuals related to the churches of ICFID or the CCC. Only two or three of these are national organizations; all the rest are local groups, including twenty identified as community Ten Days committees. The churches' grass-roots advocacy was truly becoming a voice that was heard in the land.[15]

The churches' positions on government development assistance can be summarized from the recommendations of the 1985 brief. It begins by saying that the churches seek:

> to apply to the consideration of government policy on North-South issues three central ethical concerns:
> 1. a commitment to solidarity with those who suffer.
> 2. support for reforms that will lead to greater international equity.
> 3. a desire to help Third World communities and states develop economically, to become more self-reliant and more able to avoid exploitation and dependency in their relationships with larger and richer powers.[16]

These statements reveal a very different world view from that of government, and the two themes of church development policy, solidarity and working for structural change, are both clearly present.

On the surface, it is the concern for solidarity that is most evident. The churches call for a return to the earlier target of 0.7 per cent of the Gross National Product (GNP) for development assistance — significantly higher than the existing level (Recommendation 1). But while the churches desire a greater quantity of government aid for developing countries, they also seek an improvement in the quantity of that aid.

The lion's share of Canadian aid is in the "bilateral" (government-to-government) section of CIDA. The churches argue that because this aid is given with mixed motives, it falls far short of achieving its potential in helping those most in need. Government believes that its development aid can simultaneously assist developing countries and promote the exports of Canadian business. The churches maintain that if we are seeking to bring aid to the poorest peoples and least developed countries, the two goals are incompatible. Thus, the churches recommend that CIDA untie its bilateral aid — that is, drop the requirement that 80 per cent of the funds provided for a project be spent on Canadian products (Recommendation 3). They urge a more open attitude to permitting tenders by Third World companies for components in the projects (Recommendation 2). They warn against the practice of offering Canadian aid in return for contracts for Canadian companies in Third World government projects (Recommendation 4).

The churches offer several reasons for their recommendations. Placing heavy emphasis on supplying components from Canada inevitably draws aid towards large and technically complex projects. The emphasis will be on replicating sophisticated "Western" installations (hydro dams, telecommunications) rather than on the basic infrastructure and services needed by the poor (roads, health care). In addition, spending funds in Canada means that the same aid is able to purchase less; because costs are huge here, the recipient country receives less.

At first glance, the motives of solidarity with the poor, who do not benefit from Canada's bilateral aid, are very much to the fore. Also present, however, is the churches' realization that foreign aid that ties developing countries more closely to the industrialized North will not be to their advantage as long as the present international economic system remains unchanged. Canadian bilateral aid is not helping "third world communities and states [to] develop economically, to become more self-reliant and more able to avoid exploitation and dependency in their relationships with larger and richer powers" as the churches would wish. In short, the churches are seeking structural change, and they oppose the policies underlying Canadian bilateral aid because they perpetuate the status quo.

The other recommendations point in positive directions for Canadian aid. Aid should go to countries whose governments are trying to pursue more self-reliant development and ensure that the poorest in their countries can meet their basic needs (Recommendation 5). CIDA should seek out projects that will benefit all the people in a country, "producing a wide distribution of the benefits of development" (Recommendation 6). Recommendations 9 and 10 raise the human rights concerns of the churches and urge that Canada make human rights criteria a basic co-determinant of its aid. Where human rights are "grossly and persistently violated," only emergency aid should be given.

The remaining recommendations raise additional points that are of concern to the churches. One is the possible misuse of food aid — a further example of aid given with mixed motives that sometimes destroys the food self-sufficiency of the recipient country (Recommendation 8). Another point involves the special role of non-governmental organizations within CIDA and the concern that their special contribution not be lost (Recommendation 7). This last point is expanded in some detail in Part V of the churches' 1986 brief entitled *CIDA and the NGOs*.

(A discussion for another time might explore the ambiguities within the church relationship to CIDA, for they are its clients, receiving large sums of government money each year, as well as its critics. The churches vary in their attitudes to government funding, largely according to historical positions on church and state. The comparisons are fascinating.)

Third World Debt:
Solidarity, Structural Change, and Advocacy
An appropriate way to end this section is with a brief look at the way in which the churches have tackled the issue of Third World debt. This process illustrates many of the themes of this chapter.

The churches' understanding of development as entailing far more than projects means that they see the debt crisis, like human rights abuse, as a development issue. As such, it will involve all the elements of solidarity with partners, working for structural change, involving our own people, and urging our views on government and business. We have gone through a similar process (although perhaps with less debate) in developing policy around sanctions for South Africa, the Canadian role in Central America, or even the proper function for CIDA.

The debt issue, perhaps more clearly than any other thus far addressed by the churches, illustrates the basic truth about development that we have known since the 1960s — that the root causes of Third World poverty and underdevelopment lie in global systems that are far beyond the capability of any one country to address. Despite this, the churches only began work on the issue because of appeals from their partners in debtor countries. In the Canadian context, it did not seem a major issue. True, there had been a brief period, early in the 1980s, at the beginning of the crisis, when our own banks appeared very vulnerable to a major default by Mexico or Brazil, but this danger soon passed. Yet while Canadians were assuming that the debt crisis had passed, our colleagues in Brazil, the Philippines, Zambia, and many other countries told us that, on the contrary, it was growing steadily worse. They pointed out that the drain of resources out of the Third World that began in the mid-1980s made a mockery of our development aid programs.[17] The debt issue had become a major issue of fundamental justice in relations between North and South that the churches could no longer ignore.

The Canadian churches' justice agenda was already crowded with Central America, South Africa, refugees, native people, the environment, among other issues. The debt crisis remained well down the list of priorities. GATT-fly (an ecumenical organization focused on economic justice issues) began research on the issue several years in advance of the churches' public work on the issue, as did the Taskforce on the Churches and Corporate Responsibility. It was not until late in 1987 that it became a major public focus for the churches. At that point, the churches asked the Taskforce to give it major staff attention, and at about the same time, Ten Days made it the focus of its 1987-88 action program.

The goal of the first year's program (1988-89) was to convince the banks that Canadians were aware of their involvement in loans to the Third World and were concerned that the ethical as well as financial implications of the debt crisis be taken into account. Ten Days groups were encouraged to contact their local bank managers and ask to discuss the matter. When, as in most cases, they were referred to "head office," they wrote strong well-informed letters that touched off major public relations activity on the part of several of the banks. Plans for 1989-90 include continuing the pressure on the banks from the local groups while the national churches extend the discussion to the federal minister of finance.

In retrospect, we can see there were two reasons why the churches had initially shied away from the debt crisis. The first reason was practical. It is a difficult subject, and the 1970s experience of trying to generate energy and action in the churches around the New International Economic Order (a Third World initiative to reform the patterns of international trade and finance) had not been particularly successful. Nearly everyone in the churches is a layperson when it comes to economics; most people feel incompetent to form an opinion on an economic issue, let alone approve a recommendation. Besides, economic issues seem dry and technical compared with the blood-and-sweat struggles for human rights and political justice.

The second reason related to theology. Implicit in the issue was the concept of debt forgiveness, and many felt that the churches

(perhaps especially the Protestant churches) were too closely im-
bued with the principles of capitalism to feel comfortable with
that concept. In the event, the pragmatic realities of the crisis
forced all those taking part in the policy debate to accept the
principle of debt forgiveness. What was at issue was the rationale
that we should put forward in support of debt reduction.

On the one hand, some argued that much of the debt had been
contracted by Third World dictators for illegitimate projects and
so should not be considered morally binding. They also pointed
out that excessively high interest rates in the early 1980s had
caused the debt to mushroom; they argued that the debt should
be recalculated on the basis of more normal interest rates. Others,
who perhaps hold a more optimistic view of the advocacy
process, wanted to put forward proposals that would seem
feasible to government officials and bankers, while trying to
achieve the same end result — a reduction in the debt.

The first group argued that the debt should be reduced because
much of it was illegitimate and because much of it had already
been paid. The second argued that the debt should be reduced
because there was no earthly chance that it could be paid in full
and postponing the recognition of this fact was causing untold
hardship in the debtor countries.

The first group was also concerned about Third World suffering, but (and here they echoed many voices from the partner
churches) they rejected a *forgiveness* that implied a gesture of
grace and favour on the part of the industrialized world. In short,
they sought justice, not charity. The second group responded that
justice was not likely to be done in the short term, although they
agreed that we should keep on asking for it. In the meantime, if
some measure of relief could be obtained from the bankers and
bureaucrats, on the basis of charity (and a realistic appraisal of
the situation), then the churches should argue that case to the best
of their ability.

These are two very different points of view, perhaps too glibly
described as the prophetic and the pragmatic. Yet, if the churches
were to have anything to say to the banks, and to government,
these points of view had to be reconciled. If not, common (or at
least complementary) policies could never be developed.

Accordingly, from the autumn of 1987 to the summer of 1989
the churches engaged in a drawn-out and sometimes tedious
process of building consensus. This was achieved through the
drafting, with many consultations and revisions, of the booklet
*The International Debt Crisis: A Discussion Paper Prepared for the
Canadian Churches.*[18]

Representatives of the churches who participated in this process took what they'd learned and the proposed policies back to their own structures. Several churches (the Presbyterians and the United Church) have developed their own policies reflecting that of the ecumenical paper. The rest have obtained a more general "approval in principle" from their policy-making bodies for the basic thrust of the paper.

The paper the churches finally adopted incorporates the dilemmas that a product of consensus is subject to: it is more general than a statement addressed to government should be, but more technical than an educational document for church members should be. Nevertheless, it incorporates in one document both the policy and the experience out of which it grew, most eloquently described in the statements of our partners in debtor countries. (These last, which would not normally form part of documents the churches share with the banks, drew mixed comments from bank presidents. They ranged from "Your colleagues in Brazil seriously overstate their case" to "I found what some of those Third World people said quite moving" — this from an admittedly junior executive.) Now that policy is in place, the churches and the coalitions will be arguing their positions with government and with the banks.

In conclusion, one small but significant point should be made in closing this look — admittedly in *medias res* — at the churches' work on the debt issue. An earlier version of *The International Debt Crisis* referred to this advocacy as being "on behalf of our sisters and brothers in the Third World." It described the churches' task in bank annual meetings as being a "voice for the voiceless." Strong and persuasive interventions in the Debt Study Network that revised the drafts argued that this view of our advocacy belonged to the old paternalistic "helping them in their struggle" school of thought. This section in the final version reads:

> Positive change occurs in developing countries — or in Canada — when people empowered by the Gospel take their economic and political futures into their own hands, and strive themselves to transform their lives. Our role is a supportive one, to reinforce their efforts by our advocacy with our own government and banks.[19]

Solidarity and structural change — they are the two sides of the same development coin.

Promoting "Women in Development"

One specific issue brings into sharp focus the churches' capacity to promote change, the nuances of partnership, and how the two can at times inhibit each other. It is also an issue that illustrates in a very acute fashion how urging structural change on other cultures can at some point become a new form of cultural imperialism. For these reasons, it deserves further study. The issue is the priority given to women in development projects, a whole area referred to (now that CIDA has taken it up) as "women in development" or "WID" — as in "wid-ow."

Decade for Women

During this time all UN-member countries were called upon to put into place, and then implement, legislation and programs that would enhance the lives of women. The goal was that women should move into positions of influence more commensurate with their numbers as half the world's population.

The women's decade ended with a special session of the United Nations General Assembly in Nairobi in which the Canadian government played a significant part. Representatives of Canadian churches and other Canadian non-governmental organizations took part in the NGO Forum in Nairobi in 1984. As part of its response to the women's decade, the Canadian government adopted a WID policy for CIDA. The purpose was "to help women take part in, and benefit from Canada's development assistance program."[20] In 1986 an action plan was formally launched by which this program would be put into practice.

In essence, the CIDA WID program requires that any project submitted for funding, either from within CIDA or from an NGO, must contain an analysis of the project's impact on women. The program's aim is "to empower women to build better lives, to take part in and benefit more fully from the wider development process."[21] Although this policy has been in place for several years, many agencies are still grappling with its implications. Most projects submitted for CIDA matching funds are the same as they were before WID was put in place. The accompanying analysis of the impact on women tends to be: "This project will benefit the whole community, and as women are part of the community, they will benefit along with everyone else." Where the nature of the project permits, the agency will point out that it will ease women's labour by bringing a source of water closer to the village or by increasing the supply of firewood. For many of those who worked to get the policy in place, it seems as if very little has changed.

An advance in defining the implications of the new policy was marked by a brochure issued by Partnership Africa Canada outlining its understanding of WID projects. Among other points, it notes:

> Many proposals respond to women's practical needs (for example, traditional income-generating projects or the digging of a well) and these are of course essential, but few proposals integrate a concern for meeting women's strategic needs, such as increasing women's ability to organize in order to improve their status in the community and increase their control over their own lives. Both "levels" of development work are essential to produce long-term improvements in women's lives.[22]

It is interesting to compare the churches' performance in this area with that of some of the NGOs whom we usually refer to as like-minded (CUSO, Oxfam, and Inter-Pares). How do the churches measure up in what is potentially one of the most significant frontiers of change? Not very well, according to most observers. The Canadian churches' development agencies have been no better and have probably lagged behind these others.

This will come as no surprise to those who view the churches' attitude to women with justifiable skepticism. Yet it is not what might have been expected, given the early record of the churches in this regard. Because this early period is often either forgotten or denigrated, it is worth a short digression.

The Early Missionaries and Third World Women: "Better Than Their Press"

While the primary motivation of the early missionaries was to proclaim the Good News of Christ, their preaching was very quickly accompanied by various forms of social service. An important dimension of this early activity, often overlooked, was the equal attention they gave to women.

It might be considered paradoxical that the reasons for this even-handed emphasis were theological. For while they usually accepted the social norms of their time, including the rigid role definitions assigned to the sexes, the early missionaries also believed that each individual soul, male or female, rich or poor, was equally precious, and equally in need of the Gospel message.

Consequently, they were dismayed to find that their message was denied access to half the populations of the countries to which they went. Most cultures guard their women closely, and visiting evangelists found them concealed behind walls or in inner rooms.

The sending churches soon realized that no real progress could be made in reaching women and their children with the message of the Gospel, or with human assistance, unless women workers could be found to go overseas and join in the task. In what was an unusual appeal for the time, the mission committees of the churches in Canada called on their women to form "Missionary Societies" for the purpose of raising funds and sending women overseas.[23]

Subsequently, because of the insistence of the women missionaries that girls should be taught as well as boys, separate schools were built in deference to local custom that the sexes should be segregated. Eventually, Third World women became teachers, nurses, and later scientists and doctors, only a few decades later than their Western sisters.

Christian missions not only helped women to advance, but in some cultures protected them from particularly blatant forms of oppression. The following is one illustration from among many:

> Some of the peoples of southern Nigeria celebrate the birth of twins as bringing good luck. Others believe the opposite, and, because of the fear and loathing which they feel for twins, and the women who give birth to them, they drove mothers and babies into the "bad bush" — the forest — to starve or die of exposure or the attacks of wild animals. Early missionaries in the hinterland of Calabar regarded this as one of the worst manifestations of local traditions, and several of them, including some notable women, risked their lives to protect twin mothers and their children. Eventually, at the insistence of the missionaries, the practice was prohibited by the British authorities.[24]

In contemporary justice circles it is seldom that a good word is said for the early missionary movement. Yet, despite the limitations of the roles assigned to women, this was a remarkable chapter in women's solidarity across cultural barriers. For almost a century, thousands of Canadian women worked, gave, and prayed so that other women could serve and support Indian, African, and Chinese women and their children. Moreover, although it had official sanction, the movement took place outside the clerical structures of the churches. The missionaries, the administrators, and their supporters were all, without exception, laypeople.

But while this early emphasis on women put the churches ahead of the policies of the colonial governments, it is very difficult to argue today that the church development programs that grew out of this mission history are as progressive with regard to women as those of secular or government agencies.

If we assess church development programs using the Partnership Africa Canada criteria outlined above, we see an abundance of projects aimed at women's practical needs, but very few that support their strategic needs. Churches are trying to ease the terrible burden of labour for Third World women, but, on the whole, they are not empowering them to take control of their lives.

Church development practice — as opposed to theory — here suffers from the dilemma that was touched on above. Most of our partner churches overseas are more patriarchal and conservative than churches in Canada, and most Third World church leaders, if pressed, would say such projects might be suitable to Western societies but are not needed, or appropriate, in their situations.

Promoting Change or Cultural Imperialism?
In the face of this response from our partners, how far should Canadian churches promote their own agenda for social change by enabling women to take control of their lives? In what way is this different from the cultural imperialism of the nineteenth century, which destroyed traditional African art in the name of smashing idols and put skirts on Hawaiian women?

The question of women in development programs has been a painful one for many Canadians, but, as a rule, the fear of imposing our cultural values on our partners has resulted in an uncomfortable acquiescence in perpetuating traditional roles. Few Third World women are gaining control over their lives through development programs funded by Canadian churches.

The issues would be much clearer if it were a question of complicity in oppressing or exploiting women, but this is not the case. There is no conflict on this point between Western values and the values of our church partners. The issue surfaces over cultural differences, especially where there does not seem to be a movement on the part of the women affected to change the situation. It also arises, possibly under the surface, when the partner is working in a context of oppression that dwarfs all other issues. For example, the leaders of the anti-apartheid movement in South Africa concede that they have postponed addressing a number of problems, including the place of women in South African society, until after apartheid is overthrown. In such situations, the leaders of our partner churches, unfortunately usually all men, have decided that lesser issues must wait.

Nowhere is this tension between cultural values felt more strongly than in the churches' programs in the Middle East. For many years, several Canadian churches have funded (through the WCC and the Middle East Council of Churches) an integrated program of relief and development for Palestinian refugees. Each year, a representative of the Canadian funders attends a program meeting in Cyprus, where frequently part of the agenda is taken up with a painful debate on the women's issue. Most of the European donors (the North Americans in this case are more timid) have long urged the transformation of the traditional sewing, embroidery, and baby-care classes that constitute the programs for Palestinian women into something that might fit them for the job market. (In contrast, men and boys receive sophisticated training in computers and motor mechanics.) Virtually no women are on the local decision-making committees directing these projects. The men who meet with the Western donors are middle-aged and middle class, and bear the scars of the struggle to maintain their programs. They feel that they have many problems far more significant than this one, and maintain that the women are very happy with things as they are.

In fact, however, some have argued that these programs for women may be a start towards something very significant. Because of the quiet conservative nature of the classes, Muslim families will permit their women and girls to attend them. It is the only place they go where they are not accompanied by their menfolk. Gradually, as they talk together while they work, there is an opportunity for horizons to be widened. The same techniques have worked in our own culture and in others almost as conservative as the Middle East.

Nevertheless, the feelings of the European donors on this subject have run so high that there have been threats to reduce funding unless a more progressive approach to women is adopted. The donors' power to withhold funds, which is the reality underlying the rhetoric of partnership and equality, is occasionally exercised. For the onlooking Canadians, it is clear that churches in other countries, when faced with a choice between their own deeply felt values and the autonomy of the Third World partner, sometimes choose the first rather than the second. For the Canadian churches it has usually been the other way around. The result has been warm relations with our partners, but a rather mediocre record in promoting meaningful development for women.

Reproductive Issues: The Toughest Ones of All
Perhaps the most difficult issues relate to women's reproductive roles. The "well-baby clinics," which are a feature of church-run hospitals throughout Africa, sum up the official attitude of its

churches. It is true that in many of the Protestant hospitals birth-control advice is freely available to women who already have sizeable families. However, none of the churches there have been able to come to terms with the breakdown in traditional (let alone the very recently acquired Christian) morality, which has resulted in the soaring rate of teenage pregnancies. The churches have nothing to offer these young women but sermons.

Evidently, it would be naive and wrong-headed to suggest that birth control is an answer to Africa's staggering economic and social problems. However, it is not unreasonable to suggest that those who are concerned for Africa's future (which certainly includes Africa's churches and their friends in Canada) should grapple seriously with the breakdown in social and family structures. In the process they could consider if there is a role for family-planning programs. Thus far, there is little indication that this is a priority for African churches, and their Canadian friends make only gentle suggestions. (In Asia, by contrast, there is often government and cultural support for family planning, and this support is reflected in the policies of church-run hospitals.)

While Third World churches begin to work out answers for themselves, Canadian churches seem to have backed away from the issue. There was a brief initiative in the mid-1970s, with strong participation from the Catholic bishops, to work on issues of population and immigration in a grouping called ICPOP (the Inter-Church Committee on Population). This initiative was apparently one too many in a period when a number of justice issues were competing for the energy of the churches, and it withered away. It is still present in the backs of some people's minds, but it is not on the official agenda.

This fact is noted here without analysis, except to say that the abortion debate that has raged on the Canadian social scene over the past decade has undoubtedly played a role in nudging the churches away from tackling reproductive issues, even as they relate to female and child poverty. The ecumenical consensus is still too fragile for anyone to risk putting too much effort into an issue at once so intractable and so explosive. As a result, Canadian church development agencies avoid the issue ecumenically and tend to go along with their partners in their denominational programs.

For those who see reproductive issues as solely women's issues, without the theological and ethical dimension imparted to them by the churches, this is hardly a strong position in support of lifting women's burdens. They may even see it as proof that the churches are too conservative and patriarchal to work seriously at an issue that cuts so deeply into the status quo. That may or may not be true, but whatever the reasons, there is no question that the churches, ecumenically in Canada and in overseas development programs, have ducked the question.

Conclusion

It is easy to speak glibly of "solidarity in the struggle for structural change," but the words conceal many tangled issues only partially resolved, either here or in the Third World. The hopeful sign is that the Canadian churches are fully aware that the whole development process, both theory and praxis, is still evolving.

When we speak to government about Third World issues, we talk authoritatively about what we have learned from our partners about the realities of their countries. When we speak with those partners, and with each other, we know that we are a long way from having all the answers.

III
Human Rights and Corporate Responsibility

6 • From the Gold Mines to Bay Street: In Search of Corporate Social Responsibility

Renate Pratt

In the mid-1970s Canadian churches began speaking up as minority shareholders at annual meetings of banks and corporations. They asked management to demonstrate that the presence of the company in South Africa was, indeed, ameliorating the situation for human rights for blacks in that country.

The churches' experience with their counterparts in countries like South Africa had convinced them that real development and a just peace could not be achieved as long as Canadians — whether government or private sector — provided support to the very government that had installed and perpetuated the apartheid system. The nature of apartheid and its duration provided an opening point in an extended conversation between churches and corporations on the subject of the social ethics and corporate responsibility of the boardrooms of the nation.

Renate Pratt lived in Tanzania prior to returning to Canada in the late 1960s. She was the original director of the Taskforce on the Churches and Corporate Responsibility and author of the basic document on Canadian corporate relations with South Africa, Investment in Oppression, *as well as of many briefs to government on the subject. In retirement, she serves on the board of the International Defense and Aid Fund for Southern Africa.*

— Ed.

First Steps at King and Bay

On a sunny October day in 1977 at the intersection of King and Bay streets in downtown Toronto, some two hundred people gathered for a hastily arranged service of witness amidst the towering skyscrapers of Canada's major banks. They were mourning the murder in police custody of South Africa's Black Consciousness leader Steve Biko, the outlawing on 19 October of eighteen major anti-apartheid organizations, and the banning or detention of hundreds of their members. We had organized this service in Toronto's financial district to draw public attention to the fact that Canadian banks continued by their substantial loans to South Africa to help maintain the apartheid state and its oppression.

It was a conscious decision not to have this service in front of the South African consulate or in front of a Canadian government building. This event in front of Bay Street towers symbolized the approach to justice taken by the Taskforce on the Churches and Corporate Responsibility (TCCR) to its work.[1]

Although the Taskforce continues to have a great deal to say about Canadian foreign policy, we have always maintained that our primary task is to address decisions made in the boardrooms of Canadian companies. This approach proved to be a useful reminder that, where corporate activities are associated with the perpetuation of social harm and human rights violations, they carry a "made in Canada" label, regardless of whether the situation deals with oppression in the production of South African wines, with the social costs of the economic policies of Pinochet's Chile, or with the rape of the land claimed by the Lubicon Lake Band in northern Alberta.

To explain proposals for change in corporate practice or policy that in our view might reduce oppression, we offer evidence gathered by our own churches and religious orders and by their overseas partners who are working with the victims of oppression. At times we have been able to bring spokespersons of overseas partners to offer their witness directly to corporate management and to shareholder meetings.

Where corporations are active in countries with oppressive governments, we address not only the companies in question but also the relevant government departments in order to seek clarification of Canadian policies and legislation. Where we judge that Canadian policies inadequately consider the social justice dimensions, we attempt to draw public attention to these issues and to change both government and corporate policies with regard to them.[2]

Successive Canadian governments have maintained that the promotion and protection of international human rights are important elements in their foreign policy. However, in our experience, we have observed that where there are Canadian business interests in conflict with a forthright human rights policy, the government tends to favour the former. It will be argued in this chapter that in these circumstances corporate Canada becomes the undeclared practitioner of real Canadian foreign policy.

Pioneering in Corporate Social Responsibility

Several trends in the experiences of North American churches have led many of them to become active as socially responsible investors and to exercise their shareholder rights according to church policies. When, in the late sixties, many churches in the United States joined the anti-Vietnam War protest, they became aware that their silent investments in companies such as Honeywell and Dow Chemical contributed to the very death and destruction they so fervently opposed in public statements. They resolved not to divest their shares but instead to join with like-minded shareholders and oppose with voice and vote the role of such companies in the Vietnam War. These churches calculated that the selling of their shares would result in a one-time-only public event. Keeping the issue on the public agenda of companies, in contrast, might in time win the support of other shareholders and thereby give a continuing and expanding witness to the strength of anti-Vietnam sentiments. These activities eventually resulted in the establishment of the Interfaith Center on Corporate Responsibility in New York, which has since been active in a wide range of corporate issues. The Interfaith Center collaborates closely with the Taskforce when issues overlap.

These early American church activities, of course, generated reverberations in Canada. Here, some churches had long observed certain investment principles, particularly concerning the exclusion of alcohol and tobacco companies from their investment portfolios. However, the challenge to cast the net much wider to include active shareholder participation in matters of corporate policy was indeed a pioneering task that received much reflection. The issue was debated in a variety of areas of church activity, not the least in terms of fund raising for overseas development. Here, the argument may be roughly summarized as follows: Should corporations be asked to contribute to church funds for the alleviation of human misery that may in fact be caused or prolonged by activities of the very corporation to whom the request is made? If this responsibility existed, would it not make more sense for the shareholding church to seek changes in corporate policy so that particular social ills may be cured at their source?

In the early 1970s, one issue, Canadian investment in the apartheid system of South Africa, became central to the emerging corporate responsibility theme. It had just been examined company by company by the National Board of the YWCA of Canada. The findings were issued in 1973 in the publication *Investment in Oppression*. The document had come to the conclusion that foreign investment in South Africa contributed to the maintenance of apartheid and that it created apologists for the system internationally. Several Canadian churches had co-financed the publication of *Investment in Oppression* because of their own deep interest in the issue. When, in 1975, after a couple of years of preparatory meetings, the Taskforce on the Churches and Corporate Responsibility was formally established, it was the question of Canadian corporate activity in Southern Africa that became the first major issue to be addressed by the new ecumenical coalition.

Who Sets Policy?

From its inception, an important feature of the Taskforce was its way of work. It was established to assist the churches to implement their policies in the area of corporate social responsibility. Official representatives of the participating churches and religious orders serve as links between their own decision-making structures and the Taskforce. In this way, individual member churches or religious orders have retained authority over the choice of activities in which they wish to participate, and official briefs, letters, policy statements, and the like that are produced by the Taskforce reflect the considered views and stay within the policies of its member organizations. Their representatives form a working board with subcommittees and an executive whose members are key participants in corporate management and shareholder meetings and in encounters with federal or provincial ministers and parliamentary bodies.

Although waiting for decisions from member denominations can be frustrating and time-consuming, the arrangement has served the Taskforce well; indeed it is hard to imagine how else it could function with integrity. There is a simple technical explanation for why TCCR actions cannot be divorced from those of its member institutions. Investors, including our member denominations and orders, are understandably protective about what is being said and done on their behalf. Usually, therefore, individual denominations will have made a decision about the relevant policy to be followed and about the corporate action to be taken in the name of the shareholding institution. Typically, they also designate a spokesperson to whom they entrust their proxy to represent them in the annual shareholder meeting. Thus, no one who does not explicitly have the confidence of the investing church or religious order is able to represent it at corporate meetings.

There are additional reasons why it is important that the Taskforce, in its activities, represents policy decisions of its member churches and orders. The issues to be dealt with are complex and varied. They require an ability to assimilate many different factors and to adjust to changing human situations, moving, as the case may be, between the barrios and shantytowns of Third World countries to research libraries, corporate boardrooms, and government offices in Canada. Whereas in Canada we must speak out to bring the plight of the oppressed and the persecuted to the attention of our corporations, our governments, and the media, at times when we visit states under siege, the greatest discretion is required so as not to endanger further those we wish to help. Much of the preparatory work for action is done between Taskforce staff and the members of the board, who in turn discuss the proposals with their denomination or order to seek further input and final agreement. It is this two-way flow of consultation, decision making, and action that is so essential for keeping the "ownership" of Taskforce issues in the hands of the member denominations.

Breach of Peace?

Although church participation in company annual meetings is but one aspect of TCCR activity, it is also the most public. Very quickly it gave rise to spirited objections from the business community and a number of clergy. No one associated with the Taskforce could have had much doubt that the work would create certain tensions within and without the churches. Nevertheless, the severity of the reaction came as a surprise. One of the early manifestations came at a Bank of Montreal annual meeting in 1976, when a request for a halt to the bank's South African loans aroused the wrath not only of fellow shareholders who told us in no uncertain terms where to go, but also of the chairman, who silenced us by simply switching the microphone off. (It was a decision he may well have regretted; ten minutes later we repeated what we had wanted to say at the offices of the Montreal *Gazette*.)

A sustained effort to neutralize the activities of the Taskforce was mounted in 1977 by some members of the business community and a number of clergy close to them who established the Confederation of Church and Business People. This confederation quickly attracted substantial corporate support and sought to undermine our work by accusing us of being unfair to business generally and of disseminating incorrect and one-sided information.

This sort of public opposition slowed down considerably in the mid-1980s, although the argument about the legitimacy of churches engaging in such activities continues within some denominations. At the public level, however, the right of shareholders to raise questions, even critical ones, at annual meetings of corporations is now more widely respected.

Witnesses and Evidence

So where do we get our information from? What makes us so sure that we are not unfair, unbalanced, inaccurate? We do not claim to put forward the views of the business community, which is well equipped to do this itself. Church shareholders involved in this work have committed themselves to respond wherever the decisions of Canadian corporations appear to have an adverse effect on vulnerable groups of people who have no power to affect those decisions themselves. As shareholders, the churches attempt to the best of their ability to be the voice of these people and to act in their interest when dealing with corporations. Therefore, our task is to find out as much as we can about the possible links between corporate policies and the suffering and oppression that is occurring in many lands.

Before coming to a settled view on a given situation and before making any public statement, we present what information has been gathered to the company in question, either by letter or during a meeting, so that the data can be verified or corrected and management can be given an occasion to comment. Because of the long-standing relationships that exist between the Canadian churches and their overseas partners, the most frequent information comes by way of personal visits by either Canadians who work abroad or the people directly affected who contact us.

For example, in the mid-seventies we had a visit from Desmond Tutu some time before he became archbishop and Nobel Peace laureate. We were anxious to test with him our view that further bank loans to South Africa and new investment there should cease and that any Canadian corporate activity that either aided the South African police or military should stop. When a Canadian group takes the concerns of oppressed peoples abroad, it is crucial to know that we are not seeking a change that the people most affected by it would not seek, had they access to Canadian decision makers. In a closed session Desmond Tutu told us that, although it would not be possible for the South African churches openly to support this view, they would not publicly oppose our actions in Canada and a great many would be in agreement with us. (Since the imposition of the state of emergency in 1985, Archbishop Tutu, the Rev. Allan Boesak, and other friends in South Africa have courageously broken South African law and have publicly called for comprehensive mandatory sanctions against South Africa.)

Another visitor from South Africa was a young woman from Crossroads in Capetown. In 1977 she came to tell us about the bulldozing of African dwellings erected in defiance of a South African law which requires that the families of breadwinners remain in the so-called homelands. These bulldozers, the woman told us in passing, were ordered by what was then called the South African Department of Railways and Harbours. Unknown to our visitor, this piece of information was important to us, since a number of international bank loans were being made to that particular South African government department. Moreover, a major Canadian corporation, Massey-Ferguson (now Varity), had already been questioned by us about its possible involvement in such activity. The company has never been able to assure us that, together with its South African investment partner, it has not supplied the equipment that the apartheid state used to destroy black housing such as that in Crossroads. (Typically, the defence has been that a Canadian partner in a South African joint venture is not privy to such information about the operations of the company.)

Some examples from Latin America show that in this regard as well, we benefited from information and analysis brought to us by our churches and religious orders and their Latin American partners. During the Nicaraguan revolution in the late seventies, close contact was maintained with the members of the Broad Opposition Front. We were able to obtain direct information about Canadian and World Bank loans to the Somoza regime shortly before its collapse and about conditions of work at the El Setentrion gold mine, which was 60 per cent owned at the time by Noranda Mines. Church shareholders were thus able to raise questions about these issues at annual meetings of the Royal Bank of Canada and of Noranda Mines. In addition, churches had asked the Canadian government, in September 1978 and again in June 1979, to follow the example of a growing number of Latin American states by terminating all bilateral agreements with Somoza, by indicating a willingness to recognize a provisional government, and by instituting a trade embargo to shorten the people's agony and bloodshed. The government did not do so.

The years 1977 to 1985 were marked by recurrent periods of unbearable military repression in Guatemala. We explored the possibility of a protest by Inco Limited, which at the time owned a mining complex in Guatemala and might have had some leverage with the military dictatorship, or at least might have demonstrated that its presence in the country was a positive influence for human rights. We were also engaged over several years in support action for a Guatemalan trade union at a Coca-Cola bottling plant whose leadership and lawyers had been systematically assassinated by death squads in 1978-79. Detailed information about developments at the bottling plant was supplied on a regular basis by the International Food and Allied Workers Association. This made it possible for us to act as part of a well-informed world network as we urged Coca-Cola Canada and the American parent company to agree to a fair settlement. The flow of direct information and contacts remained critical throughout the Guatemalan terror until the time a settlement was achieved.

At times, it was important for the people struggling in Latin America to get their information to far more Canadians than those sitting around the TCCR's table. Therefore, in 1980 we co-sponsored a special conference called the Human Rights and Social Justice Conference on Latin America. During the three days of deliberations, guests from Brazil, Bolivia, Nicaragua, El Salvador, and Guatemala among others gave evidence and helped some seven hundred participants to explore the impact of human rights violations on the people living in the area and their aspirations for development. Although they had been invited, no political representative of the government participated and no official from External Affairs attended. This was in sharp contrast to the attendance of ninety representatives of the various levels of federal and provincial governments at a major trade-promoting business conference organized by the Canadian Association — Latin America and Caribbean (CALA), which took place in Toronto at the same time.

In the face of the argument that economic development ameliorates the situation for human rights, the Taskforce, like most other organizations, needed to monitor the evidence from the most celebrated test case — Chile — to see if the claim could be substantiated. The Taskforce was able to monitor the wealth of information about social and economic conditions in Chile after the military coup in 1973 because of particularly close relationships between its member denominations and religious orders and the Chilean churches and human rights groups. As corporate investment in and bank loans to Chile became a major concern for the Taskforce from the mid-seventies onward, members of its board paid extended visits to obtain first-hand information about the social cost to the poor of Pinochet's economic austerity measures. Chilean human rights lawyers and trade unionists continued to visit Canada. They briefed us on the plight of the hundreds of political prisoners and disappeared persons and on the rise of unemployment and the deterioration of employment conditions.

As environment issues began to crowd the TCCR agenda in the mid-1980s, it quickly became clear that they too had their international dimensions. A Filipino environmental group, for example, has turned to the Taskforce for help regarding a Canadian company. Since 1975 Marcopper Mining Corporation, 39.9 per cent owned by Canadian Placer Dome (until 1987 Placer Development), had been dumping tailings into Calancan Bay, off the Island of Marinduque. The company had thereby practically destroyed the livelihood of the community of fishermen in the bay. With the collaboration of several scientists from the International Marinelife Alliance, the TCCR was able to have an on-the-spot examination of the situation, followed by an exchange of consultative visits between members of the Taskforce and staff of the Filipino environmental organization. After discussions with the management of Placer Dome, a number of our members submitted a proposal to the 1988 shareholder meeting asking for approval of an independent assessment on the adverse effects of the Marcopper waste dumping. Management advised shareholders to defeat the motion and the proposal lost. The following year Professor Zenaida Uy, head of the Filipino human rights coalition, Bayan, accompanied the senior finance officer of the United Church of Canada to the Placer Dome annual meeting. "Thousands of subsistence fishermen and their families in Marinduque," she told the shareholders, "have had their food source killed by the dumping" — a statement that was rejected by Placer Dome's president. At time of writing, this particular struggle continues.[3]

Such are the stories from the "underside" that we have compiled and that complement our own research concerning investment, loans, and Canadian government policies and actions. The Taskforce is not, of course, the only organization compiling such data; indeed, we are often indebted to other Canadian and international organizations and to investigative journalists for their meticulous research. However, the Taskforce is the only organization that offers such documentation to the actual or the potential corporate actors. We do this in cases where, in the opinion of church shareholders, a corporate decision may make a significant difference — for good or ill — to the conditions of life in a specific area.

In most cases the first step is discussions with senior management to review the evidence and to encourage the company to consider church proposals for modification or reversal of its decisions. In some cases, negotiations continue over many years, as they did over the issue of bank loans to South Africa and to Chile. If presentations or formal proposals to annual shareholder meetings are contemplated, these would be part of such negotiations. Although most encounters with the business community involve a certain amount of tension and sparring, some relationships evolve into greater appreciation of each other's positions. During our very first management meeting, one bank president told us that neither he nor any of his senior officers had any experience in dealing with people like us, that nothing in his training had prepared him for such encounters, and that there was no structure in the bank to accommodate and deal with our concerns. He was sufficiently intrigued, he said, that he was prepared to engage in exchanges of views with regard to the social and political impact of the bank's international loans, and he did.

In other instances our presentations have caused a great deal of resentment that appears to rankle even after the grounds for the controversy are removed. Between 1975 and 1980, for example, the Taskforce had opposed Noranda Mines' unconditional plans to become the first large international investor in Chile after the 1973 coup d'état. The coup's particularly brutal nature had evoked international aversion and outrage. We argued that a major investment by as important a mining company as Noranda would lend a mantle of respectability to the repressive junta and thus prepare the path for other foreign investors. In requesting Noranda to make its investment in the Andacollo project conditional upon the restoration of civil and human rights in Chile, we had sought and received widespread support from the On-tario and Quebec federations of labour, the National Board of the YWCA, and scores of other organizations and important individuals from across Canada. Towards the end of 1980, Noranda announced that it was suspending the project for "business reasons."

Sometime later, we read with interest a case study (about which we had not been consulted) on the church/Noranda controversy entitled "Noranda-Andacollo, 1980." It had been prepared for their students by Professor P. Killing of the University of Western Ontario and P. Richardson of Queen's University. The introduction was by Alfred Powis, chairman and chief executive officer of Noranda Mines at the time. It contained this astonishing outburst:

> We might have dropped this venture three years ago when we were in tough financial shape and cutting back non-essential projects, if it had not been for the complaints mounted against us by the Taskforce on the Churches and Corporate Responsibility. We found their presumption in telling us not to invest in Chile very annoying, and were particularly upset with the protests they organized at our annual meetings and at the occupation of our Montreal office.

Shuttle between Business and Government

The one constant preoccupation of the Taskforce is social justice and an end to human rights violations against the poor and powerless. If, in our quest for corporate social responsibility, approaches to corporations promise fruitful negotiations, this route is preferred. Such corporate co-operation on a social justice issue would simultaneously assist in the alleviation of a specific social harm while setting a precedent for the particular corporation and for corporate Canada in general. We were, for example, anxious to see Canadian corporations and banks adopt codes of corporate conduct that would contain commitments to social responsibility principles that were precise and concrete enough that they could be understood by employees at all levels and could be applied and monitored throughout a company's domestic and international operations.

However, we discovered early on that with few exceptions, most corporations and banks, despite numerous, often quite congenial discussions, were reluctant to enter into such co-operation with us. They were more interested in convincing us that their enterprises, far from inflicting or perpetuating social harm, represented "engines for change" that would in time restore human rights and benefit everyone. Even where the evidence seemed incontrovertible that unconditional business confidence in a human rights violator regime strengthened the arm of the regime and prolonged repression, the business people we met with always felt their argument was unassailable, that the corporation acted as a good corporate citizen and was not violating any law in Canada or anywhere else, including international law, with which some were completely unfamiliar.

In all such cases, it was important, therefore, to determine for ourselves exactly what was the position of the Canadian government and what legislation governing corporate conduct was relevant. These questions led us to new frontiers of discovery, revealing in some areas non-existent or inadequately enforced legislation; in others we uncovered fine-sounding policy statements and international commitments that, after some probing, turned out to be political mirages. They lost all meaning once senior public servants had instructed us just why those statements were never quite applicable in the concrete cases we brought to them. Several examples come to mind.

United Nations Security Council and Namibia
In 1978 the Canadian government had accepted United Nations (UN) Security Council Resolution 418, which obliged states to observe a mandatory arms embargo against South Africa. We discovered that, notwithstanding the mandatory nature of the embargo, no Canadian law exists that governs the monitoring and enforcement of this important and unique UN measure. Instead, the government insists that it enforces the embargo by applying the Export and Import Permits Act and that no specific legislation is required.

Ford in South Africa
Until the mid-eighties we considered the Ford Motor Company and Alcan Aluminium Limited to be in violation of the UN Security Council's mandatory arms embargo, at least in spirit if not in letter. Ford South Africa, then a subsidiary of Ford Canada, had contracts to supply vehicles to the South African police and military. About this fact there was no dispute. We had photographic evidence of black political prisoners being herded into Ford vans. We had discussed this matter with the company, which feared that terminating these contracts might jeopardize contracts with other South African government departments and even risk a consumer boycott of Ford cars. In 1981 we therefore proposed to the secretary of state for external affairs that since it was clearly the intent of the arms embargo to deprive the South African police and military of international supplies, the Canadian government was bound to tell Ford Canada that its subsidiary was in violation of the arms embargo and that it should cancel such contracts.

The Canadian government was unmoved. The secretary of state for external affairs replied that the government was very doubtful Ford could be judged to be in violation of the arms embargo, since Resolution 418 referred to "the sale and transfer of equipment and related material *to* South Africa" (emphasis added). As the vehicles were manufactured in South Africa, the Canadian government felt it would not be right to put pressure on the company to suspend those contracts. It thought our request to be unrealistic and in conflict with Canada's rejection of extra-territorial jurisdiction. There was no recognition of the moral and practical reasons that presumably had motivated the Canadian government to support the UN's mandatory arms embargo under Article 7 of the United Nations Charter (under the article, South Africa was threatening international peace). (Ford ultimately divested its South African holdings in 1987.)

Alcan in South Africa
The second case concerned Alcan's 24 per cent partnership in Hulett Aluminium Limited of South Africa. Alcan had been one of our earliest discussion partners, even from the days prior to the formal establishment of the Taskforce on the Churches and Corporate Responsibility. Because of the company's involvement in strategic industries and the major role aluminum plays in modern weapons systems, there had been a near certainty for years about Hulett's involvement in South Africa's military-industrial complex. This suspicion had been deepened by two factors. First, the South African armed forces' journal, *Paratus* (June 1980), reported that Hulett's South African chairman was serving on the South African prime minister's Defence Advisory Council. Second, Hulett had been designated a "national key point" industry under the National Key Points Act (1980), reserved for industries important to South Africa's military. Key point industries must comply with requests from the armed forces to store military equipment on company premises and to train company militia units in readiness for serious racial unrest. Alcan itself minimized its military involvement in South Africa. For all they knew, we were told, Hulett might be producing aluminum lunch boxes for soldiers or, at the most, insignificant quantities of specialized materials that could be used for military equipment. The company resisted our repeated requests for a review and full disclosure by its board of its military involvement in South Africa.

We put the case of the key point designation to the Canadian government and asked that it disallow as normal operating expenses, for purposes of Canadian tax deduction, taxes paid to the South African government on military contracts and costs incurred through the requirement of the South African Key Points Act. However, no such thing could be done. The Canadian government felt that it could not properly or effectively use Canada's tax laws to prevent companies' compliance "with legal obligations placed on it by the South African Government."[4]

The Canadian government showed no interest at all in the possible weapons' components Alcan and its South African partner might be supplying to the South African government.

Presumably this was for the same reason advanced by the government in the case of Ford Canada: namely, that by manufacturing military goods for the apartheid government in South Africa rather than importing them from Canada, Alcan was not violating the mandatory arms embargo. The cases of Ford and of Alcan made it clear to us that the Canadian government was not in the least concerned about the possible and effective circumvention by Canadian companies of the arms embargo resolution. Instead, it was engaged in legalistic sophistry to demonstrate that the wording of the resolution precluded any need for action on the part of the Canadian government.

Following the 1984-85 popular uprisings throughout South Africa and the imposition of a state of emergency, the Canadian government finally issued several sanctions measures. These included a ban on equipment sales from Canada to the military and police. We filed a formal shareholder proposal with Alcan asking the company to apply this same restriction to its South African operation. If this was not possible, it should dispose of its South African investment. In the negotiations over the proposal, senior Alcan management assured us that the benefits to their black workers far outweighed in significance Hulett's negligible sales to the military. They informed us that they would oppose our proposal at the shareholders' meeting for this reason.

It took a personal visit to South Africa to finally learn the facts about the company's involvement with the South African arms industry. In early 1986 I acted as resource person to an official delegation of Canadian Catholics, whose members were guests of the Southern African Catholic Bishops' Conference. During a meeting with Hulett's workers, we learned that the company produced a variety of military components, such as casings for rocket shells, aluminum fins for bombs, specialized sheet metal for armoured plating, and explosive powder for both civilian and military use. These materials, we were told, were sold to South Africa's state-owned Armaments Production Corporation, its subsidiaries, and affiliates.

Returning to Canada, we issued a news release relating what had been disclosed to us. One week before the March shareholder meeting, a senior Alcan officer phoned the Taskforce to inform us that Alcan Canada was about to announce an agreement to sell its South African interest to Hulett's parent company. In the final analysis, we could rely neither on the Canadian government's new get-tough-with-South Africa policy nor on Alcan's assurance that its involvement in military commerce in South Africa was insignificant. Only the courage of South African workers and the determination of the members of the Taskforce brought to an end this Canadian complicity with the South African defence industry.

The Pillage of Namibian Resources

South Africa's continued and illegal occupation of Namibia prompted us to request that the Canadian government and Canadian mining companies recognize United Nations Decree No. 1 (1974). In 1966 Canada had supported a UN resolution that terminated South Africa's mandate to rule Namibia and declared illegal South Africa's continued occupation of the country. Decree No. 1 sought to protect the natural resources of the people of Namibia until an internationally recognized government could decide how Namibians could best benefit from them. Canadian companies with investment in Namibian resource industries were Falconbridge (which sold its mine in 1983) and Rio Algom, which had a 10 per cent interest in the Rossing uranium mine and a seat on its board of directors.

Successive Canadian governments refused to recognize Decree No. 1, and Canadian companies were able, with no adverse consequences, to deplete Namibia's non-renewable resources. On the contrary, although these companies operated under concessions from the illegal administration and paid taxes to it, they were allowed to deduct taxes paid to the illegal regime from their Canadian taxes. Far from simply tolerating such activities, the Canadian government itself participated in this profitable plunder. It issued import permits for uranium mined in Namibia and continued to be involved in processing this uranium through its crown corporation Eldorado Nuclear Limited right up to the start of the implementation of the UN plan for Namibian independence in 1989. None of this, according to Canadian governments since 1966, conflicted with Canada's policy of regarding South Africa's administration of Namibia as illegal.[5]

In our experience with government ministers and corporate management, few issues have elicited responses as unforthcoming as those related to Canadian policies on Namibia. Searching for an answer to why this should be so, I am reminded of a throw-away remark made in 1975 by a junior official working in the office of the secretary of state. Seeing us out of the building after a meeting with the minister, he speculated that the government would never accept Decree No. 1 because essentially it asked on behalf of Namibia what Canadian native peoples were unsuccessfully demanding in Canada: no resource development before land claims are settled. Fourteen years later and in view of all we learned about the forty-year struggle of the Lubicon Lake

Band for a land-claims settlement in northern Alberta, this remark still remains the most likely explanation.

The Invisible Sanctions against South Africa

For about a year and a half in 1985 and 1986, the Mulroney government appeared determined to provide domestic and international leadership in progressive policy changes regarding the apartheid state. His government announced a series of measures that in part resembled policy recommendations the Taskforce had offered over the previous decade. However, in contradistinction to the Taskforce's recommendations, none of the government sanctions, which were announced with considerable fanfare, had legislative backing. They therefore lacked any means of enforcement and proved too feeble to withstand the efforts of determined opponents to undermine them. The enormous surge in Canada-South Africa trade figures for 1988 and 1989 bears this out. By 1989, we are left with fluffy public relations exercises designed to divert public expectations away from the promise of further sanctions in order to save face for the government and preserve the remnants of a progressive image.

It is perhaps an amusing footnote to this gloomy section to quote the indefatigable Glenn Babb, South Africa's ambassador to Canada between 1985 and 1987. Writing in Peter Worthington's February/March 1987 issue of *Influence*, a glossy magazine for the upwardly mobile Canadian male, he comments favourably that "the Department of External Affairs went to considerable lengths to find out from businessmen how sanctions could affect them in the way of imports and exports. Most of these businessmen rejected interference in their affairs and spelled out the consequences for them."

However, for "Ottawa," Babb reserved some rather extravagant language, which, in the light of our persistent disagreements with government policies, misrepresents both our position and that of the Mulroney government. Surely Babb was not reflecting the thinking of External Affairs officials when he wrote: "Ascertaining the losses Canadian business would suffer was an exercise in futility. Ottawa was merely going through the motions before applying sanctions that the Task Force on the Churches and Corporate Responsibility (TFCCR) [sic] had already, long before, decided for the government."

Private Loans and Public Debt

Flush with petro-dollars that had flowed into the international banking system after the abrupt increase in petroleum prices in 1973, bankers from all Western countries attended annual meetings of the International Monetary Fund (IMF) and the World Bank with only one intention: to lend, lend, lend. At these and other financial get-togethers billions of dollars were dealt into the treasuries of Third World governments, particularly those of Latin American regimes with often threadbare credit-worthiness and a track record of alarming instability. In 1981-82 the party was over; a worldwide recession drove up interest rates and borrower after borrower found that they could not repay the loans that were now falling due.

During the intervening years, the TCCR had been engaged in an intense discussion with Canadian bankers, presenting evidence of gross and systematic human rights violations by governments seeking Canadian loans, and pressing bankers to apply social criteria to their loans policy and to withhold loans to repressive regimes.

South Africa

The case of bank loans to South Africa and to Chile best illustrates the point. In 1974 an unknown employee of the European American Banking Corporation made available to the Interfaith Center for Corporate Responsibility printouts of multimillion-dollar loans made by Western bank syndicates to the South African government and its state agencies. For the first time we began to appreciate the substantial role of private bankers in international politics, previously hidden from minority shareholders behind the screen of client/banker confidentiality.

We spent the ensuing decade gathering evidence of loan involvement and making the case to the major Canadian banks in private and public meetings that their continued lending was but a vote of confidence in the apartheid regime, ensuring the continuance of the status quo. The banks tenaciously defended their right to extend loans to South Africa on the grounds that these were perfectly legal — although, they said, client/banker confidentiality prevented them from revealing such loans (indeed, they argued that they were even prevented from telling us when they had not made loans!). They scoffed at our suggestion that South African president P.W. Botha was a bad risk; governments, they said, do not default. In any case, they did not want to get mixed up in politics and they thought that at least some loans to the South African government would benefit the black population.

The proposition was swiftly rejected by our South African friends, whose history provided no evidence for this.

Having returned to the major Canadian banks year after year since 1975 with our updates on South Africa's oppression and with persistent requests that loans should no longer be made to the apartheid state, we take some credit for making the task of the Mulroney government easy when, in 1985, it requested and received the banks' agreement to a voluntary ban on new South African loans. Beginning with the Royal Bank in 1978, most of the large Canadian banks had established increasing restrictions on South African loans, which by 1985 amounted to a virtual no-new-loans policy.

Chile

After the bloody coup d'état in Chile in 1973, international outrage grew over the junta's unceasing human rights violations. Bilateral and major multilateral aid to Chile declined. Towards the end of 1975, several donor governments began to attach human rights criteria to their Chilean aid programs. It was at this stage that General Pinochet turned, successfully, to private banks for support. By 1977, more than 80 per cent of Chile's total borrowing was accounted for by private bank loans and suppliers' credits. The five major Canadian banks (the Royal Bank of Canada, the Bank of Montreal, the Canadian Imperial Bank of Commerce, the Toronto-Dominion Bank, and the Bank of Nova Scotia) were heavily involved in this lending spree. We estimated from public sources that between 1976 and 1982 when the Chilean economy collapsed, these Canadian banks had participated in consortia loans to Chile amounting to a total of at least U.S.$2.231 billion.[6]

As with Canadian bank loans to South Africa, the TCCR attempted to prevent this increasing involvement of our banks with the brutal regime in Chile. We owed it to our partners in Chile to do our best to shorten their agony and to expose the regime's violent acts. We did not want our bankers to conduct business as usual with this unusually bloodthirsty regime. The banks, for their part, were expressing confidence in the introduction of free market principles in post-coup Chile. The extent of their Chilean loan participation showed that theirs was not only the role of an interested observer. We argued in vain in closed meetings with management and in the public arena of shareholder meetings that in addition to the appalling human rights violations, the economic growth of Chile under Pinochet was favouring the interests of the elite and was exacting high social costs from the majority of the population. Ordinary Chileans now faced increased unemployment, decline in real income, reduction in social services, including health care and education, and removal of state subsidies on basic food stuffs.

With the influx of foreign capital, corruption among the rich and the powerful increased. In 1982 the Chilean regime was forced to intervene to save several large banks from collapse. In a dramatic reversal of its free market discipline, the junta took charge of the banks' overdue loans and bad debts, totalling about U.S.$1 billion. Nevertheless, our suggestion in 1982 that Pinochet's Chile, like Botha's South Africa, was a bad risk drew this bristling rebuke from a senior banker during a shareholder meeting: "We think if there is one thing of which we are capable, it is assessing loan risks.... We would not be involved in Chile if we had reason to believe that we are risking the bank's funds unwisely, so we're perfectly satisfied with our exposure in that particular country."[7]

This was the year that saw the end of voluntary loans to Chile and the beginning of endless rounds of involuntary loans as that country fell behind in its interest payments. "Involuntary loans" is the bankers' euphemism for loans made to debtors so that they can service their debt.

Guatemala

Private sector loans frequently dwarfed, or replaced in importance, official transfers through foreign aid programs. Loans to Guatemala between 1977 and 1985 provide a classic example of this phenomenon. During those years, Guatemala saw some of the most brutal human rights violations in the entire hemisphere. The country was rocked by a succession of military coups, which by 1984 had brought four different generals to power in as many years, each as corrupt as his predecessor, creating a public relations nightmare for their Western backers. The situation was so unstable and dangerous that the Canadian government had suspended its project aid and withdrawn its aid personnel.

In 1981 the TCCR was touched by these events directly when a founding member of the Taskforce, Sister Noel O'Neil of the Sisters of St. Joseph (Toronto), had to flee from Guatemala after a grenade had been hurled into her convent and her name had appeared on an army death list. Also in that year a Roman Catholic lay missionary from New Brunswick was murdered by death squads.

It was therefore with amazement that we learned in October 1981 from *This Week*, a Guatemalan business newsletter, that several Canadian banks were participating in a sizeable loan for a major road network in Guatemala that was to serve the military and its commercial interests. The TCCR felt that by stepping in where Canadian aid would no longer go, the Canadian banks were undercutting Canada's foreign policy position. On several occasions Canada had initiated or supported resolutions at the United Nations Commission on Human Rights chastising the Guatemalan regime for its continued and systematic human rights violations. The Taskforce also judged the banks' loans to be totally irrational in view of the inherent instability and corruption of these successive military regimes. Five months after the loan agreement was concluded, another coup brought a new general to power. He promptly cancelled the road project and threw its executive officers into jail on charges of corruption. The Guatemalan people, already bludgeoned by the military, now had to shoulder the financial burden of repayment. The ousted regime, which had signed the original agreement, had guaranteed the loan. In the view of the international bankers, they were doing nothing illegal in demanding their due.

The Bank Act and Foreign Policy Implications
When in 1978 the Canadian Parliament began its decennial revision of the Canadian Bank Act, we saw an opportunity to take our concerns about Canadian bank loans to repressive regimes to the House of Commons Standing Committee on Finance, Trade and Economic Affairs and to the Standing Senate Committee on Banking, Trade and Commerce. We proposed that in the interest of public and shareholder accountability a revised bank act should include provisions for uniform and equitable disclosure of loans over $1 million by Canadian banks to foreign governments or their agencies. We also proposed that in order to preserve the principle of client/banker confidentiality, such disclosure should only be made thirty days after a loan agreement had been signed. Referring to loans to South Africa and to Chile, we argued that such loans had major foreign policy implications, since they sustain repressive regimes unacceptable to our government and to large numbers of concerned Canadians. Such regimes, we suggested, are able, at no risk to themselves, to ignore diplomatic reproaches from governments:

> Significant loans to foreign governments are an important, at times a crucial element in the determination of some governments of their social, political and economic systems and in the formation of Canadian foreign policy responses to them.... In many ways, such loans or the absence of such loans, are as and sometimes more significant in Canada's foreign relations than are foreign policy stands by the Canadian government.[8]

Our policy proposal was rejected by the Standing Committee. Had it been accepted, it is just possible that faced with disclosure, banks might have shied away from or would at least have reduced lending to the most unsavoury and unstable regimes. As the generals and dictators were gradually replaced by fragile democratic structures in such countries as the Philippines, Brazil, Argentina, Guatemala, Nicaragua, and Bolivia, their governments and people might have been less burdened today by crushing international debt incurred by their erstwhile predecessors. Dictatorships and repression might not have lasted quite as long; official corruption might have been less profitable; and the pool of money leaving these countries (for overseas bank accounts!) might have been smaller. Alas, the uncurbed lending spree continued until the recession in 1981-82.

A particularly cruel irony is visited upon the poor and the marginalized in most debtor countries. Under their corrupt and oppressive governments, they had endured unemployment, wage controls, and cutbacks in both social services and food subsidies. The poor had not benefited at all from the international bank loans that had sustained their rulers. Now, as these heavily indebted states seek help from the International Monetary Fund, they face identical policy demands — cutbacks in social services and food subsidies — as essential conditions for IMF credits. Thus, the suffering of the poor continues, this time because their governments have to meet interest payments on loans that were imprudently contracted by both borrower and lender.

Fifteen years ago when international bank loans flooded the markets, the TCCR had asked for the inclusion of social criteria in the banks' loan policies and for greater prudence in the choice of their clients. We submitted briefs to our government and participated in parliamentary hearings to argue the case of the poor and the victims of oppression in order to obtain for them a modicum of protection and relief. Today, the tide has gone out. Where bankers had welcomed and with their loans supported the promotion of free market policies, they are now looking to their governments for relief from loan losses. In this they are successful. The Canadian government allows the banks to deduct from their taxes requisite increases in their reserve funds against possible default by major debtors. In other words, Canadian taxpayers partially underwrite losses incurred by Canadian banks for loans from which they had no benefit and about which they were neither informed nor consulted. No parallel relief mechanisms have been devised to shield the debtor countries and the poor within them from the hardships of loan repayments.[9]

Is It Worth the Trouble?

At this point one might conclude that this chapter does little else but demonstrate how small the impact of church shareholders has been in their call for justice and how disproportionate are the efforts that must be made to influence the business community or the policies of the Canadian government. Judging the achievements of the Taskforce on the Churches and Corporate Responsibility on an incremental basis, however, presents a far more optimistic picture. Recognizing that corporations like the churches are major social institutions that contribute to the shaping of society's values and aspirations, the member churches of the Taskforce had set out to awaken or to reinforce within the Canadian corporate community a commitment to corporate social responsibilities. They launched this long-term program by approaching the corporations with specific and concrete social injustices to which the corporations were contributing. Few would have predicted in 1975 that this initiative would endure and would expand to the kind of activities that could only be sketched in the preceding pages. The novelty of this work had provoked anger and opposition in powerful sections of the church and of the business community that might, in the early years, have overwhelmed us had it not been for the resolve of the first board to stay its course. Thus, important pioneering work was accomplished. Few today continue to question the legitimacy of the effort to be a socially responsible investor, with a concern for social ethics and for the impact of financial decisions on a whole range of people.

An important factor in this change has been credibility. Because the Taskforce is one of the few organizations in Canada that directly addresses the social consequences of corporate activities, a wide range of national and international organizations and media rely on the Taskforce for accurate information. Granted, the corporations, banks, and departments of government with whom these questions have been raised have at their disposal financial resources and staff contingents far in excess of those of the Taskforce. However, we have as our most valuable human resource our partners and friends in the Third World who tell us about conditions of life and about the impact of companies in their countries. They provide us not only with important evidence, but their stories also deepen our covenant to act on their behalf. To win their confidence and to build credibility for our organization in Canada have been major achievements.

Finally, we realized from the start that whatever influence we would exert on Canadian foreign (or domestic) policy would have to be done by means other than quiet lobbying. We had to win public recognition before we could hope to be listened to seriously by the Canadian government. To the extent that the quality of the work of the Taskforce has gained it recognition, the government and its public service have come to accept the TCCR as a critic of consequence.

However, to do justice to the moral task requires more than intellectual credibility. To win the widest possible understanding and support for our concerns, our submissions to government seek to be self-explanatory, containing a narrative background, the bases for recommendations offered, and the recommendations themselves. Such briefs are certainly written for the government, but they are also designed with an eye on their value for public education. Thus, even if government remains unresponsive and the primary objective of the brief has not been achieved, the story will have been told in a way that is generally instructive about the activities of the government. Lifting a corner of the curtain that commonly conceals the more complex entanglements of government and corporations may not be the least of the accomplishments of the TCCR.

7 • The Good Samaritan Stops at the UN: Canadian Churches and the Struggle for Human Rights

Tim Ryan

Since the United Nations (UN) was established, member nations have been trying to work out their own consensus on the basic standards for the treatment of people by states and their agents. The enormous gap between the UN covenants on human rights and the actual experience of victims of torture and disappearance has fostered a worldwide human rights network in which Canadian churches have participated. The task of this network has been to hold states accountable for their treatment of their own citizens and to prod other states into an assertive role in protecting the voiceless of the world from violations by their own governments.

The Canadian churches have created specialized organizations to help them document the real situation for human rights in countries where people are at extreme risk. They have also developed a means of accompanying states as they gather at the UN from year to year to review their achievements in advancing the cause of human rights. It is an exercise in truth telling, neighbourliness, and human solidarity on a global scale.

Tim Ryan is director of the Ecumenical Forum of Canada and a priest with the Scarboro Foreign Mission Society. He worked as a missionary in Brazil for many years. On his return, he served as director of the Inter-Church Committee for Human Rights in Latin America, where he was responsible for fact-finding trips to Central and Latin America and for assessments of country situations and preparation of Canadian church briefs to government and to the United Nations.

— Ed.

Human Rights and Moral Commitment

The human rights work of Canadian churches has drawn together a broad spectrum of religious bodies in which the majority of

Canadian Christians have membership. Structurally, the work on human rights in Latin America, Africa, Asia, and other parts of the world has been a triumph of ecumenical co-operation. In this work, the churches have wed a specialized and structured social action in defence of human rights with a faith perspective and moral commitment. In a religious sense, the work has been a way of making concrete Jesus' call to be neighbour to the one who had been beaten and robbed on his journey; however, in our world being neighbour is less a matter of taking the victim to the nearest inn than it is a question of accompanying him into the labyrinthine corridors of the United Nations and External Affairs, in search of protection.

The approach of the churches has been grounded in their religious and moral perspective, in contrast to the secular and legal approach of other organizations. As sponsors of specialized human rights organizations, their expertise was only secondarily in human rights and only tangentially in foreign policy. The expertise of the churches was primarily rooted in experience. Their connections with church counterparts in other countries brought them into daily contact with people who had been tortured, arbitrarily arrested, or made to disappear. Having had that direct experience, churches approached questions of human rights from the point of view of the victims of violations, rather than from an academic or diplomatic perspective. Nevertheless, the churches have acquired a certain institutional experience and history in human rights work that amazes one sometimes.

The experiment with specialized human rights organizations began in the early 1970s, but its roots lie much deeper in the personal experiences of individuals who have been changed and converted by the experience of people in other countries of the world. Travel has given that opportunity to many more people than in the past. Also, church people who served overseas — and their children — brought back a knowledge of life in other cultures that goes back generations. Over time, these missionaries brought into the Canadian church a changed and rather sophisticated analysis of the experience of people abroad, as well as of our own experience. They helped bring about a realization in Canadian churches that one thing Canadians could do to support the struggle for human rights around the world was to change those aspects of life in Canada that hinder or advance the pursuit of human rights in other countries.

People who had had such an experience overseas also brought to the Canadian churches a certain tactical realism. They recognized that change does not come about with hit-and-run tactics.

As valuable as a church leaders' brief or a mass rally might be, it takes more sophisticated tactics to create the kind of impact on social structures that will change them. What was called for was radical social engagement, rather than idealistic moralizing.

To move themselves beyond hit-and-run tactics, churches created specialized human rights organizations. They were generally organized geographically: the Inter-Church Committee for Human Rights in Latin America (ICCHRLA); the Canada-Asia Working Group (CAWG); the Inter-Church Coalition for Africa (ICCAF); and more modest committees working on human rights in the Middle East, the Caribbean, and the Helsinki region.

The mandates of these committees and organizations differ, but at bottom they can all be described as groups that try to contribute in practical and concrete ways to the struggles of peoples in Latin America, Asia, and Africa to overcome human rights violations and to advance towards greater social justice and full human development.

Today, the human rights work of these groups goes on in a regular cycle that brings the real life experience of violated people in other countries to the attention of the Canadian government as it addresses particular foreign policy questions and, ultimately, to the attention of the other governments that gather annually at the United Nations to review the situation for human rights around the world. The role of specialized organizations like the Inter-Church Committee on Human Rights in Latin America, the one I know most intimately, is to hold up the experience of people who have been tortured or have had relatives disappear against the rhetoric of governmental claims that all is well in this country or that. It is a work of truth telling and calling the responsible to account in full view of as many of the people of the world as can be persuaded to watch.

This kind of work is carried by two distinct tasks: monitoring the human rights situations and working out strategies for an effective Canadian contribution to securing human rights around the world.

Getting the Story Straight

Human rights organizations like the ones in Canada depend on an independent and objective pursuit of the facts of a human rights situation and on bringing those facts forward in such a way that they get public attention. Often a very difficult situation simply does not register in the consciousness of Canadians. In a complex world, geographical distance may make it slip from view. In such a situation, the greatest enemy of human rights is the simple lack of attention. People who do not know what is going on miss the opportunity to express the fact that they care about it. In turn, people who are being cruelly repressed can be left isolated and disempowered because no one knows their story.

The existence of worldwide organizations of churches, as with many professional groups, means that a basic network exists between people whose lives would normally be contained within the boundaries of their own countries. Information about bad human rights situations can be passed around that network through the regular meetings of the committees and assemblies that make world organizations work. The network means that people with a commitment to one another hear the story of human rights violations from the point of view of the violated, even when their story might not yet be getting the attention of the world media.

Once a situation has been identified, however, the critical task for a human rights organization like the ICCHRLA is getting to the facts. This is often very difficult, for any number of reasons. Distance is the most obvious. Fact-finding missions can be important but are also very costly and in some situations are simply not possible. Civil strife and anarchistic conditions in a country may mean that the information systems are not working, much less the other services that make it possible for Canadian human rights workers to meet with their counterparts and the victims of abuses in the country. Language can also get in the way at times, especially with indigenous groups or others that may be under attack. Beyond that, interpretations of events by groups both inside and outside the country representing particular interests can blur the facts of a case. Yet solid, irrefutable information is critical to the work of bringing the real situation for human rights before those responsible for upholding international law and the commitments to human rights it is supposed to represent.

This need for facts has forced groups like the ICCHRLA to build links with as many human rights organizations as possible in each country: churches and church human rights groups, specialized human rights organizations, organizations created by victims and their relatives, and every other kind of group active in human rights work. The point has been to multiply the sources of information and to use critical investigative techniques so that the facts on the human rights situation can be as free as possible of ignorance, manipulation, and political or ideological bias. People who experience violations or are threatened by abuse depend on absolute truth and accuracy as a minimal defence.

Governments, including our own, are often heavily influenced by information supplied by other governments. A government accused of carrying out, or at the least tolerating, serious human rights violations will have its own special interest in discrediting individuals who have charged them. Some will resort to human rights rhetoric in an effort to be seen as saying the right things on the international stage. Others will admit that human rights violations occur, but that they are necessary in order to create the conditions for progress in the country.

The special relationship between governments created by the norms of international diplomacy creates another problem for human rights groups. The details of the story of human rights abuses need to be put on the table and their interpretation tested in the light of the international standard agreed to by the member nations of the UN. If the Canadian government is to be expected to take diplomatic action on a particular situation — despite the protests of a particular state — the facts need to be correct or the people themselves will be in danger of fading from the view of governments like ours.

Getting the facts on the record, however, is not only laborious; it is also extremely sensitive. Details must be verified by several sources. Human rights workers need to know the strengths and weaknesses, as well as the interests, of the sources of their information. More than that, they have to remember that they are dealing with the testimonies and the photographs of people whose relatives have suffered terrible loss. Each person and each situation matters. The people involved are not just "cases," nameless victims of a concept known as "human rights violation," or even examples of trends in the human rights record of this country or that. The human rights workers have to take up the horrifying experience of real people and bring it forward as a public witness in the spirit of human solidarity.

The means for ferreting out the facts of a story are actually quite ordinary. Reading is one of the most important. Much of the information about violations is available through printed material. Daily newspapers often tell a great deal about violations, as do reports of human rights organizations, academics, unions, professional organizations, and even commissions of inquiry. The flood of information has to be culled, weighed, and compared. Claims have to be verified and conclusions drawn.

Although the story of human rights violations may well be in sources available to virtually all of us, the threads of the story appear one strand at a time. They move past us day after day in such a way that they become fragments of information rather than a story whose meaning we can discern. That means that human rights workers must spend a great deal of time piecing together bits of stories that have emerged gradually. They are at one level "readers" for the Department of External Affairs and the UN, readers who watch for the story of what is happening to the people most at risk within a society.

Visits to countries where violations are going on are also important. In fact, Canadian churches have encouraged the Canadian government to broaden its own direct contacts within countries and to increase its sources of information to include a broad range of grass-roots, credible, and independent sources of human rights information. Human rights workers may need to go to refugee camps to take the testimony of people who have fled a massacre or a war. Or international observers might be requested by the churches or other national organizations of a country to witness major events, such as elections.

The United Nations itself can provide important pieces of the human rights story through a special type of visitor known as a "Special Rapporteur." These people are appointed by the UN to go to a particular country to investigate a very serious situation and to report back to the UN Commission on Human Rights (UNCHR) on behalf of the international community.

The reports of Special Rapporteurs can be extremely helpful in putting human rights violations in the public spotlight. They also have some obvious limitations. Governments accused of violations have to co-operate with the Special Rapporteur if they wish to remain in good standing with the UN, but countries with the worst records and little need for international approval may refuse to co-operate. Or reports may be written with less concreteness than the situation requires. Still, a rapporteur can play an important role in opening up the facts in a particular country and placing the information available from non-governmental organizations (NGOs) on the collective table.

Developing Strategies in Support of Human Rights

Once the facts of the human rights situation have been gathered, the question becomes, To whom does this information go and how do we get the people with responsibility to hear it? In the early days of this work, the churches tended to convey much of the information they had by every means possible: letters to the minister of external affairs; meetings arranged between victims of violations and government officials; dossiers to members of Parliament for use during Question Period; briefs to the Canadian delegation to the United Nations Commission on Human Rights; and so on.

At some point during the 1970s, the Canadian churches and their partners in Latin America began looking for a particular role that Canadians could carry out in support of human rights work inside particular countries. Human rights groups in Latin America were quite sophisticated about what they could do domestically, but they were also sophisticated enough to understand that there were other hands that could assist them outside their country. The United Nations was the obvious place to put those hands to work, partly because it was one arena that was always available, even when their domestic situation had been closed down by severe repression. Latin American colleagues decided that UN work was an important supportive strategy and began asking people in other countries to become involved. It was a significant step for Canadian churches because it allowed them to move from assisting people overseas in a sporadic fashion to forming a network of human solidarity.

For Canadian churches, the priority was clear: they needed to use whatever clout the Canadian government and other Canadian actors might have in Latin America to support a change in the human rights situation. The churches in ICCHRLA considered Canadian corporations and investments in the region, as well as strong bilateral ties between Canada and violator nations, as points on which to press for action on human rights. Since these were relatively few, it made more sense to press for Canadian action in a multilateral arena like the UN Commission on Human Rights. That was one place where Canadian foreign policy had the potential for making Canada an actor on the world stage in support of people's struggles for human rights.

Gradually, the churches worked out a way of accompanying the UN process as a key strategy of their human rights work. The point to the exercise was to inform and to have an impact on Canadian policy and practice at the UN, as well as to work directly within UN structures to have an impact on other governments as they assessed the global human rights agenda and the records of the countries coming before them each year.

There were two main channels for working. The first was the Third Committee of the General Assembly. The second was the UN Commission itself, which meets each year for six weeks in February and March. The process is much the same each year. The human rights workers bring their factual assessments of the country situations to the arena where those countries will be considered by their peers — other governments — and judgements will be made. Those judgements might range from passing a resolution with a negative judgement against the offending government, naming a rapporteur to study the situation and report back, or recommending that member nations of the UN change their behaviour towards the offending country (by stopping arms shipments, for example). These actions would not actually change the human rights situation in the country, but they would place some small limits on the freedom of the government to violate the rights of its own people with impunity.

A Voice within the United Nations

Canadian churches have no particular interest of their own to advance by participating in the UN Commission on Human Rights process. The point has been to help provide "a voice to those who have no voice" and to ensure that those with the power to make decisions hear that voice as they vote. This has sometimes meant ensuring that people from violator countries get to Geneva themselves. Early on in their work on the UN Commission, the Canadian ambassador to the UNCHR, Ambassador Yvon Beaulne, recounted his own experience in that arena. He reported that at one point the American and Chilean delegations were seeking support for a resolution that would end the work of a UN working group on the disappeared. That year a group of relatives of the disappeared had travelled to Geneva to monitor the proceedings. "Somehow," the ambassador said, "when it came to the crucial vote, it was impossible to vote for ending the group because we knew the Grandmothers of the Disappeared were in the gallery and their eyes were upon us."

The UN Commission is an intergovernmental process and therefore relatively inaccessible to the average victim of human rights abuses — especially people who have no money of their own to dedicate to the task. Some international non-governmental organizations have been granted consultative status with the commission. For Canadian churches, the link is through the Commission of the Churches in International Affairs (CCIA) of the World Council of Churches (WCC), which has NGO status with the UN.

It is a rare occasion when the most victimized people are able to speak for themselves to the UN Commission. When Chilean student Carmen Gloria Quintana told her own story at the UNCHR, she became in the world press a representative of the thousands of voiceless people who will never get to put the facts of their cases on the table. Carmen Gloria described her experience of being attacked by Chilean soldiers as she and a companion walked towards a student demonstration; they were beaten, doused with gasoline, and set alight by the soldiers.

Carmen and her family had fled to Canada, where staff of the ICCHRLA met her in hospital in Montreal. Because churches declare that their place as religious communities is with the victims, the Canadian Council of Churches (CCC) was asked to pay for Carmen and her mother to travel to Geneva so that she could tell her own story before the UN Commission. The CCC agreed, but it took more than a plane ticket to get her story into the official record. As an individual victim, Carmen Gloria had no right to speak; an NGO had to request time on the agenda and appoint her as its spokesperson. The World Student Christian Federation (WSCF) agreed to do this. Beyond that, Swiss medical authorities were initially reluctant to let her into the country because local doctors — for fear of liability suits — were unwilling to carry out the medical treatments prescribed by her Montreal doctors.

Nevertheless, when she recounted her story for the delegates, a dozen ambassadors rushed forward to embrace her. The Chilean delegation had asked for the right to respond, but thought better of it when they saw the reaction of other delegates. And the American delegation dropped the resolution it had been circulating that had offered praise to the Chilean government for its progress towards democracy. Instead, a resolution condemning human rights abuses in Chile was adopted.

Anecdotes such as this one might suggest influence and power. In reality they are brief moments of humanity in a world with the capacity to make thousands disappear daily and to burn every student who happens to get in the way. But even that brief moment is better than nothing. It is a way of making a public demonstration that the people who suffer at the hands of their governments matter and that we in the rest of the world know what is going on and who is doing it. The facts of the story matter.

With so few victims actually able to confront the delegations meeting at the UN Commission, it has been important to find ways to stimulate as many delegations as possible to take an active role in restraining human rights violators. ICCHRLA was the first of the Canadian churches' human rights organizations to commit time and energy to the UN process. ICCHRLA set out to focus its information on human rights in major briefs on disappearances, torture, arbitrary arrests and detentions, and attacks on civilians in Chile, Argentina, El Salvador, Guatemala — most of the places in Central and Latin America where human rights violations were going on. It presented its information to all delegations, key media, and non-governmental organizations. It also arranged for Canadian church observers to be in Geneva during the UNCHR's meeting.

The flurry of activity around the time of the meeting made human rights issues newsworthy in Canadian papers, as church delegates sent home information on the efforts of one country to avoid a Special Rapporteur or of the American delegation to get Chile removed from the agenda of countries for review. At the end of the annual session, the Canadian church delegate would hold a briefing session for the media on the outcome of the UNCHR meeting, on the performance of the Canadian delegation, and on situations still untouched.

Gradually, it became clear that the Canadian delegation had poor information on specific situations or no instructions from the Canadian government to support a particular judgement on, say, Guatemala. This meant that more people than the members of the Canadian delegation needed to be made aware of the facts of human rights violations and to be pressed to take those facts into account in forming and implementing government policy. Otherwise, there was little hope of achieving consistency between Canadian rhetoric on human rights and actual performance on the international stage, as well as back home.

From the churches' point of view, there was a clear need for a series of mechanisms for taking human rights seriously and inserting them into the decision-making process in Ottawa. Over the years, a regular cycle of human rights gatherings has been developed, in which a large number of Canadian human rights organizations now participate. Typically, the work year within Canada begins for the churches with a meeting between their human rights workers and the Canadian ambassador to the UNCHR, plus staff of External Affairs. The objective is to share views on the accomplishments and failures of UN human rights work during the past year and to develop a shopping list of the situations that need special attention during the months before the next meeting of the UNCHR. The churches have pressed the ambassador to request information from officials of the Canadian government responsible for geographic areas. The point has been to increase Canadian capacity to gather independent information so that Canada can make its own assessment of serious situations, rather than rely on information supplied by violator regimes or even simply the American government.

In January of each year, the Department of External Affairs gathers together what some call the "human rights family": non-governmental organizations, the minister for external affairs, the Canadian delegation to the UN Commission on Human Rights, and area desk specialists, among others. At this meeting, the facts are in. What is at stake for human rights workers is getting a commitment on the part of the government to support a resolution on Country X or the appointment of a Special Rapporteur to a country or a special theme or even a preferred wording for a new human rights standard being developed by the UNCHR.

Over time, the NGOs pushed for a written government statement of the position it was willing to see govern the activities of the Canadian delegation in Geneva. A written statement had become important, as church representatives realized that although in many meetings officials and civil servants had nodded in apparent agreement with the churches' argument, once out of Ottawa they had done nothing to support a stronger approach to human rights; sometimes, in fact, they had supported the erosion of human rights by silence at the wrong moments.

The in-Canada phase of the Canadian churches' work on the UN process has become critical to closing the loop between Canada's statements of international commitment to human rights at the UN and its actual behaviour back home vis-à-vis people's struggles to have international commitments realized in their own countries. As important as international commitments are, church human rights organizations began looking for more than a correct vote at the UN. They began looking for greater explicitness on human rights in Canadian foreign policy. They also began looking for mechanisms of accountability for people charged with implementing Canada's commitment to human rights. Parliamentary committees needed to demand such accountability of government officials; they also needed to press for a transparent decision-making process on Canada's relations with human rights violator regimes, rather than a hidden process, often involving decisions on arms sales and so on, conducted in cabinet.

El Salvador: A Case in Point

El Salvador is one of the countries on which Canadian churches have filed major reports annually throughout the 1980s. Like other human rights organizations, the churches document the details of serious cases, such as the torture and killing of an entire group of people. However, the report is more than a listing of those who have disappeared, have become political prisoners, or have been killed. It also assesses trends in critical areas, such as the rule of law in the country, the government's actions to restrain death squads, and the impact of the war on civilians.

The 1987 meeting of the UN Commission on Human Rights was a particularly important occasion for human rights workers for several reasons. The U.S. government was taking an extremely partisan position in its reporting on human rights violations in El Salvador. Its open support of a military victory by the government and its aid commitment of almost two million dollars a day meant that victims of violations in El Salvador were not likely to find the American delegation drawing attention to their situation at the UNCHR meeting. In addition, the Canadian government had restored bilateral aid to El Salvador in 1986. Having decided that the Duarte government had the situation sufficiently in hand to merit renewed aid, the Canadian government also appeared to be under a certain pressure to look positively on the human rights record of El Salvador. Furthermore, two competing approaches to human rights were being advanced in the continuing debate over whether or not El Salvador had gotten the situation under control. Those who took a political approach argued that conditions in El Salvador had improved so dramatically that the government should be commended and that it was no longer necessary for international organizations to monitor the situation. Those who took a humanitarian approach argued that the kinds of violations that continued were an affront to human dignity and were as serious as under the previous regime.

The Canadian churches' assessment of the situation for human rights in El Salvador in 1987 was therefore an important one. The report was based on information gathered through fact-finding trips by Canadians and through excellent investigative work by numerous human rights organizations in El Salvador, including the Legal Protection Office of the Roman Catholic Archdiocese of San Salvador, the Salvadoran Non-Governmental Human Rights Commission, and the Federation of Co-operative Associations of Agricultural Production in El Salvador, among others.

The evidence gathered confirmed that fewer Salvadorans had been victims of torture and assassination at the hands of death squads during 1986; there had also been fewer civilians killed in indiscriminate bombing attacks by the country's military than in the previous year. The year 1986 had clearly seen improvements over the early eighties, but then those had been the bloodiest years in the country's history. The churches were not willing to give El Salvador a clean record, however, because of overwhelming evidence that the root causes of the violations had not been removed and that, in fact, systematic, if somewhat less grotesque, violations of people's dignity and of the principles of international law continued.

The experience of members of the Federation of Co-operative Associations of Agricultural Production in El Salvador illustrated the relationship between human rights abuses and the underlying social and economic conditions of the majority of the people of the country. In the first four months of 1986, approximately fifty people who were members of some of the organizations making up the federation were captured by the military or security forces. While many were released within a week of their arrest, some were held as political prisoners, four were killed, and one "disappeared."

These attacks occurred in the wake of government accusations that groups like the federation were "front organizations" for the guerrilla forces, while others were being manipulated by Marxist-Leninists. The churches found, however, that the impact of the continuing war, the 1986 earthquake, and government cutbacks in key areas of social investment were the sources of the social ferment in El Salvador in 1987. The government itself estimated that 30 per cent of the population was unemployed and 35 per cent underemployed. Meanwhile, the basic basket of consumer goods cost four times the average monthly wage of people employed in commercial, industrial, and service sectors and seven times the average wage of agricultural workers. Nearly 500,000 people had been displaced from their homes by the seven-year war and nearly 300,000 had had their homes damaged or destroyed in the earthquake.

In those circumstances, the social unrest was not surprising to the church team that visited El Salvador. People of El Salvador, ground down by the civil war and decades of economic deprivation, organized assemblies of people seeking fundamental change in their society, including communities of earthquake victims and groups of displaced people, as well as the more customary labour and agricultural organizations. Relatives of those members of the federation who were arrested or killed formed part of one of the organizations in El Salvador that worked most consistently for fundamental change in the country. The political prisoners and the people assassinated were indeed victims of human rights violations, but they were also victims of a more fundamental resistance on the part of the government to groups that have sought change through political and non-military means over the years. In their pursuit of fundamental human dignity and basic needs, the people of El Salvador were caught between government and guerrilla troops that did not recognize international law and human rights covenants; they were also deprived of the protection of the law because of a judiciary hampered by corruption, fear, and the socio-political chaos of the country.

Given these more fundamental problems in El Salvador, the Canadian churches urged the government to review the human rights situation again before any additional bilateral aid was granted. They also asked that the Canadian delegation to the UN General Assembly and to the Human Rights Commission take an active role in getting support for a resolution expressing concern for the continued human rights problems in El Salvador, as well as support for a continuing role for a Special Rapporteur in that country, whose task is clearly and critically defined.

The report prepared by ICCHRLA became the official record of the churches' assessment of the real situation for human rights in El Salvador, to be placed beside the declarations of the Salvadoran delegation and other interested parties in order that the merits of the cases made could be judged and a resolution adopted by the UN Commission on Human Rights. The Canadian churches, therefore, needed to make sure that country delegations as well as non-governmental organizations participating in the UNCHR had copies prior to the February meeting. They also had to ensure that the Canadian delegations and the key people in the federal government had seen the report and had had a chance to discuss the evidence for the key points on which it differed with the official assessment of External Affairs.

The 1987 consultation between External Affairs and the non-governmental human rights organizations followed what has now become a customary format. Government officials offered their assessment of the 1986 meeting of the UN General Assembly and noted the general issues that would affect the 1987 meeting of the UN Commission on Human Rights (in this case, a review of the status of the international covenants on human rights, the Convention on the Rights of the Child, a "Draft Body of Principles" aimed at protecting people who have been detained or imprisoned, and the UN's financial crisis). Officials gave an overview of the proposed agenda for the convention, many of the items routine by now and on some points unrelated to any serious effort to end abuses.

The heart of the matter, however, for the ICCHRLA was the discussion between External Affairs and the non-governmental organizations on the country situations to be discussed at the UNCHR meeting under agenda item 12: "situations which appear to reveal a consistent pattern of gross violations of human rights." Government officials, including people responsible for the area desks within External Affairs and those associated with multilateral organizations like the UN, offered the official assessment of the human rights situation in countries of particular concern in the UN or within the non-governmental community in Canada. In 1987 the list included Ethiopia, Uganda, South Africa, Egypt, Iran, Iraq, Israel, Lebanon, Syria, Afghanistan, India, Indonesia, Korea, Pakistan, Philippines, Sri Lanka, Vietnam, Chile, Cuba, El Salvador, Guatemala, Haiti, Nicaragua, Peru, and a CSCE update for Europe.

The government statement on El Salvador acknowledged that there had been a decline in death squad activity, disappearances, and bombings of civilians since the early 1980s, an observation confirmed by the report of the UN Special Rapporteur on El Salvador. The statement also noted that there was a great deal of room for improvement, including an end to the attacks on civilians by both parties to the civil war, an end to the detentions of human rights workers in the country, and a thorough reform of the country's judicial system to make it deal adequately with human rights violators under the principles of international law. The statement addressed the issue of Canada's renewed aid to El Salvador in the light of the continuing human rights violations. It argued that renewed aid was part of Canada's effort to ease the extreme human suffering created by the major earthquake in late 1986.

The churches were concerned that the Canadian delegation should recognize how much the fundamental situation in El Salvador had deteriorated, despite actual decreases in the numbers of individual human rights violations. They also wanted a commitment from the government that the Canadian delegation would support a renewed mandate for the Special Rapporteur rather than give an implied endorsement for the Duarte government if the rapporteur were dropped. The annual consultation included major time for dialogue between External Affairs and human rights groups, where the differences in their assessments could be tested. The churches have generally set out in the hope of persuading the Canadian government to take up the mandate that all states have within the UN: to recognize the legitimate interests of sovereign states and to pursue the member states' collective responsibility to citizens of any state who are victimized by their own government.

After the Canadian consultation, the action quickly moved to Geneva, where country delegations worked at reaching conclusions that could be supported by the majority of members at the end of the six-week session. The Canadian Council of Churches sent two observers to join other churches on the official observer team of the World Council of Churches. Their job was to meet with delegations, to make sure they had the reports, to explain details, and to seek strong leadership on behalf of the people who were most at risk in each situation.

The results were mixed for the ICCHRLA's work on El Salvador in 1987. The resolution that was finally adopted by the UN Commission took a stronger stand against violations than the one of the previous year, despite a glowing report by the Special Rapporteur. El Salvador remained on the commission's agenda. The Canadian delegation, led by Gordon Fairweather, was active, especially with European delegations, and gave a strong and pointed speech. Three Canadian MPs, members of the Parliamentary Standing Committee on Human Rights, participated in the commission. The Irish delegation gave a speech that quoted directly from the ICCHRLA briefs, and other delegations were seen consulting the materials before they gave their speeches.

Still, there were few dramatic moments regarding El Salvador in 1987. The interventions in Chile, Sri Lanka, and East Timor were more immediate that year. Clearly, too, the reports of special rapporteurs on the peace process allowed the human rights situation in particular countries to be viewed more positively than was warranted, according to the research of human rights organizations. The outcome of these interventions in El Salvador (as well as Guatemala and other countries on which the churches presented briefs) indicated how very difficult it is to provide real protection to people at risk of disappearance, assassination, and torture in countries where the fundamental causes of economic and social inequity continue and where civil war not only contributes to violations but delays the fundamental changes that would undercut the social conflict in which abuses flourish.

At one level, the UN process is an exercise in truth telling. It takes the commitments made by states to protect the rights of all people and holds these up against the hard evidence of real people's lives. At another level, though, it is an exercise in using what leverage Canada has to support the people in many countries of the world who struggle to hold their own governments to account and secure the protections they have been promised. In going through this process for over a decade now, Canadian churches have found that the UN process is also a means of sharpening our commitment to a reformed and transparent political process within Canada. At its simplest, the UN process — whether in Geneva or in Canada — has to do with giving and keeping one's word to one's neighbour.

8 • From Oppression to Promise: Journeying Together with the Refugee

Kathleen Ptolemy

When the violation of their rights has become unbearable, the citizens of scores of countries have taken the world community at its word and sought a safe place to hide from those who would torture, kill, or imprison them. They have not always found the door open wide. In the eighties, refugees have been forced to settle by the millions in refugee camps while they waited for a civil war to end or for a Western country to grant them the right to asylum that is enshrined in international law.

Like other Canadians, church people became deeply involved in settling refugees when the Chilean, the Indochinese, and Central American movements took place. Out of that experience in settlement, they gained a concrete understanding of how fragile the right to asylum is for a person fleeing for his or her life. In an effort to have international commitments embedded in domestic law, Canadian churches have prepared briefs to government, have sent delegations to the UN, and have reluctantly gone to court to challenge the current law, which most affects the person seeking asylum.

Kathleen Ptolemy is the director of refugee programs for the Anglican Church of Canada. She served as the founding director of the Inter-Church Committee for Refugees, where she represented the churches in international refugee consultations, in field missions to protect refugees in camps, in discussions with government and with other non-governmental organizations, and with the UN High Commission for Refugees.

— Ed.

A Refugee Movement at its Birth

Late one night in May 1981, two Canadian churchmen sat down to prepare a theological statement for the delegates to a consultation on refugee resettlement in Stony Point, New York. Their work gave perspective to a movement about to be born among Canadian churches.

Here are some excerpts:

> It is not merely that we who live in lands of resettlement, have the power to give or withdraw our ministry to refugees, but that in the refugees we can come face to face with Christ in his passion, that we may share in the joy. So we are caught up in the great challenge of journeying together with the refugees. Yet more: the refugees cast the penetrating light of judgement on our own societies — on the paradox and the hypocrisy of giving onerous aid with one hand, yet supplying weaponry to repressive regimes with the other; on the black-out of concern and compassion by racism, self-protective attitudes and self-serving immigration policies; on the complicity in making the means of mass suffering and tolerating attitudinal and systemic grounds for exploitation....
>
> Journeying together with the refugees on the road from oppression to promise requires that we courageously name the powers that tyrannize millions of people. We must expose the roots of injustice. We must address ourselves with energy to international aid and questions of justice, to violations of human rights, to immigration policy, and to racism in our societies. We must support peoples in their struggles towards self-determination in their call for land reform and job creation.

For those who were there, that midnight effort framed the basic perspectives on the refugee work of the past years. Today the existence of over fourteen million refugees worldwide and far more internally displaced people reminds us of our dismal failure to end war, human rights violations, and underdevelopment. But wonderful things have happened on the way. Thousands of refugees have been protected, resettled, and reunited with their families by the efforts of Canadian people, including church people. And a network of informed and caring Canadians has built a refugee advocacy movement that is unequalled anywhere. Refugees have informed, challenged, and given passion and energy to this work.

The roots of our work had begun much earlier with the September 1973 coup in Chile. Then came the Indochinese refugee movement of the late 1970s and the Central American refugee crisis, which erupted in 1980. The issues that were identified and the principles that were developed during that period have continued to shape the direction of the advocacy of Canadian churches on refugee questions in the eighties.

Refugee Movements to Canada

In the aftermath of the September 1973 coup in Chile, Canadian churches became deeply involved in advocating for the human rights of the thousands of Chilean political prisoners and refugees who sought help. The advocacy was effective. Canadian links to missionaries in the area provided the basis for an informed and persistent appeal to the Canadian government by grass-roots Canadians. A milestone in Canada's emerging refugee policy was achieved: refugees fleeing from right-wing dictatorships were recognized as representing a legitimate refugee movement. The Chilean movement, along with the program for Asians from Uganda from 1972 to 1973 and the small Tibetan program in 1970, marked the first clear expansion away from the classical postwar refugee movements, which included the Hungarian and Czechoslovakian movements of the fifties and sixties. The roots of a global refugee policy had become established.

As the Chileans arrived, a Canadian refugee advocacy network began to form. The number of church members directly involved with refugees, and therefore with the policies and practices of the Canadian government, rose dramatically. People learned about Canada's refugee-determination procedures through first-hand experience with Chilean refugee claimants. They learned about Canadian selection criteria and procedures when they sponsored refugees themselves. Some witnessed the pain of people whose flight to Canada was deterred by visa restrictions. These direct experiences with people from Chile laid the groundwork for church advocacy on refugee rights — the right to leave and to return to one's country and to seek and find protection in Canada.

Southeast Asians made up the next major wave of refugees. Since 1975 over 115,000 refugees from Vietnam, Kampuchea, and Laos have resettled in Canada. Few Canadians will forget the peak years of 1979 and 1980, when over 60,000 Indochinese refugees — the boat people — arrived in Canada, compelling a community outreach of truly magnificent proportions. Across the country, refugees were welcomed, fed, clothed, and set on their way to making it in Canada.

Many Canadians were deeply and permanently affected by the experience. The refugee's trauma of flight and fear dug deep into the consciousness of people who had never been connected with any comparable situation. Refugee sponsors learned — some for the first time — about the realities of poverty in Canada. Searching for affordable housing for the refugees they had sponsored, coping with the intricacies and frustration of our social security and welfare systems, experiencing the racism of some potential landlords and employers — all these and more were part of the refugee-resettlement package. Some sponsors were transformed by the experience as they uncovered the inequities and structural problems that characterize our own society.

The desire to help was intense, prompted in large part by the compelling scenes of escape and terror in the media coverage. For the front-line people who were planning to receive refugees, the needs were clear. Information and advice on a wide range of resettlement issues were urgently required, and these were sometimes produced in time to be useful. Many relied, however, on common sense, good will, and inventiveness to bridge cultural and communication barriers. All in all, the resettlement effort succeeded and earned Canadians the prestigious Nansen Medal in November 1986.

For the national churches, supporting the initiatives of the local churches was an easy matter, both in principle and practice. Each denomination could look back on its own history as an immigrant or refugee people; they also had a solid biblical basis upon which to encourage acts of good will to refugees.

While Canadian churches were engaged in sponsoring Indochinese refugees, other major movements erupted in Afghanistan, Iran, Iraq, Sri Lanka, El Salvador, Guatemala, Ethiopia, and Uganda, among others. Church people became inundated with compelling pleas for sponsorship from every corner of the globe. And they discovered that while it was a relatively simple matter to sponsor an Indochinese or Eastern European refugee, the same could not be said for other refugee groups. This discovery meant that another major policy issue had moved from the domain of a few immigration officials to the public realm. How are refugees selected for admission to Canada? Why are refugee claimants from Eastern Europe and Indochina presumed to be refugees while others have to meet stringent refugee criteria? Why will Canada admit only a few hundred African refugees and almost no Afghan refugees when their respective communities comprise over half the world's refugees? Why can a refugee be refused admission to Canada simply on the basis of the place from which he or she applied? Why are there no refugee application forms, just immigration application forms? Why, in other words, are there different standards and procedures for people with equal needs for protection and a new life? Who gets in and why?

When Canadians responded to the plight of Indochinese refugees, they did so out of compassion. Indeed, very few public concerns were raised regarding the root causes of the Vietnamese refugee situation. When the refugee crisis erupted in Central

America in 1980, the Canadian church response took a substantially different shape. For some years, Canadian church organizations such as the Inter-Church Committee for Human Rights in Latin America (ICCHRLA), Ten Days for World Development, Project Ploughshares, and GATT-fly had been building a network of informed people who were committed to working for change in the areas of human rights violations, structural injustices, militarism, and underdevelopment. These people wanted to know why Salvadorans and Guatemalans were forced to flee their homelands. Given the closeness of Central America, they could see at first hand how the foreign policy of a country can shape one's view of and response to a refugee situation. They saw refugees as part of a large global game — pawns in superpower political manoeuvres.

The response of the Canadian churches to the Central American refugee situation could therefore be much broader in scope than had been possible in the Indochinese refugee crisis, which focused completely on refugee resettlement in Canada. Personal testimonies by refugees and travellers to Central America intensified Canadians' awareness of the motivation for flight and of the lack of security in first-asylum countries, such as Honduras and Mexico. In the networks that existed across the country, people began to grapple with this new refugee movement and its complex interplay with political, social, economic, and cultural phenomena. Refugees from Central America became more than people who needed a new home in Canada. They were seen as victims of systemic oppression, people whose basic rights had been denied. They were not people who had opted for a permanent future outside their home country, but people who were waiting for a chance to return home. They were refugees, not immigrants.

Church energies went into a wide variety of activities: urging the Canadian government to adopt a better foreign policy in Central America; providing protection to refugees in Central American refugee camps; assisting refugee claimants in Canada; resettling refugees in Canadian communities; advocating for increased refugee quotas for Canada; and pushing the United Nations system to provide more adequate protection and material assistance to refugees.

Putting Policy Issues on the Public Agenda

Meanwhile, there was urgent need for certain policy issues to be addressed, and churches felt compelled to get together to discuss matters of common concern. The Refugee Concerns Project of the Canadian Council of Churches (later, the Inter-Church Committee for Refugees or ICCR) began meeting formally in January 1980. The timing was good, for it was during those early years of 1980 and 1981 that major government refugee-resettlement policies and programs were being formulated. The church coalition, though very new and uncomfortable with itself, was on hand to influence those policies and programs.

And the government, itself caught up in the throes of a major refugee-resettlement phenomenon, accorded the churches some recognition as a legitimate voice of concern. Trips by church people to Ottawa for consultation with government officials began at this time and have continued on a regular basis.

The issues that were identified by the churches through the Indochinese refugee-resettlement experience have not changed substantively over the past ten years. The first brief of the Refugee Concerns Project Committee in 1980 recommended, among other things:

- that refugee quotas be separated from immigration levels;
- that refugee levels be determined on the basis of the refugees' need;
- that resettlement programs be uniformly available to all refugees;
- that private sponsorship be maintained as a vehicle to ensure refugee admissions over and above government quotas, and not in place of government quotas;
- that levels for Latin America be increased in the light of the situation and our regional concern;
- that refugee selection be based on need for protection rather than immigration factors;
- that the Joint Assistance Program — a combined government assistance and private sponsorship program — be given high priority for difficult resettlement cases;
- that selection procedures be made more flexible and efficient and that urgent cases be moved immediately;
- that visa requirements not be imposed on countries with serious human rights violations; and
- that joint consultation and shared decision making become the operative norm.

The issues raised by the Inter-Church Committee for Refugees in its May 1989 brief to Immigration Minister Barbara McDougall are almost identical. Little has changed. The differences between refugees and immigrants are still not clearly understood or reflected in public attitudes. Refugees still are assessed by immigration officers on the basis of both refugee and immigration factors. Refugee-resettlement programs still lack uniformity and universal access for all refugees. The Joint Assistance Program, initiated by the churches to provide special support for the most needy refugees, is still not effective. Tensions over the proper balance between government-assisted and privately sponsored refugees continue. Overseas selection procedures are in acute need of reform and procedural streamlining.

Still, the ten years of briefs and delegations to Ottawa between 1980 and 1990, all fuelled by first-hand experiences with refugees, have not been futile. Some goals have been achieved. The federally funded Host Program now enables government-assisted refugees to benefit from the friendship and support of a host group as they settle in. Additional government-funded services for privately sponsored refugees have reduced the financial burdens on sponsorship groups. A special joint assistance program for vulnerable women refugees has been set up. Many churches across the country have accepted the fact that sponsoring one Indochinese refugee family was the beginning, not the end, of their refugee ministry, and they have continued in their work with repeated offers of sponsorship and other resettlement services.

Contentious Issues

Despite the progress made on particular issues, several contentious issues remain on Canada's agenda for the refugee movement, as is the case in several other countries. Such issues include the refugee's right to asylum in Canada, the refugee-determination process, the refugee's protection rights, the adequacy of the international system for protecting refugees, and the need to make Canada a genuine country of first asylum.

The Right to Asylum
One of the earliest contentious issues to emerge was the refugee's right to flee his or her own country. When Chileans sought refuge within the Canadian embassy compound in Santiago, the Canadian government chose not to grant any right of diplomatic asylum. However, when Canadian churches pressed the government to respond humanely to these people and to the thousands of political prisoners, it created a special "designated class," an administrative device that allowed the government to select, under refugee criteria, people who were still inside their country.

(Refugees are, by definition, people who are outside their own country.)

This particular designated-class mechanism has been a mixed blessing, especially when paired with a visa requirement. When the program has been applied to political prisoners in Chile, Argentina, and El Salvador, it has indeed given people under government detention a chance to obtain release and resettle in Canada.

However, the government has also used the designated-class mechanism to justify removing its visa exemption for people from some refugee-producing countries. Chile was a case in point. When the visa exemption was removed in 1979, the Canadian government tried to offset criticism by pointing out that Chileans could simply go to the Canadian visa officer in Santiago and apply for refugee status under the designated-class regulations. No doubt some people have been helped through this program, but many more have been afraid even to consider this escape route. Most people who fear persecution in their country are reluctant to present themselves publicly to a foreign embassy, which is assumed to have locally engaged informers. Most people are also afraid of revealing the details of their refugee claim while still in their country, and even if accepted, they fear waiting for months in a dangerous environment for health, security, and passport clearances. Critics of this "in-country" processing of refugees claim that the benefits for a few do not outweigh the disadvantages for the many who are trapped in their countries because there is no fast way out.

The Canadian government points out that it has no responsibility to protect people trying to flee countries of persecution to Canada. Hardliners in government claim that no refugee has the right to enter Canada without prior immigration processing abroad. The churches have opted for a position that declares that Canada is a logical and accessible country of first asylum for many refugees and that bureaucratic obstacles, such as visa requirements, should not be used to prevent them from leaving their countries to seek protection in Canada. They have argued that Canada does have the right to control its borders through the use of visa requirements, but that a visa should not be required for nationals of any country for whom Canada is "logical and accessible" and where there are serious human rights violations.

Thus, the churches were silent when visa exemptions were removed from countries such as India, Sri Lanka, and Bangladesh because Canada is not easily accessible to those countries. But protests were loud and clear when visas were imposed on

Guatemala and Chile, the argument being that Canada has particular obligations towards refugees fleeing countries that are "connected" to Canada through geographical and/or airline proximity.

The churches' debate over the visa requirement was extremely important. It had to balance the rights of the state with the rights of refugees to seek and enjoy in other countries protection from persecution. The human rights imperative, in constant tension with the "sovereign right" of nations to control their borders, will continue to dominate the churches' work.

Who Gets in and Why?

The issue of who needs and who "deserves" protection by Canada continues to provide room for debate, both within the churches and within the government. For years the Canadian government has allowed for the admission (subject to further screening on immigration factors) of two classes of refugees: (1) Convention refugees (as defined by the UN Convention Relating to the Status of Refugees), determined to be in need of third-country resettlement (for example, a Ugandan refugee living in an asylum country where he has a serious protection or resettlement problem); and (2) people who qualify as a "designated class of person," identified by parliamentary regulations to be in refugee-like situations and of concern to Canada. People who fall into this category are nationals of Eastern Europe and South East Asia. From time to time, the government also "designates" and recognizes certain classes of people as Convention refugees, even if they are not yet outside their country (for example, nationals of El Salvador, Guatemala, and Chile).

Much has been written by critics outside church circles about the political bias that is inherent in this two-pronged selection policy. Up until 1988, the majority of people who entered Canada under the refugee program were members of those designated classes who are not required to pass the Convention refugee test. Most of these people came from Communist countries.

The churches have tread very carefully around this issue of political bias and unevenly applied standards. One temptation was to take a purist approach and advocate that all refugee admissions meet the UN Convention refugee test of living outside one's country and being unwilling to return to it because of a well-founded fear of being persecuted for reasons of race, religion, nationality, membership in a particular social group, or political opinion. However, whose interests and needs would be served by this position?

At the heart of the dilemma for the churches is the human reality of thousands — millions — of people who may or may not be refugees in the Convention sense, but have nonetheless left their countries, are unlikely to return for a variety of reasons, and therefore need a place to go. Solutions need to be found for these people. Many experts argue that most of these people would fit into a liberally applied Convention definition; others argue for the need for a broader definition of refugee, one that would provide for an administrative response to these "grey area" people who have left their countries for the foreseeable future and require some humane resolution to their situation. These people present one of the most alarming and unresolved global issues of our time. Millions of people — not officially found to be refugees — are living in limbo, sometimes illegally. They are unable to get on with their lives, to restore their family units, or to get on economically and socially in their host communities. A huge powder keg is brewing and the problem is largely unacknowledged. A new approach is sorely needed.

Protection Rights in Canada

Two other major policy issues for the Canadian churches were born in the Central American experience: (1) What protection rights does a refugee have? (2) What is the responsibility of the UN system to refugees?

The issue of protection rights became pressing in late 1981 when the Canadian churches began sending Canadians into refugee camps along the Honduras-Salvador border. This effort came about because of a desperate appeal from Honduran church agencies, which were unable to prevent killings and continuing repression of refugees and agency workers alike at the hands of Honduran military and Salvadoran paramilitary forces. The Hondurans felt that lives could be saved if a group of people were present on the scene who were able and willing to confront authorities, report to the media, and expose atrocities.

Church meetings in Canada were rife with tension. Was it appropriate to send untrained Canadians into life-threatening situations in Honduras? Who should be responsible for protecting the refugees? What constitutes protection? Despite these concerns, over forty Canadians participated directly in this effort. They volunteered their lives to stand with the refugees in Honduras. They went, returned, and created an overwhelming testimony of compelling information on the security problems of the refugees. Many thousands of Canadians participated indirectly in the Central American refugee crisis through the testimonies of refugees and the eyewitness accounts of Canadians returning from the camps. Those close Canadian contacts with Salvadoran refugees in Honduras and the reports prepared by each observer provided the basis for the Canadian churches' decision to move onto the international lobbying ground of the United Nations High Commission for Refugees (UNHCR).

At that time, many people saw the UNHCR's protection role in strictly legalistic terms: recognition of refugee status. People who were recognized as Convention refugees had the right not to be deported or returned to the frontiers of territories where their freedom would be threatened by persecution. Therefore, the focus at the time was on granting refugees the legal recognition of their right to be protected from deportation or "refoulement."

However, that protection was cold comfort to people whose primary concern was their physical security. The host government of the country where they sought asylum should have assumed this responsibility, but if it had not, as in the case of Honduras, then just who should have done so? The issue was technically difficult but practically simple: the office of the UNHCR had been given the responsibility to protect refugees. Refugee workers insisted that this must include protection of life itself, as well as legal protection.

The Inter-Church Committee for Refugees went to Geneva in October 1982 to make its concerns known to the executive of the UNHCR. The Canadian churches' recommendations for strengthening the UNHCR's protection of refugees in the region were not radical, but they were timely. Shortly afterwards, the UNHCR placed "roving protection officers" along the Salvadoran border in Honduras to facilitate safe arrivals, and staff presence in the camps themselves increased. Problems did not disappear, but there were some improvements.

Today the UNHCR publicly promotes a much broader description of its protection mandate. In an address given to a conference on "Human Rights and the Protection of Refugees under International Law," Fiorelli Capelli, head of the UNHCR Europe and North America Section, articulated two additional protection principles: respect for the physical security of refugees and respect for their other basic human rights.

Pressures on the International Protection System
The authority of the UNHCR is critical to the protection and well-being of at least fourteen million people in the world today. That authority is moral, and not legally enforceable. Most countries that receive refugees have become signatories to the appropriate global and regional conventions. However, as in the Central American experience, enforcing these conventions can be

extremely problematic. It is the spirit of the conventions that succeeds or fails.

Despite enormous efforts by many deeply committed but demoralized people working within the UNHCR system, the agency's protection mandate has come under serious pressure in recent years. The "fortress mentality" of many countries of the West — essentially closing their borders — has forced the UNHCR into an uneasy complicity with states that use questionable tactics to deter refugees (for example, detaining asylum seekers when no crime has been committed; using visa restrictions and penalties on airlines and other transport carriers to deter arrivals; inadequate refugee-determination procedures; and expelling asylum seekers).

In other parts of the world, the UNHCR finds it increasingly difficult to put an end to military attacks on camps, raids and abductions by pirates, forced returns, boat push-offs, and so on. Many critics argue that the Third World countries are simply following the lead of Western countries — that they are no longer prepared to accommodate the vast majority of the world's refugees when they see Western countries failing in their small burden-sharing responsibilities towards the very few refugees who try to enter the West in search of protection.

In addition to its protection problems, the UNHCR is facing a severe financial crisis because of the reluctance of key states to give adequate financial support. Even basic care and maintenance for refugees can no longer be assured. Administration, leadership, and management problems abound. Whatever the reasons, the refugee system is losing ground in its efforts to protect refugees.

The initial response of churches around the world has been a practical one: to press governments to fulfil their financial responsibilities to the UNHCR. A second response is their effort to bolster the protection of refugees through other United Nations bodies, such as the UN Commission on Human Rights.

Canada: A Country of First Asylum

A few decades ago, Canada, well protected geographically from the world's refugee "hot spots," was not a country to which refugees fled in large numbers. Other countries were more logical choices for a fleeing refugee. The growth of the airline industry and the Chilean coup changed that. Although the numbers of Chileans who came to Canada in search of protection was small — 173 in 1977, 251 in 1978 — they formed the largest block in overall totals of 522 and 685 respectively. Because of the church links between Canada and Chile, the Chilean refugees in Canada engaged Canadian church people in their struggles to claim asylum here.

Until the present Immigration Act was proclaimed in 1978, there were no legislated procedures by which to implement Canada's obligations to protect refugees in Canada. Indeed, Canada did not sign the 1951 Geneva Convention and the 1967 Protocol until 1969. The churches' direct experience with the Chilean refugees drew them into the mid-seventies parliamentary debates over proposed refugee-determination procedures. The principles that have guided church action were laid out at that time. They stipulated that the person claiming refugee status should:

- have the right to appear in person and present his or her case before the people who make the decision;
- have the right to know and to respond to information that can be used against him or her;
- know the reasons for the decision in his or her case; and
- be assisted to obtain competent legal counsel.

The government incorporated very few of the churches' principles or suggestions. Instead, it opted for a procedure that assumed that refugee claimants to Canada would be few and far between, a handful of foreign students and defectors, for example. The process enshrined in the 1976 Immigration Act required a hearing before an immigration officer, a verbatim transcript, a recommendation by the Refugee Status Advisory Committee on the basis of the transcript, and a decision by the minister of employment and immigration. People who claimed refugee status had appeal rights, including a redetermination by leave before the Immigration Appeal Board and appeal on judicial grounds to the Federal Court of Appeal.

When the 1978 procedure was implemented, the problems refugee workers had expected became realities. Lawyers and refugee claimants looked to the churches for many things, including expert testimony on country conditions and advocacy against the deportation of people refused status wrongfully. It was inevitable that the churches should become involved as major actors to reform a system that was inhumanly slow and fundamentally flawed in providing fair and speedy decisions.

The churches began putting forward briefs critiquing the system and suggesting appropriate reforms as early as 1979. Under the auspices of the Canadian Council of Churches, a "Concerned Delegation," made up of church, legal, labour, medical, and humanitarian organizations, began presenting briefs and meeting with ministers and senior immigration officials to clarify problems and press for structural changes. The most receptive minister during that period was Lloyd Axworthy. In February 1982 he organized a symposium to consider the issues. His message and his actions gave hope that fundamental reform was imminent. Immigration officials, however, still refused to support the need for change. They argued that Canada would be swamped with abusers; that Canada would become a magnet for hordes of refugees if the system were reformed; that the taxpayer would not tolerate the costs involved in providing an oral hearing for refugees. However, many staff and members of the Refugee Status Advisory Committee, as well as of the Immigration Appeal Board, supported the need for reform.

A pilot project was established in 1985 that allowed for some refugee claimants to have a type of hearing before a member of the Refugee Status Advisory Committee. Some optimistic people were convinced that this small pilot project would lay the necessary groundwork for the eventual incorporation of a full oral hearing into the legislated procedures for determining one's refugee status.

Meanwhile, other events were beginning to control the agenda. The numbers of refugee claimants were rising dramatically. In 1978 the Refugee Status Advisory Committee received 685 claims. In 1982 the number was 3,441. The backlog of undetermined cases grew. The buildup could easily have been corrected with the infusion of additional resources and the streamlining of administrative procedures, a course recommended at that time by a government task force. But the buildup was not corrected, with the result that some people who were clearly not refugees began to claim refugee status simply to prolong their stay in Canada.

A group of Sikh refugee claimants, whose cases had not been accepted at the determination and redetermination levels, carried their concerns over the unfairness of the system to the Supreme Court of Canada. The Canadian Council of Churches, with the voluntary services of expert immigration counsel, intervened. In a historic decision, *Singh et al.* (June 1985), the Supreme Court affirmed what had been known for years: the existing system failed to provide a fair hearing on life-and-death matters. The only remedy available to the courts was to insist that all claimants refused at the first level have the right to a full redetermination of their claim before the Immigration Appeal Board. The system became severely bogged down under the strain, and the government was compelled to act. In May 1986, Walter McLean, the junior minister of immigration under Employment and Immigration Minister Flora MacDonald, announced the basic thrust of the proposed "reforms." Instead of a simple oral hearing before a decision-making body, and an adequate appeal, the government introduced a complex, multi-tiered system designed to screen out most applicants before their refugee claim could be heard.

After months of fierce debate and efforts to change the proposed legislation in the initial stage, Bill C55 was introduced in the spring of 1987. It was even more restrictive than Walter McLean had suggested. Years of calls for reform had culminated in legislation designed to return most refugee claimants to those countries through which they had travelled en route to Canada.

Witness after witness appeared before parliamentary committees of the Commons and the Senate. Hours were spent with key political figures in an effort to convince them that protecting refugee rights would not destroy the country, but would strengthen our social and moral fibre as a nation and also deter abusers. Campaigns were launched to deal with claims that refugees were immigration queue-jumpers at best and terrorists at worst. The 1987 arrivals of Sikh refugee claimants by boat generated further public debate. A media extravaganza filled an otherwise quiet summer. Everyone became opinionated on the subject of refugees. Undercurrents of racism surfaced.

The government pressed its advantage, introducing yet another piece of draconian legislation. Bill C84 was introduced on the pretext of a national emergency created by the arrival of a boatload of Sikhs. Some amendments to the bill were made, after long and arduous struggles by a united group made up of constitutional lawyers, refugee experts, UNHCR officials, and members of the Refugee Status Advisory Committee and the Immigration Appeal Board. However, the victories were small. The government was determined to send out a tough message to the rest of the world. The Senate, after achieving some modest gains, gave in, in view of other pressing issues before it, including the Meech Lake Accord and the Canada-U.S. trade agreement.

It was very difficult to participate in those months of hearings and maintain faith in the ability of the parliamentary system to ensure good law. When government chose to ignore virtually unanimous criticisms of the legislation — including its denial of fundamental rights guaranteed by the Charter of Rights and Freedoms, some hard decisions had to be made.

In this process, churches had learned that the legislative process does not, in and of itself, guarantee fundamental rights. We learned that many politicians do not believe in the importance of protecting the rights of strangers in our midst, and we learned that the courts will play an increasingly important role in defining the moral and legal shape of our society. And so the decision was taken by the Canadian Council of Churches to challenge the new legislation before the courts. On 3 January 1989, the council filed a statement of claim that called into question the constitutional validity of some eighty provisions of the amended legislation.

The decision to proceed with a court action was not taken easily. In a letter dated 12 September 1988, David Woeller, general secretary of the Anglican Church of Canada, noted:

In response to requests by its member churches the Canadian Council of Churches has determined to set up a project to seek to remedy in the courts, the constitutional defects of the two Bills. Although this is not an unprecedented action (the Canadian Council of Churches intervened in a 1985 case regarding the rights of refugee claimants), it was not taken easily. The process is long, difficult, and will require great commitments of energy, expertise, and financial resources. The overriding reason to go the next step is very deeply rooted in our social justice commitments to stand with the oppressed and persecuted. Although some of the flaws inherent in these Bills will be tested in the courts by other parties, the churches are concerned to speak for those who have been summarily removed from this country and are unable to avail themselves of due process.

Persons other than those directly affected, i.e. the refugee claimant, may bring an application to review legislation before the courts. The Canadian Council of Churches can seek standing as a party which has a good possibility of satisfying the court that it has a genuine or a direct interest in the subject matter of the legislation....

The areas on which the counsel for the Canadian Council of Churches will concentrate are those that have life-threatening implications for refugees. The major Charter section which will be involved is Section 7, which requires that where a person is deprived of life, liberty or security, principles of fundamental justice must be applied before the deprivation occurs.... there is a strong feeling of optimism that the Challenge to the Court is not only very necessary, but also winnable! The consequences of not trying are too serious to allow abandoning the cause of refugee protection now. So the challenge continues, since the importance of the issue has not diminished.

The decision to launch a court action marks a profound moment in the life of the churches in Canada. Emilio Castro, the general secretary of the World Council of Churches, wrote in a letter of support (10 February 1989) wrote:

At the same time, we have been encouraged and inspired by the Canadian churches' numerous attempts to speak out on behalf of the refugees and asylum-seekers. We have followed the advocacy efforts of the Inter-Church Committee for Refugees with great care and have shared information about your efforts with churches in other parts of the world. As you now embark on court action to challenge the government's law, we want to assure you that you have our complete support in this endeavour. Churches around the world are watching not only the court challenge and the government's response, but also are taking courage from your leadership in this important area.

As you know, the current trend is clearly toward more restrictionist policies on the part of western governments toward those forced to flee their homelands to seek security and peace. Indeed, the Central Committee of the World Council of Churches stated in August 1988 that the churches are called to speak out on behalf of refugees as part of their prophetic mission.

It is likely that the court action will proceed well into the nineties. The Canadian Council of Churches had hoped to have the proceedings under way to deal with the substance of concerns during 1989. However, the government mounted challenges against two preliminary issues, claiming that the church was not an appropriate body to represent refugee issues before the courts and that there were no justifiable concerns. These questions of "standing" and "cause of action" were heard in the federal Supreme Court in March 1989. On 26 April, Mr. Justice Rouleau found in favour of the churches on both counts and ordered the government to present its defence within ten days. The statement of defence was produced in November 1989. An appeal by the government of the preliminary motion decision was to be heard in early 1990.

It is true that gains have been made. Canada has acknowledged its responsibilities as a country of first asylum. Yet the struggle continues to ensure that the procedures we have in place actually allow people who flee in fear for their lives or their security to claim that right to first asylum in Canada. Whatever legislation we have in place, people will continue to become uprooted from their communities, their cultures, their climate, their language, their roots. Journeying with the refugee will continue to challenge us and test our faithfulness to the God who requires that we enable the uprooted to become subjects, and not objects, of their own history.

9 • The Christian Churches and Foreign Policy: An Assessment

Robert O. Matthews

The Canadian churches have focused a great deal of effort on achieving changes in Canadian foreign policies that will put this country squarely on the side of human rights and peace. After twenty years of attempting to influence government policy, the churches have seen only modest results. The reasons lie as much with the nature of the political decision-making process in Canada as they do with the churches themselves.

Robert O. Matthews is a professor in the Department of Political Science at the University of Toronto. He was co-editor, with Cranford Pratt, of Human Rights and Canadian Foreign Policy *(McGill-Queen's University Press, 1988), and has written or edited many other publications. He represents the Canadian churches on the World Council of Churches' Commission on the Churches in International Affairs in Geneva, Switzerland. This article is adapted from an article by Professor Matthews published in the* Journal of Canadian Studies *in 1989.*

— Ed.

Foreign Policy from the Periphery

With increasing vigour over the last two decades the mainstream Christian churches have campaigned publicly and have lobbied the federal government to ensure that Canada's foreign policy and programs better reflect a concern for human rights and social justice. Although they have become increasingly sophisticated and systematic in approaching this task, the churches have not had much direct impact on public policy. They sit on the periphery of the policy process. While they have had reasonable success in gaining access to policy makers, their influence on actual government policy has been marginal. Despite their relative ineffectiveness as an interest group, however, the Canadian churches have not been deterred from performing what they consider to be an important component of their responsibilities. Even if exchanges with the government and its officials do not result in dramatic shifts in policy, they highlight the underlying nature of government policy, provide educational material for the churches' broad constituency, and contribute to the evolution of a Canadian public opinion that will be more responsive and sensitive to human needs internationally.

Historical Development

The churches have not always expressed so forcefully their views on human rights, nor have they always assumed an adversarial role in their relations with government. In the area of foreign policy, the churches tended to focus their attention on peace and disarmament issues in the 1950s, adding development questions to their agenda in the 1960s, as well as a general concern for "achieving universal acceptance of the primacy of general human rights standards, by which the actions of nations can be judged and influenced."[1] Their concerns therefore reflected the broader concerns of the world community.

Initially, church-government relations were almost collegial. For the most part the churches issued statements that were then either forwarded to Ottawa by letter or presented directly through visits, but little or no attempt was made to engage in a sustained exchange of views. Only at the churchman's seminar, an annual event held in Ottawa, did church representatives have a real opportunity to question the government's foreign policies. Even then, during these seminars the churches tended to behave rather like any "group of Canadians who 'whisper in the king's ear' when he needs advice on foreign policy."[2]

Towards the end of the 1960s, the approach of the Canadian churches changed as they began to focus on foreign policy issues. Influenced by contacts with churches of the Third World in the World Council of Churches (WCC), the Protestant churches in Canada chose to stand beside "the poor, the oppressed, and the marginalized." The result was a sharp distinction between their stand and the government's.

This shift was also influenced by the Canadian government's policies in regard to the Vietnam War and South Africa. These were the two issues that first drove home to many Canadian church people that there were important elements of Canadian foreign policy that distressed them. Many churches and church leaders became critical of the United States' conduct of the war in Vietnam and of what they came to see as Canada's complicity in it. They expressed this concern by helping American draft resisters who sought safety in Canada, by participating in public protests, and by speaking out against government policy. Regarding South Africa, the government's White Paper *Foreign Policy for Canadians* aroused some church people because it emphasized economic growth at the expense of social justice. The White Paper tried to balance Ottawa's revulsion for apartheid with the "better than normal opportunities for trade and investment in the growing economy" of South Africa.[3] "The Black Paper," one of the earliest critiques of the government paper, argued that Ottawa seemed prepared to sacrifice principles for what were at best negligible gains,[4] and offered an alternative policy responsive to cosmopolitan values.

It was apartheid and Third World demands for the equal application of the United Nations' New International Economic Order that prompted Canadian churches to organize systematic programs in the field of foreign policy. The first of such efforts was Ten Days for World Development, an educational program that grew out of the belief that Canada was not doing all it could and should to close the gap between rich and poor nations. Through Ten Days, the churches tried to mobilize Canadian public opinion in support of changes in public policy that would strengthen Canada's contribution to a just and compassionate world. The other organizations created by the churches analyzed Canadian policy and practice and put forward proposals for making both the policy and its implementation more consistent with international human rights standards.

Inter-church Coalitions as Instruments of Action

The Christian churches have chosen, for the most part, to pursue their human rights work through inter-church coalitions rather than through the Canadian Council of Churches (CCC). Coalitions are preferred because they permit the full involvement of the Roman Catholic Church.

The inter-church coalitions have proved to be a very effective instrument for pursuing human rights. In the first place, they have enabled the churches to mount programs that no single church could possibly consider. Only the United Church and the Anglican Church employ people with a specific responsibility in the field of human rights. Thus, the coalitions allow the various denominations to combine their limited resources to undertake significant programs in this area.

Secondly, the coalitions bring together Protestants and Catholics in parts of the world where their unique skills, experience, and direct contacts broaden and strengthen the overall effort. This is particularly noticeable in Central and South America, where the Catholic Church's presence is so much more extensive than that of the Protestant church. The coalitions also provide concrete support to local churches and groups pursuing human rights on a scale that is broader than church-to-church relations in that part of the world would allow. At the same time, through the coalitions, partner churches in Latin America, Africa, and Asia can find a wider audience and a more influential champion for their point of view than is available through their own denominational counterpart in Canada. Finally, the coalitions enable the churches to speak with one voice.

The Churches' Methods

The advocacy techniques used by the churches fall along a spectrum from the most direct approach to government, such as a telephone conversation with a cabinet minister, to the most indirect method, such as public education. In effect, all of the churches' advocacy work is directed at influencing the government and its policy, whether the method is direct representation through church leaders or stimulation of broader representations by church members across the country.

Direct Approach to Government

The churches have focused their most sustained efforts on direct approaches to the federal government. The approach may be to the cabinet or to individual members of the government, as well as to different levels of the bureaucracy. The more significant the question, the more likely the churches are to contact a member of the cabinet rather than a civil servant.

The churches make most of their approaches to the Department of External Affairs and its minister. They are paying increasing attention to other branches of government, however. The Inter-Church Coalition for Refugees (ICCR) deals more frequently with the Department of Immigration than it does with External Affairs. The Taskforce on the Churches and Corporate Responsibility (TCCR) has increasingly sought to communicate with the slightly more obscure areas of government that deal with international economic issues, such as the Export Development Corporation and Canada's representatives on the international financial institutions (IFIs), the World Bank and the International Monetary Fund. TCCR is not averse to talking to External or to Finance, but it is very much aware of the extent to which decisions are made and implemented outside the glare of public scrutiny.

Whatever level or branch of government the churches may address, they do so for a number of reasons. In the first place, through exchanges with government officials, the churches are able to clarify what government policy actually is or is supposed to be.

Equally important is the need to open the eyes of government to the day-to-day reality facing the majority of people in the world. Often the Canadian government's information on local situations is sadly inadequate and slanted in favour of the most powerful within foreign societies. Canadian officials and members of Parliament (MPs) have tended to hear from certain groups within Canada — notably, the military and business communities — more than others. The churches have corrected that imbalance by ensuring that the government has the chance to hear the views of other groups and sectors of society. Many of the inter-church coalitions invite visitors from different areas of the world and arrange that during their stay in Canada they meet with officials and politicians in Ottawa. These visitors can range from exiled political leaders, to church spokespeople, to peasant leaders. The Inter-Church Committee for Human Rights in Latin America (IC-CHRLA), for instance, estimated that it had helped to organize fifty such visits during one three-year period.

The churches submit to the government evidence they have amassed from a variety of sources. In a sense, the churches brief the government, providing officials with information that they might otherwise not possess or might possibly ignore. The detailed briefs that ICCHRLA and the Canada-Asia Working Group (CAWG) submit to Ottawa in anticipation of the annual meeting of the United Nations Commission on Human Rights (UNCHR) illustrate this important function.

The churches also openly press for changes in current policies. They may focus either on an emergency situation, such as the obvious needs of refugees in Chile in 1973, or on a long-term problematic issue, such as apartheid in South Africa. Through verbal and written submissions and through direct consultation, the churches can propose alternative policy options to replace those presently in place. At the annual consultation in Ottawa between non-governmental organizations (NGOs) and government officials, the churches and their NGO colleagues are able to open up a broad discussion on Canada's international human rights policies, to review the government's actions or inactions, and to press for needed changes.[5] They thus perform the function of policy advocacy.

Thirdly, the churches are anxious to monitor what the government actually does. By attending key sessions of United Nations bodies, the churches can monitor the government's performance in these international arenas and report back to their support groups at home and to the media. GATT-fly, a coalition for economic justice, played this monitoring role effectively at the World Food Conference in 1974, at the fifth special session of the UN General Assembly, and at the fourth session of the UN Conference for Trade and Development (UNCTAD) in Nairobi. Similarly, Project Ploughshares attended the first and second special sessions of the UN Conference on Disarmament. Finally, since 1981, the Canadian churches have sent an observer to the UNCHR as part of a WCC delegation.

These operations with the government are closely interrelated with the churches' public education work on human rights issues. That work is better informed, more immediately relevant, and more effective because of the knowledge and experience gained from the direct lobbying activities.

Approaches to Parliament and Parliamentarians

Sometimes the churches have addressed their message to Parliament as a whole or to individual MPs, either as a substitute for a direct approach to the government or as a parallel instrument to a direct approach. Most often a brief — carefully drafted and well argued — is presented by a select group of church leaders. For example, ICCHRLA, ICCR, and TCCR each submitted a brief on different aspects of Canadian policy to the subcommittee on Latin America and the Caribbean of the Standing Committee on External Affairs and National Defence.

However, the churches cannot simply submit their briefs and leave the results to chance. The ground must be properly cultivated beforehand and maintained afterwards. When overseas visitors go to Ottawa, they are taken to see members of Parliament as well as government officials. Information is also circulated to MPs, though often on a selective basis. Church leaders and church staff meet and correspond with a select group of MPs, such as members of Parliamentarians for World Order. Individual parliamentarians have also gone on fact-finding missions organized by the churches to see a particular situation for themselves. The churches hope that the result will be a well-informed and sympathetic audience within Parliament when a brief is submitted. Although the numbers of MPs may be small, their influence can be strong in practice.

Creating a Favourable Climate of Opinion

A less direct approach used by the churches involves "going public" or voicing aloud their opposition to government policy and mobilizing public support for an alternative. An example of this tactic was the press conference on Central America organized by the churches on 23 March 1982. At the conference a statement signed by many prominent church leaders was released to indicate the churches' disapproval of the Canadian government's inability to detach itself from U.S. policy in Central America. The church leaders also expressed their displeasure that Prime Minister Trudeau had refused to meet with them over this issue.

Creating a favourable climate of opinion also refers to the long-term educational work of the churches. The research and the resource materials produced by the coalitions inform the educational programs of the churches. By a lengthy, indirect process, this can have an impact on government. The more successful the churches' educational work, the more effective are their lobbying efforts. A well-informed and highly motivated public will press for a shift in government policy in line with the churches' point of view.

Each church uses different educational techniques. In general, however, they include the following: public meetings involving people whose rights have been violated; exposure tours in which Canadians go to church educational centres to observe first-hand the impact of human rights violations on people; major conferences for educational and strategy-building purposes; educational materials to support the efforts of local human rights educators within the church; and publication of up-dated information in reports, church publications, pamphlets, and books.[6] These activities broaden and deepen church members' understanding of the root causes of human rights violations and of the role that Canada and Canadians play in that process.

Advocacy with the Private Sector

The final set of church activities that can be described as advocacy relates to the private sector. The focus of church policy in this area is upon private Canadian institutions, not government. Yet, the government sets the ground rules or the framework within which our private institutions operate. Ultimately, the government is responsible for and affected by what its corporate citizens do.

Through their involvement in another country, private Canadian institutions may help to sustain human rights violations that the Canadian government itself has condemned. For example, direct investment or the extension of credit may provide financial support or moral legitimacy to regimes that openly violate the rights of their people. In focusing attention on this adverse impact of Canadian businesses, the churches hope to convince our corporate leaders that foreign investment does not necessarily ameliorate the human rights situation in a country. They also hope to convince Canadian bankers that extending credit to repressive regimes may, in fact, help keep them in power. The churches identify the effects of Canadian investment and credit on the most vulnerable people within a country experiencing serious human rights violations. They then lay out the evidence before management in letters and at private, closed-door meetings. If these discussions fail to move senior management to revise policies, the churches raise the issue at the public level by posing questions and introducing resolutions at annual shareholder meetings. As a last resort, they can divest their shares.

The direct targets of the churches in such circumstances are the corporations in which they are themselves investors. However, the churches contend that the actions of the private sector cannot be treated in isolation from government policies and relations between states. What our private institutions do abroad can strengthen, undermine, or affect in other ways what the government's policies seek to achieve. Therefore, the churches argue, the government should ensure that the policies of Canada's domestic institutions abroad are consistent with the standards set for their behaviour within Canada.

In response to pressure from the churches, senior management of Canadian corporations argue that their corporations are not violating any laws in Canada or in the country where they are being challenged. Their operations are consistent with existing Canadian policy and with the rules of the present international economic system. They help make it run effectively and they benefit from it. The churches contend that since the present order is itself the cause of poverty and repression in the Third World, Canada should contribute to building a new international economic order, including appropriate institutions and codes of behaviour. In the light of their experience in the Third World, Canadian churches believe that the government must alter the framework of rules and regulations within which corporations and banks operate if these latter cannot be persuaded to change their ways.

Evaluating the Churches as Lobbyists

Assessing the churches' impact on the government's human rights policies is a difficult task at the best of times. In the first place, the policy decisions the government takes are usually the result of a complex interplay among various pressures, some international and some domestic. Within Canada the churches are not the only group working actively for human rights. They work as colleagues with many other concerned groups in Canadian society. Ottawa is also subject to pressures from outside the country that would either encourage the government to promote human rights or discourage it from promoting them. It is not possible to know exactly what effect any of these specific sources of pressure have on Ottawa's final decision. Any assessment is an exercise in judgement and interpretation.

In the second place, the churches' human rights goals are themselves an obstacle to assessing the churches' effectiveness as lobbyists. The government tends to view the concern for human rights as one of several, often competing, foreign policy goals. It also tends to view the struggle for human rights as a humanitarian, apolitical process. The churches, however, approach human rights as all-embracing. They see the struggle for human rights as a political process that seeks the fuller liberation of society and its members.

Since the government and the churches approach human rights from such different perspectives, their standards for evaluating the effect of the churches' advocacy work also differ. Some observers argue that the churches' lobbying has been successful when a political prisoner is released from jail as a result of public pressure or when Ottawa closes down its trade office in another country in protest against human rights abuses. The churches, however, usually conclude that these are desirable outcomes but that, by themselves, they are inadequate.

Finally, the government may not make certain decisions because it fears negative reactions from the public. While the churches have helped set boundaries for politicians, it is nearly impossible to assess "non-decisions," since these are invisible. Still, there may be occasions when an observer or participant is able to conclude legitimately that the churches or other groups have prevented the government, at least for the moment, from adopting a particular policy.

Even the churches are not able to agree among themselves on the value and effectiveness of the kind of advocacy work they do in the human rights field. There are at least three distinct views. Some church people feel that a great deal can be accomplished by working directly with officials in government. In this view, lobbying activity can be effective if it is done discreetly and if one sets realistic targets.

A second view, held widely in the churches, is that the government is not likely to be responsive to the churches unless their demands are limited in scope and overlap with other government interests. In this view, government may respond positively if public opinion favours the policy initiatives being called for by the churches.

People who hold this view do maintain direct contact with government and Parliament, but they place greater value on their educational and representational activities. Direct contacts with government help the churches in their work because the discussions reveal the political issues that are at stake, the woefully inadequate performance of the government, and the need for changes in government policy. Even though their efforts have little immediate effect, church people with this view of church-government relations feel the need to express publicly their solidarity with the powerless, with those whose rights are violated, and to remain consistent with their own values. The people in this group argue that as long as government policies fall short of the values the churches are seeking, they are obligated to voice their beliefs — in effect, to act as the "conscience of society." For this group the churches must remain faithful to their role as an alternative voice in the world community.

Within the churches, a third group takes the more radical position that the economic and political structures of society must be transformed by mobilizing workers and peasants in the Third World and ordinary people in Canada to take direct action. This is the position GATT-fly adopted in the mid-1970s, once it gave up its initial task as lobbyist.

My own assessment of the churches as lobbyists closely reflects the approach of the second group above. The churches have had some successes. The government has, for example, increased the number of refugees it was prepared to admit into Canada, both from individual countries and in global terms. It has changed the procedures by which refugees are processed. It has voted affirmatively at the United Nations Commission on Human Rights on resolutions that were particularly critical of El Salvador and Guatemala. But all of these policy initiatives were very limited in their actual achievements. They fell far short of the churches' overall goals and expectations. They can also be easily reversed, as the recent government policy on refugees illustrates.

In three policy areas, however, some observers argue that the churches have had a substantial impact on government policies: South Africa, Central America, and the integration of human rights into the policy-making process.

South Africa

In the fall of 1977, the government announced that, among other things, it was removing all Canadian trade commissioners from South Africa. At a conference sponsored by the Canadian Institute for International Affairs, in 1982, External Affairs official Harry Carter argued that various domestic pressure groups had had a "considerable" influence on Ottawa's decision to revise its earlier policies towards South Africa.[7] Carter cited the churches, academics, labour organizations, and such other groups as Oxfam and the Toronto Committee for the Liberation of Southern Africa. Nevertheless, my examination of the factors affecting this decision suggests that international events and pressures had a far greater impact than did lobbyists within Canada.

Ottawa was forced to take some step on South Africa in response to the dangerous situation created by the collapse of the Portuguese empire, the increasingly violent struggle in Zimbabwe, and the situation in South Africa itself. The South African government was tightening its policy of apartheid in response to the growing resistance of the black majority. Canada's allies had already taken a more forceful stance on the South African question, including the United States under the new Carter administration. Canada could not afford to maintain the status quo any longer, particularly once its position became more visible as it assumed its seat as a newly elected member of the United Nations Security Council. In my view, it was international pressure, rather than the articulate voice of lobby groups at home, that led Ottawa to harden its policies towards South Africa. Lobbying by the churches and other groups simply permitted the government to act in the full knowledge that its policies would at least have support at home. The actions Canada eventually undertook were largely symbolic and were a pale reflection of what human rights activists had themselves called for.[8]

Even the more forceful policy of the Mulroney government can not be explained by church and other interest-group pressure. The Mulroney government decided — belatedly — to put Ottawa's 1977 policies into effect and to establish new sanctions for three reasons: international pressure, particularly from Canada's Commonwealth partners in black Africa; the fear that civil war in South Africa would play into the hands of the Soviet Union; and the prime minister's personal commitment to the cause of change in South Africa.

Church coalitions, particularly the Taskforce on the Churches and Corporate Responsibility, did play a role in sensitizing Canadian opinion to the crises in South Africa, to the adverse impact that Canadian banks and corporations have had on the black majority in South Africa, and to the importance of a more forceful Canadian position on the issue. The church coalitions also served as an important source of ideas for the Conservative government when, between June and October 1985, it conducted public hearings, casting about for possible policy alternatives.[9] However, it is unlikely that the Canadian government would have taken the steps it did under pressure from the churches; the international pressure cited above was critical.[10]

El Salvador and Guatemala

Another policy area in which Canadian churches and other groups appear to have made their influence felt concerned human rights in Central America. As the situation in Central America deteriorated from 1979 onwards, Canada found itself drawn into the affairs of a region that it had traditionally ignored. By 1981 Canada was openly supporting and even initiating resolutions in the UNCHR and the UN General Assembly that condemned the governments of both El Salvador and Guatemala for their persistent and gross violations of human rights. By itself, this was not especially noteworthy. Canada had not hesitated in the past to single out for public censure countries that had atrocious human rights records. In November 1981, however, Ottawa was adopting a new approach. It expressed its opposition to the human rights violations in El Salvador and Guatemala by announcing that it would cancel its bilateral assistance programs to those two countries. This was an unusual step for Canada to take. Previously, the government had resisted cutting off aid, on the grounds that this kind of action would "penalize the less fortunate for the errors of their governments."[11] Canada has only rarely cut off its aid programs. In bringing its aid to a halt in El Salvador and Guatemala, Canada presumably ran afoul of its principal ally, the United States, which under the Reagan administration was anxious to shore up the military regimes in both countries with material and diplomatic support.[12] Clearly, then, here was a case in which pressure from groups within Canada, articulated most forcefully by the churches in their various submissions to government, led to the adoption of a positive human rights policy by Ottawa.

From the churches' perspective, however, the government's human rights policies in Central America do not deserve such a high rating. As with South Africa, the shift in Ottawa's policies looks better on paper than it really is. The churches see the new policies as extremely cautious, falling far short of what they would have liked. Even the government's motives for halting aid to El Salvador and Guatemala are unclear. The government has stressed to the churches that this step was taken in response to the massive and persistent human rights violations in the two countries. Elsewhere, however, it has said that conditions in the two countries at the time meant that Canadian aid personnel were in jeopardy. Both motives may have played a role in Ottawa's decision to cancel these bilateral aid programs.

Following the elections in El Salvador in 1984, the new Conservative government of Prime Minister Mulroney announced its intentions to renew bilateral aid to El Salvador. Non-governmental organizations, including the churches, did not share their government's view that an elected government in El Salvador could reduce human rights violations and reform the country's legal system. The evidence of continuing human rights violations was too great. Therefore, the churches, among others, urged the Canadian government not to renew bilateral aid to El Salvador. Despite the pressure, Ottawa went ahead. In June 1985, Monique Vézina, minister of external relations and international trade, visited El Salvador as part of a trip to Central America and informed President Duarte of Canada's intention to extend to his country an $8-million line of credit.[13]

This decision and the subsequent decision to renew aid to Guatemala as well confirmed for the churches their assessment of government practice. Whether the government was Liberal or Conservative, concern for human rights did not constitute an essential purpose or guiding principle of Canada's foreign policy.

The Standing Committee on Human Rights

In the churches' view, if human rights issues are to be taken seriously in this country, Canada should move beyond its valuable efforts at the UN Commission on Human Rights. Canada should ensure that its concern for human rights is embodied in its policies and votes in IFIs, in its decisions concerning military sales and security assistance, in its distribution of foreign aid, and in its development of foreign political relationships.[14] Unfortunately, it has been Ottawa's practice to compartmentalize human rights, to limit its consideration of human rights to specialized international forums. In doing so, Ottawa necessarily finds itself in active and continuous conflict with the churches.

One stream within the NGOs' work on human rights has focused on a set of proposals aimed at integrating the human rights commitments made by Canada into the foreign policy work done by the relevant ministries of government, as well as by Parliament. For some years, the churches called for an annual parliamentary hearing on the status of human rights violator countries, particularly those with whom Canada has extensive aid, trade, and financial relations.[15]

In February 1986 the government established the Standing Committee on Human Rights. This committee would appear to be a third example of church influence on Ottawa's policy making in the human rights area. The churches certainly welcomed the committee's establishment, but they were extremely doubtful about its mandate and its effectiveness. They feared that the committee's focus would be limited largely to domestic considerations, such as the review of the reports from the Canadian human rights commissioner, the privacy commissioner, and the access-to-information commissioner.

While it may have been expedient to hold hearings on economic sanctions against South Africa, one has to wonder whether similar hearings will be held with respect to other countries that are both guilty of human rights violations and of particular interest to Canada. In fact, the committee's subsequent work on development assistance was troubling. In its response to the report of William Winegard's review of Canadian development assistance, the government rejected two of the committee's major recommendations. The committee's first recommendation was that the Canadian International Development Agency (CIDA) should establish a framework paper on human rights, with an appropriate country classification grid. The second was that CIDA should work with the Department of External Affairs to prepare an annual review of Official Development Assistance as it relates to human rights issues. This review would be tabled in Parliament each year and referred to both the Standing Committee on External Affairs and International Trade and the Standing Committee on Human Rights. The government argued that neither the establishment of a grid nor the preparation of annual reports to Parliament would serve the foreign policy interests of Canada.[16]

It is still unclear whether the Standing Committee on Human Rights will become an effective instrument for the pursuit of human rights. To do so, it would need to monitor the full range of the Canadian government's foreign policy, investigate the extent to which human rights concerns are truly reflected in it, and have full access to relevant information. If this were to happen, the goal of integrating human rights in the day-to-day work of foreign policy decision making and practice might be advanced. If this is not done, the committee will serve simply as a stage on which Canada's politicians are able to make grandstand plays before the public.

In Conclusion

It is to be expected that the government may often take human rights positions that the churches will criticize. After all, the churches are a major repository of ethical values in our society. Governments, while not unresponsive to values, are subjected to a great many other pressures as well. There will always be a gap between the government and the churches on these issues, but why is that gap as large as it is, despite widespread public opinion favouring human rights?

The International System

When churches and other groups complain about the unresponsiveness of government to their demands, the government's constant refrain is this: as long as the world is organized into competing sovereign states, there are bound to be "constraints on our international activities, particularly in the current environment of distrust, disillusionment and insecurity."[17] By this line of reasoning, the churches' failure to attain their human rights goals is an indirect result of the existing world order.

The international system does set limits on individual and collective efforts to enforce the human rights standards agreed to by states. Despite these agreements and the efforts of the United Nations, most states are still reluctant to discard the principles of sovereignty and of non-intervention in the internal affairs of other states.

Canada's ability to pursue an active human rights policy is constrained as well by its own diverse and sometimes conflicting national goals. States have their own legitimate ends, of which human rights is only one. There are inevitably times when a government may have little choice but to sacrifice or at least to moderate its concern for human rights in view of other pressing concerns, such as national security, world peace, national prosperity, the aims of world development, pressure from privileged economic groups, or the desire to avoid offending a powerful ally. And of course, while statesmen may and often do concern themselves with the rightness of what they do, they cannot ignore the effects of their actions either.[18] In deciding how best to promote human rights around the world, a state must concern itself with the effects of its actions on the human rights violator, on those whose rights have been violated, and on its own interests.

Canada shares these priorities with other states. Taken together, they may require that Canada moderate its pursuit of a world free from human rights violations. However, the conflicts between foreign policy goals are not always as acute or as damaging to its interests as Ottawa is apt to claim. The concern for national security, world order, and economic growth are often exaggerated and misperceived, while the importance of justice or human rights is underestimated.[19]

The international system can and does impose limits on a state's ability to pursue forthright human rights policies in the global arena. However, the international system does not prescribe specific policies. The choices about which policies to pursue are made by Canadian leaders, not the international system. The decisions they make reflect the importance they attach to human rights considerations relative to other values. The fact that the churches disagree with government choices and that the churches' preferences are largely ignored is more the result of other factors than it is a symptom of an international system that discourages ethical behaviour. For the most part, the churches' policy recommendations have not been naive, unrealistic, or insensitive to the other concerns that must be considered by government. And since other states have and, in some cases, still do pursue a more forthright human rights policy than does Canada, Ottawa's timid and cautious conduct cannot be attributed to the international system alone.

The Canadian Political System

In very general terms, the Canadian political system acts as a severe restraint on the ability of non-governmental organizations to affect policy, particularly foreign policy.[20] The dominant position of the Executive, together with the practice of party solidarity, means that cabinet rather than Parliament is one of the most effective points of access for interest groups. Equally important to the policy-making process is the bureaucracy, which provides advice to cabinet ministers and is responsible for administering legislation once it has been passed. The result is a political process that "operates primarily through the relatively closed, disciplined and hierarchically organized structures, the party system and the bureaucracy, which reach an apex in the cabinet."[21] Such a system is not very receptive to demands from the outside public. If interest groups are to have any impact on the policy process, "they must maintain close connections with one of the principal policy structures, especially the bureaucracy, and avoid any type of action which might place those connections in jeopardy."[22]

A relatively closed, self-contained system of political decision making limits access to the policy process. The churches do maintain contact with middle and upper levels of the bureaucracy and, from time to time, communicate with members of the cabinet. However, they usually make these approaches in reaction to a particular policy announced by the government. They have made some progress in establishing more continuous and regularized contacts. Churches and other groups have met regularly with Canada's ambassador to the UNCHR and related External Affairs staff. By providing detailed and reliable information, the churches have managed to have some impact on the positions adopted by Canada in Geneva. Still, these conversations do not yet amount to a genuine consultation. Even if they did, they would be severely limited by time and by the fact that so many different types of human rights concerns can be placed on the agenda.

What the churches want is an annual public forum in which participants can review the human rights situation in countries of special interest to Canada, assess the policies of the Canadian government towards those countries, and debate the relationship between human rights and other aspects of Canadian foreign policy. Whether the Standing Committee on Human Rights will fulfil that goal remains to be seen.

Until now, it appears that the churches have been kept at arm's length, leaving government to make policy choices on its own, shielded from public view. Yet not all groups in Canadian society have been excluded from policy-making circles. The government's continued opposition to the overall thrust of the churches' human rights proposals contrasts sharply with its responsiveness to the business community and its interests. Whether it is the result of pressure from the business community or close identification with it, the government exhibits a "corporate bias" in its foreign policy.[23]

Clearly, the fact that the Canadian political system is surprisingly closed does not explain why decisions made by policy makers do not reflect the ethical judgements of the churches. Since other pressure groups manage to reach and influence policy makers, the explanation for the weakness of the churches must lie elsewhere.

Characteristics of the Churches as Lobbyists

The influence any interest group has is likely to be related to some of its own characteristics, particularly its legitimacy and its available resources. In the eyes of the government, the group's legitimacy is probably most important. If Ottawa views church representatives as "radicals," as idealists, or as "unrepresentative" of their broader constituency — and all of these claims have been made — then they are unlikely to get an open and fair hearing. Their influence is bound to be limited. To be effective, interest groups must be seen to represent their constituency and to share the values and standards of government officials and politicians.

Frequently government officials have suggested that church statements and pressure represent the views of a small radical fringe within the church. Therefore, government does not have to take their lobbying activities seriously. It is true that statements by the churches can carry different levels of authority. The higher the policy-making body that issues church policies, the more representative the policies are likely to be. But even statements issued by ecumenical coalitions stay within the policies adopted by the churches, even though they are not directly issued by each specific church. For the most part, the groups engaged in human rights are agents or instruments of the churches.

The positions adopted by most church bodies on human rights cannot be dismissed as unrepresentative of their wider constituencies. Nevertheless, their views do differ markedly from the government's. They are in substantial opposition to many aspects of Canada's foreign policy. The churches have become a "counter-consensual" group, that is, a group that adheres to values largely at odds with the government's. The churches believe, for instance, that Canada and Canadians have an obligation "to act internationally against widespread starvation, extra-judicial execution, systematic torture, or extensive detention without trial."[24] They argue that such actions should not be limited to quiet diplomacy or relegated to the UNCHR and kept out of the deliberations of the IFIs and decisions on foreign aid, international trade, and foreign investment. They also argue that "the struggle for human rights, even of the individual, is at root a struggle for the liberation of the entire community."[25] In short, the churches argue that a genuine concern for human rights cannot be a purely humanitarian one, as the government maintains; the human rights issue is fundamentally political in nature.

As counter-consensual groups, the churches should not expect the government to respond favourably to many of their recommendations. Still, the government cannot totally ignore the churches, as they are "too respectable and too substantial"[26] and their lobbying is, for the most part, extremely well organized and based on thorough research. But since the human rights goals of government and churches are often so far apart, the failure of government to respond to the churches should come as no real surprise.

The international system does set limits on what any state can hope to accomplish in the field of human rights, especially a state of Canada's size. This influence alone cannot explain the unresponsiveness of the government to the churches' lobbying. Canada's leaders could adopt a more forthright human rights policy if they so wanted. In my view, the two most influential determinants are, first, Canada's political economy, the maintenance of which requires that the government be particularly responsive to the interests and needs of the corporate sector, and second, the values of the churches themselves, whose views on what human rights policies Canada can and should pursue place them in substantial opposition to the government. In their lobbying efforts the churches will have to content themselves with marginal changes wrung from the government by means of hard work and the amassing of incontrovertible data on human rights abuses. Although such "victories" cannot be dismissed as unimportant, the churches may choose to concentrate more of their time on public education, sensitizing Canadians to the churches' cosmopolitan values and attitudes.

Appendix 1

Canada's International Relations: An Alternate View

Canadian Council of Churches

Excerpts from a brief submitted by the Canadian Council of Churches to the Special Joint Committee on Canada's International Relations, November 1985.

(Editor's Note: In 1985 the Canadian Council of Churches presented a major brief to the Special Joint Committee on External Affairs and National Defence, as part of its participation in a major review of Canadian foreign policy. What follows are the key sections describing the principles the churches wished to see forming the basis of our foreign policy and a list of over sixty recommendations of concrete steps that Canada could take to give real life to those principles.

The statement also included sections on geographic issues pertaining to, among others, Latin America, South Africa, the Caribbean, Asia, the Helsinki region, and the Middle East.)

Chapter 1
An Enhanced World Role for Canada

The recent Green Paper on "Directions for Canada's International Relations" refers several times to the dynamics and interdependence of international life. Despite this recognition of what we believe to be the reality of the world in the late twentieth century, the major focus of the policies outlined in that paper is a narrow emphasis on Canada's need to become economically competitive, and to secure itself against external threats — specifically from the Soviet Union.

Our response grows out of a deep concern that Canada, like most other states, is engaged in the pursuit of its narrow self-interest at the expense of the broad long-term imperatives of global survival. In contrast to the Green Paper's image of a world of egotistical states, each pursuing its own competitive course and intent on achieving its own security, we are inspired by a vision of a world in which peace, prosperity, and justice are indivisible.

The churches are firmly committed to the belief that the security of Canada cannot be established independently of the security of other countries, or on the basis of an unjust world order. We know that ultimately our prosperity depends on all other peoples prospering as well. We know that there can be no true and lasting peace without justice for men and women everywhere. We believe that our humanity can only be fully realized in a world in which human rights are respected every-where, and in which all peoples are assured of their basic needs.

We know that the world which we are describing is an ideal, but we believe that we have no alternative but to work towards making it a reality. In fact, it is in the interest of Canada, as of all middle and small-sized countries, to pursue such a reality. It is the less powerful states that suffer most in an international arena where the rules for equitable relations between states are allowed to break down. We believe that Canada can play a constructive and mediating role on the world stage. The pages which follow contain specific recommendations for Canadian policies which we believe would be helpful steps leading to a more truly just and peaceful world.

The chapters which follow deal with areas in which the churches have particular concerns. There are, however, two basic issues which we wish to address in this introductory chapter. They are: (1) the need for Canada to have an independent foreign policy; and (2) the importance of Canada's maintaining its support for multilateral institutions.

1. An Independent Foreign Policy for Canada

One of the questions raised by the Special Joint Committee on Canada's International Relations (Themes for Phase Two) is "What historic and geographic factors, natural and human resources and traditions in-fluence Canada's foreign policy?"

Evidently, a major factor influencing our foreign policy is our close proximity to the great power to the south, with whom we share a continent and four hundred years of history. The United States is a great and good neighbour; the lives of our two nations are inextricably inter-twined, so much so that a markedly anti-American foreign policy is unrealistic. And yet, we maintain that Canada is, in the best sense, a "friend of the United States" when it maintains a little distance. Canadian effectiveness on the world scene is diminished if we are in-variably seen as closely identified with American policies. Moreover, there are occasions when our assessment of a situation requires us to take an independent position. One example will illustrate our meaning.

The American analysis of the situation in Central America seems to be almost wholly in Cold War terms. Their determination to resist the development of "other Cubas" has led them to adopt policies which are rapidly militarizing the region, are lending support to brutally repres-sive regimes and are driving movements seeking to redress economic and political injustices into the arms of the eastern bloc. Independent observers of American policy in the area can see that they may in the end bring about the very result they are seeking to avoid. The friends of the United States can be most helpful by encouraging the peace process and by doing all in their power to address the root causes of the unrest.

Canada can play the role of friendly critic. She can attempt to con-vince the United States of the values of multilateralism. She can also interpret the United States to other countries. Although she is a member of NATO and the western bloc, Canada is still regarded by most coun-tries as friendly and non-threatening. As such, Canada can sometimes find acceptance for proposals which, if they came from the United States, would be viewed with suspicion. This gives Canada an advantage on the world political scene which it is our responsibility to exercise in the most constructive way possible.

Canada has a natural affinity in size and outlook with the Nordic countries, the Netherlands, Australia and New Zealand, and can work with those countries in establishing good relations with other blocs. It could be that there is potential for a "small power bloc" of western nations which could find partners in the non-aligned world. The futility of superpower rivalry and the stalemate caused by the division of the United Nations into three opposing camps, East, West, and non-aligned, is painfully clear. For this reason, there may be a role for a new alignment of smaller states, friendly to the United States but not threatening to either the eastern bloc or the non-aligned countries. As a leader in such a bloc, Canada could play a very constructive and creative role.

2. The Importance of Supporting Multilateral Organizations

As a small country in world terms, Canada's interests are well-served by a multilateral approach to international issues. The major powers may be able to act unilaterally or bilaterally, but most nation states including ourselves make our most effective contribution as part of a larger effort.

The section of the Green Paper on the UN system and multilateralism raises a number of questions. We are in general agreement with the Green Paper's view that the UN "helps to substantiate and validate Canada's position in international affairs and provides a vehicle for the exercise of our influence." The paper raises the question to what extent the UN furthers Canada's current and prospective interests and priorities in light of the fact that the United States no longer attaches the importance to the UN that it once did. As we have indicated, it is our strong belief that Canada needs the United Nations, and should put a high priority on the task of revitalizing it.

As we noted above, we believe that Canada should be seen as pursuing its own policy initiatives on the world scene. We recognize that the United Nations system with its rigid pattern of voting blocs is inhibiting to initiatives from many countries, Canada included.

We wish to congratulate the Canadian government on its recent successful participation in the UN Assembly to mark the end of the Decade for Women. We are aware of the high esteem in which Canada's contribution was held by the delegates of other countries, and consider this an indication of the notable role Canada can play on the world stage.

However, we have a concern about Canada's participation in the UN system, which can be summed up in the observation: "Canada has a role to play in the UN, but doesn't play it." (Quoted from a representative of another country in an article, "Canada at the United Nations," by Peyton V. Lyon, International Perspectives, September-October 1985, p. 17.)

Participation in the UN Assemblies often becomes an almost perfunctory ritual in which the content of every speech or intervention can

be predicted in advance. This breeds a cynicism which we have sometimes seen expressed by External Affairs officials as an implied attitude
of "What is the point of a Canadian intervention when it probably won't
succeed?" While not underestimating the problems, we strongly believe
that cynicism leads to apathy which, if shared by many of the potential
leaders of the UN, will spell its death-warrant. We firmly believe that
would be a tragedy not only for the developing countries but also for
Canada and other countries of the western world.

For this reason, we welcomed the appointment of Mr. Stephen Lewis
as Canada's Ambassador to the United Nations. We commend him for
the energy with which he is representing Canada and the enthusiasm
with which he defends the organization against its numerous critics. Our
perception is that Canada is again, in the mid-1980s, establishing a
significant place for itself in the United Nations.

We support Canada's efforts to reform some institutions, notably
UNESCO, from within. The withdrawal of the United States and other
countries from UNESCO does not solve any of the problems of that
organization but rather creates new ones. (We were saddened to hear
recently from a church partner in St. Lucia of the cancellation of an
excellent literacy program in his country because of the cut in UN-
ESCO's budget.)

The paper also raises the question of Canada's role as part of the UN's
peacekeeping efforts. Elsewhere in this brief we express our conviction
that peacekeeping is a highly appropriate role for Canada's armed forces
to play. In answer to the specific question asked: we would advocate a
return to the practice of UN sponsorship of peacekeeping operations,
and we would like to see additional Canadian resources devoted to this
enterprise.

Canada's avowed support of the United Nations may face a severe
test if the United States does in fact cut back on its financial support.
Countries like Canada, some of which are already contributing more per
capita than the United States, may be asked to contribute even more in
order to make up for the shortfall in the UN's revenue. We would urge
that Canada indicate its willingness along with other countries to assume a greater share of the expense of maintaining the UN and its
organizations.

Turning to Canada's other multilateral involvements, we note the
increasingly significant part which we are taking in the Commonwealth
of Nations. At this moment in history, Canada, together with Australia
and New Zealand, is playing a constructive bridging role between the
United Kingdom and the third world members. We commend the Prime
Minister on the leadership which he showed in the recent Commonwealth meeting in the Bahamas, where the question of sanctions against
South Africa proved so divisive.

We are surprised in fact, in light of the very prominent Commonwealth role played by Mr. Trudeau over many years, the excellent beginning made by Mr. Mulroney, and the positive emphasis we know is laid
on Commonwealth connections by our diplomats in Africa and Asia,
that the Commonwealth tie is given only a few lines in the Green Paper.

We believe that there are many constructive initiatives possible within the Commonwealth; it is potentially very valuable as an alternate forum to the UN, where the lines between the western countries and the third world are very sharply drawn.

We welcome Canada's recent initiative in supporting other Commonwealth governments as they implement programmes of mass immunization against six childhood diseases. This is a good example of interaction in the relatively small forum of the Commonwealth where Canada's initiatives and contributions can have a real impact.

Canada's bilingual character makes it a desirable centre for further studies and cultural exchanges for the large majority of the countries in the developing world. This is reflected in the programmes Canada supports through the Commonwealth and our participation in La Francophonie. We are very well equipped for leadership in this field. We would urge that Canada continue to make this a priority....

Chapter 2
Canada and the Third World: Aid, International Trade and the International Financial Institutions

I. Introduction

Over the last several decades, Canadian churches have actively engaged in relief and development activities in many third world countries. In this they have been part of a widespread movement of concern and commitment in Canada that has actively sought to express its solidarity with the world's poor. This movement has embraced many groups, whose positions have not been identical. Nevertheless, three concerns have usually been central to their positions and activities.

1. An acceptance that we Canadians have obligations which extend to those beyond our borders.
2. A recognition that the international order persistently works to the advantage of the rich and powerful within it; equity and justice towards the less developed countries will therefore require concessions from the countries of the North.
3. An emphasis in development activities on helping communities of poor people and poor countries to meet their basic needs more adequately, and on assisting them to gain a greater control over the forces and institutions which determine their economic progress.

The Canadian NGOs were not alone in their advocacy of these central propositions. The second proposition above, that there are obligations of justice and equity which call for concessions by the North, was at the core of the demands of the third world in the mid- and late-1970s for a new international economic order. The validity of this claim was unambiguously supported by Prime Minister Trudeau in his famous speech in 1978 at Mansion House, London, by the Brandt Commission in 1980, and by the Parliamentary Committee on North-South Relations in its report in 1980.

The third proposition, that development assistance should concentrate upon helping poor people and poor countries to meet their basic needs, was very widely championed in "development circles" by the mid-1970s as it became more and more clear that without special care much development assistance might fail to be of any value to the poorest within the countries being aided. It was the International Labour Office that gave to the concept of basic needs its most persuasive definition. The ILO also agreed, and it was a view that received wide endorsation, that the objective of development assistance was to assist poor people and poor countries to be able themselves to meet their basic needs. The Declaration of Principles and Programmes of Action adopted by the 1976 World Employment Conference of the ILO includes this authoritative statement (from Annex B in *Employment Growth and Basic Needs: A One-World Problem*, prepared by the ILO, 1976):

. . . .

2. Basic needs ... include two elements. First, they include certain minimum requirements of a family for private consumption: adequate food, shelter and clothing, as well as certain household equipment and furniture. Second, they include essential services provided by and for the community at large, such as safe drinking water, sanitation, public transport and health, educational, and cultural facilities.
3. Basic-needs-oriented policy implies the participation of the people in making the decisions which affect them through organizations of their own choice.
4. In all countries freely chosen employment enters into a basic-needs policy both as a means and an end. Employment yields output. It provides an income to the employed, and gives the individual a feeling of self-respect, dignity and of being a worthy member of society....
6. In developing countries satisfaction of basic needs cannot be achieved without both acceleration in their economic growth and measures aimed at changing the pattern of growth and access to the use of productive resources by the lowest income groups. Often these measures will require a transformation of social structures, including an initial redistribution of assets, especially land, with adequate and timely compensation.

CIDA came close to embracing a similar attitude toward development in 1975 with the publication of its policy paper, *Strategy for International Development Co-operation 1975-80*. That paper in many ways marks the high point of CIDA's ability to give a primary emphasis to helping poor countries and poor peoples to meet their basic needs. However, this paper was never an authoritative guide to CIDA policy, and certainly, it did not reflect the attitude and values of the Departments of Finance, and of Industry, Trade, and Commerce. Almost from the date it was published, there was major erosion of CIDA's ability to pursue the objectives set out in the strategy paper as other, and lesser, objectives were quickly required of CIDA. This erosion is well-known, and has been authoritatively documented by the North-South Institute in its *In the National Interest* (Ottawa, 1980).

Over the past decade CIDA's concern with basic needs and with projects that will directly help the poor has declined as its interest in large-scale projects and in the newly-industrializing countries has grown. In contrast, the churches, along with many of the major non-governmental organizations working on aid, have moved in quite the opposite direction. The development which they are concerned to promote is less and less seen in terms simply of an expanding gross national product for the countries they seek to assist, and more and more in terms of increasing the capacity of these countries to meet the basic needs of their peoples and of achieving more just international economic relations.

For example, the 1985 *Action Goal and Objectives* of Ten Days for World Development urged the Canadian Government "to develop and strengthen policies that will support the development of just, self-determining and participatory societies...." The target of this recommendation is Central America, but the perception of development which informs the recommendation has universal applicability. The Inter-Church Fund for International Development (ICFID) has recently issued a similar definition of development. It is:

> ...a process of continuous change by which any country or sector of population seeks to advance itself both materially and spiritually by: (a) transforming its productive structure to serve its needs more adequately, (b) establishing new and more just social relationships; (c) acquiring adequate and appropriate political and administrative institutions; (d) renewing is own culture to achieve a better quality of life.

With a greater sensitivity to the multiple dimensions of genuine development has come also a greater awareness of the complexity of the causes of underdevelopment. ICFID, for example, observes that:

> There is increasing exploitation of the poor by the rich. Global resources, sufficient for the satisfaction of every human need are controlled and enjoyed by a powerful few....

The Canadian Catholic Organization for Development and Peace in its 1982 statement on basic principles pursued this theme further.

> ...Underdevelopment is in large measure caused by rich countries, and it is rich countries which create obstacles to development such as militarization and control of prices and markets. Development of the Third World is also the responsibility of the richer countries such as Canada and demands much more than financial aid....

The Canadian churches have also applied these values in assessments of specific Canadian economic policies towards the third world. Examples of this are the recent Canadian Council of Churches' submission on the government discussion paper, *Export Financing*; and the statements by church representatives to the Special Parliamentary Committee on North:South Relations. In addition, church representatives have been active participants in the preparation of such statements as the paper on Canadian development assistance which was published in 1979 by the Canadian Council for International Co-operation and the 1981 and 1984 statements by the Group of 78.

This paper develops further the positions taken in these earlier statements. We are seeking to apply to the consideration of government policy on North:South issues these central ethical concerns:

1. a commitment to solidarity with those who suffer;
2. support for reforms that will lead to greater international equity;
3. a desire to help third world communities and states develop economically, to become more self-reliant and more able to avoid exploitation and dependency in their relationships with larger and richer powers.

These three concerns are the basis of our recommendations with regard to aid, to trade, and to the international financial institutions (IFIs). Some of our recommendations seek to stop the erosion that has already occurred in the aid and trade policies of the Canadian government and in the activities of the IFIs. Others seek to move beyond this immediate, damage-limiting objective to suggest policies that would promote greater international equity and provide greater concrete assistance to the least developed countries. Finally, there are recommendations which even more clearly go beyond the intentions of the present Government and give concrete expression to the churches' concern that we respond more generously and imaginatively to the needs of the poorest, including their need to gain a greater control over the circumstances of their lives.

II. Development Assistance Policies

It is urgently necessary to reverse the trend in Canadian aid policies which has involved over the last ten years a significant retreat from the policy statement of 1975. We therefore recommend that:

1. The Government of Canada should restore 1990 as the latest date by which it commits itself to reach the target of .7% of the Gross National Product for its development assistance expenditures.

This recommendation is only the beginning of a revitalized aid program for Canada. Indeed, by itself, and without other reforms it might be of limited value. However, it is a desirable first step. We have been promising the third world that we accept this target for nearly two decades. Let us begin by withdrawing the announcement that Canada would

delay until 1995 the final achievement of the target for its aid expenditures of .7% of the Gross National Product. Let us reinstate 1990 as the
date by which this target will be reached.

2. **CIDA should immediately permit tenders from other third world
   countries in relation to the development assistance projects admin-
   istered by its bilateral programs....**

3. **Canada should rapidly and progressively untie its bilateral aid, that
   is, permit the countries being assisted to use competitive international tenders for projects financed by Canadian aid.**

This will significantly increase the real value of Canadian aid to the
recipients. Regulations presently require that Canadian goods and services constitute 80% of bilateral projects. This requirement has been estimated, even by Presidents of CIDA, as adding an additional cost
averaging between 20 and 25%. There is a second important consequence to this untying. As long as Canadian aid is as tied as it now is,
Canada can do little to assist many of the projects which are most likely
to help meet the basic needs of poor people. Activities such as the
provision of rural water supplies, tertiary roads, low-cost urban housing, rural dispensaries, and agricultural extension services cannot be
provided if 80% of the inputs must be Canadian in origin. The selection
of the projects to be assisted by Canada is thus severely skewed in
the direction of capital-intensive, large-scale, technologically complex
projects.

4. **CIDA funds should not be used, directly or indirectly, in association
   with export credits to secure capital contracts for Canadian firms.**

This practice has developed and become common in recent years. It is,
indeed, the most important innovation in Canadian aid policies in recent
years and the most damaging. Canadian bilateral aid had long been in
large part tied to the purchase of Canadian goods and services. To this
self-serving practice was then added the promotion of Canadian trade....
  This new emphasis has two main implications. The first is that more
aid should be given to the newly industrializing third world countries,
for their markets are potentially far more important to Canadian exports
than were those of the least developed. The second implication is that
Canadian aid should be used in a variety of ways to help secure for
Canadian firms substantial orders, particularly for capital goods. The
techniques used are several and they are complicated. But their central
characteristic is that CIDA assistance is made available on the condition
that a commercial project associated with the aid project is awarded to
a Canadian firm. The results are obvious. Aid is drawn towards projects
that are large and capital-intensive. Aid is also by this device more likely
to be awarded in higher income countries for it is they who are most
likely to have the large capital projects capable of being financed in these
complex ways. First the previous government and more recently the

present government have announced their intention of devoting one-half of all increases in aid spending to a mechanism which would achieve this same end.

We do not deny the legitimacy and importance of trade. However ... it is shabby to present as aid funds spent in the promotion of Canadian exports. To propose, as the government is proposing, that 50% of the increase in CIDA's budget should go to the new aid-trade facility is effectively to use these funds for trade promotion. It thus undermines the meaning and value of the government's acceptance of .6% of GNP as the target for aid expenditures.

In addition to the above recommendations, which seek primarily to check the erosion of the integrity of CIDA's development assistance which has occurred in recent years, we add these further recommendations, which would lead CIDA in imaginative and desirable fresh directions. Many of these additional recommendations are corollaries of the conviction so widespread amongst both church and non-church NGOs, that we should be seeking to promote development which involves much more than an expanding Gross National Product.

5. **Canadian aid should be directed in particular to those countries whose governments are seriously endeavouring:**
   a) to pursue a more self-reliant development strategy, and
   b) to ensure that the poorest in their societies are able to meet their basic needs....

6. **In selecting the projects and programmes which are to receive Canadian support CIDA should take especial care to search out those activities which will "produce a wide distribution of the benefits of development..., enhance the quality of life and improve the capacity of all sectors ... to participate in national development efforts." (Quoted from CIDA's 1975-80 Strategy Paper.)...**

7. **Special care should be taken with CIDA to ensure that the NGOs are not treated as agents for the implementation of government policies and that NGOs' aid programs are not regarded as mere extensions of government-to-government assistance....**

8. **The Canadian government should commission a major review of CIDA's use of food aid....**

9. **The Canadian government should establish basic human rights criteria as one of the important co-determinants of Canadian aid policies....**

10. **Where it is clearly determined that basic human rights are grossly and persistently violated by a state, that state should receive no Canadian government-to-government assistance, except for emergency relief aid....**

III. Trade Policies

The churches' recommendations in the area of development assistance dealt first with measures to check the damaging disintegration which has occurred in recent years. Our recommendations with regard to trade policies also begin with remedial measures, for in recent years there has been an erosion also in the openness of access which Canada gives to manufactured goods from the third world.

However, trade policy issues are more complex than those of aid. In recent years, the export of manufactured goods from third world countries to western countries such as Canada has become controversial, with clear implications for domestic manufacturing and employment. There are a number of mutually re-inforcing factors at work.

They include: the high levels of unemployment; the increasing importance of trade to western economies; the great increase in global planning and global sourcing by transnational enterprise; the speed at which at least a few less-developed countries are moving through the various stages of industrialization. All of this means that governments such as the Canadian government are bound to be concerned about the employment and investment consequences of third world industrial exports upon their own domestic economies.

Low-cost manufactured imports are not nearly as important as technology in generating structural unemployment. The invention of new products and, even more, of new manufacturing processes has always been the primary cause of structural unemployment, from the invention of the spinning jenny to the moving production line to robotics and micro-electronics. Nevertheless, low-wage imports, though a far less significant cause of unemployment, are a highly visible source of unemployment and are easily targetted. In devising public policies to manage this structural unemployment, it is important to recognize that some of the possible responses to these low-cost imports have disproportionate and substantial negative consequences for the third world. For this reason, the churches believe Canadians have an obligation to promote employment and growth in Canada in ways that do not impose any special burden on the countries of the third world....

The churches recommend that:

11. **Canadian policies designed to deal with structural unemployment due to low-cost imports shall not be negatively discriminatory against third world countries and, except possibly in rare exceptions, shall be transitional in nature. These policies, called industrial adjustment policies, should be designed to facilitate the transfer of capital and labour to industries in which Canada can maintain a comparative advantage rather than to perpetuate and entrench a declining industry at increasing cost to Canadian consumers and to the third world exporters.**

The record to date is far too clear: country-specific protectionist measures are used primarily against the weakest of those countries that are selling in Canada. Non-discriminatory trade rules, that is international rules that rule out protectionist measures that are specific to one or a limited number of countries, are therefore of particular importance to the less-developed countries for they (and East European countries) are almost always the main targets of such measures. For similar reasons, safeguard measures should also be transitional in order to ensure that they are being used to facilitate an orderly adjustment to the appearance of the third world products rather than to block their way permanently.

12. **Manufactured products from poor countries should not be excluded from Canada merely on the grounds that they come from low-wage societies.**

To accept that goods can be excluded merely on the grounds that they come from low-wage societies would be to aspire to a two-tiered system of international trade in which manufactured goods were almost exclusively produced by already-developed countries; any such exclusion would deny poor countries what is often their one comparative advantage, their low wages; it would entrench what would constitute a policy of trade apartheid.

However, in order to protect the interests of labour both in Canada and the third world, much more effort is required to ensure that employers, both multinationals and indigenous capitalists, do not exploit third world labour in the manufacturing of goods for export to Canada. This does not mean that they must pay wages equivalent to Canadian wages, for that would mean that they could never be in a position to export. However, it should mean that the exporting companies are meeting basic standards relating, for example, to safety regulations, to child labour and to hours of work and that their wages are comparable to or better than the wages of other workers in that national economy. To that end:

13. **Canada should itself enforce a fair labour practices code upon its trading partners, and should press for the introduction and enforcement of such a code internationally.**

14. **The Canadian government should formulate vastly improved domestic policies of industrial adjustment....**

15. **Canada should strongly support the General Agreement on Tariffs and Trade, and should seek to ensure that it reflects the needs of the poor countries more than it has in the past....**

16. **Canada should acknowledge that the present international economic order works to the persistent comparative disadvantage of poor countries, and should support and play an initiating role in international efforts to promote a new and more equitable international order....**

17. Canada should be ready to negotiate long-term commitments to purchase commodity exports from third world countries that are seeking to plan their economies and need the security of such commitments-to-purchase as Canada could offer....

In concluding these recommendations relating to international trade, we would underline that we value an ordered, non-discriminatory multilateral trading system. We see it as being as important in that arena as is the UN in the arena of international political issues.

However, we are not thereby intending to recommend to third world countries that they should pursue an export-led development strategy, relying on manufactured exports as their "engine of growth." For many of the less-developed countries and for most of the least-developed amongst them, such a development strategy is unlikely to be advantageous. The development agencies of the Canadian churches tend instead to suggest an emphasis on food self-sufficiency, on rural development, and on community-based and community-strengthening projects.

Nevertheless, all third world countries desperately need foreign exchange for essential imports and all seek international markets for their produce and goods. These recommendations, if implemented, would help to ensure that they are fairly treated in the international trading arena.

Finally, it is important to note that these recommendations are also in Canada's national interest. They would contribute to a more just and therefore more peaceful international order and they would help to strengthen the international structures and framework of rules whose strength and efficacy are as much in Canada's interest as in the interest of the third world.

IV. The International Financial Institutions (IFIs) — The World Bank, the International Monetary Fund (IMF), and the Regional Development Banks

The history of the International Monetary Fund, the World Bank and the regional development banks can be seen in one of two rather different ways. They can be seen as institutions created by the major capitalist states to manage the international economic order in capitalism's interest. They can also be seen as rather inadequate and still fragile international institutions which are all the world has to accomplish important international tasks which are as much in the interest of mixed economy states and socialist states as capitalist states. The truth is that both of these perceptions are correct. These institutions do serve the interests of capitalism. They are dominated by the major capitalist states. However, their two major functions are certainly important also to the less-developed countries. The provision of short-term credits in hard currencies to countries facing unanticipated severe balance of payment problems (the IMF) and the provision of long-term loans for major developmental projects (the World Bank and the regional development banks) are activities needed by any international economic order. Though the less-developed countries have had much to criticize in the operation of these institutions over the decade, it has very much been the case in recent years that they have been their champions while the United States has sought with success to limit severely their funding and to constrain their activities.

Five developments in recent years must be noted as background to the recommendations of this paper. They are the following:

First, the International Monetary Fund has been intimately involved in the negotiating and management of the various agreements relating to the very severe debt crises which have engulfed the economies of a number of newly-industrializing countries. This has had an adverse impact on the resources and the energy that the IMF has devoted to the problems of the less-developed countries which have been so enormously affected by the global recession.

Second, neither the World Bank nor the IMF has come forward with facilities to provide credits and loans adequate to the needs of the less-developed countries that face major structural adjustments that are not temporary and cannot be completed in a short number of years. This is a major failure of creative leadership by these institutions, a failure partly due to the preoccupation, just mentioned above, with the debt crisis of a few major NICs.

Third, there has been a vast and depressing asymmetry in the reaction of the IMF to the continuing international debt crisis and the global recession. The Fund, and the international community more generally, has no capacity to influence the policies of the United States, whose enormous defence expenditures and massive budget deficits are the main cause of the abnormally high interest rates which, in turn greatly intensify the debt burden of third world countries and retard a global economic recovery. In contrast to this inability to influence policies in the United States, the Fund bears down heavily upon the poorest countries, insisting upon policy changes that have the most adverse impact upon the welfare of their poor.

Fourth, since 1980, the United States policy towards these institutions has been particularly unhelpful and unconstructive. The United States has sought to influence the decision of these institutions about loans and credits to governments that are out of favour in Washington. Even more important, the United States, as part of its general irritated reaction to the UN family of institutions, has been a major opponent to adequate augmentation of the IMF quotas and the resources for the International Development Association, the concessional finance arm of the World Bank. American policy continues to be unhelpful, but in recent months it appears as if the US now sees the possibility of bending IMF and World Bank policies to serve the goals that they, the Americans, have defined. Recommendation 20 speaks to this latest development.

Fifth, there is a marked tendency on the part of each institution to use the very powerful leverage which they have over third world governments-in-need to secure the adoption by third world governments of internal trade, monetary, public finance and public sector policies which reflect a strong pro-capitalist, pro-market ideological bias and a marked disregard for the welfare of the poor.

The Canadian government has continued to be a strong supporter of the international financial institutions. Canada has opposed the efforts of the United States to limit their effectiveness. Canada has also on several important occasions, in one or another of these institutions, voted in favour of credits or loans which the United States was opposing. However, CIDA, External Affairs, and Finance have tended very much to accept unquestioningly the IMF/World Bank view of the causes of third world development problems and have supported efforts to mobilize multilateral pressure on governments that try to stand against the policy pressures placed upon them by the IMF and the Bank. Canada has thus contributed to, rather than moderated, the western ideological common front, which faces any third world country seeking to pursue a development strategy that challenges that ideology....

The churches recommend that:

18. Canada should join like-minded middle powers of the west and influential developing countries in a concerted effort to ensure that the World Bank and the IMF become much more responsive to the needs of the poorest countries....

19. Canada, nevertheless, should view with great caution the recent American effort to integrate more closely still the lending policies of the international institutions and the major international banks....

20. Canada should work to ensure that the conditions attached to the credits extended by the IMF are carefully revised so that their burden does not fall primarily upon the urban poor and the rural landless....

21. Canada should seek to ensure that the arrangements for "rescue operations" suggested as ways of dealing with the debt crises of such countries as Argentina, Chile, Mexico, and Brazil do not leave the poor of these countries to carry the main burden, and to that end should support international negotiations to set the terms of a complete recasting of the debt relationships so that there will be a genuine sharing of the burden which avoids the imposition upon the debtors of socially, economically, and politically destructive burdens....

22. Canada should support the calling of a new "Bretton Woods" Conference so that the structures and responsibilities of the major international financial institutions can be freshly renegotiated....

23. Canada should urge the World Bank to make major and serious efforts to ensure that their support is available to governments seriously striving to promote development and the welfare of their

people along lines that seem to contradict the present ideology that is dominant within the World Bank....

24. Canada should urge the IMF and the World Bank to use their undoubted leverage to ensure that no government receives assistance from them if that government seriously abuses the basic human rights of its citizens....

25. Canada should instruct its Executive Directors of the international financial institutions to incorporate immediately human rights criteria as a co-determinant of how they vote on proposed credits and loans from these institutions....

Chapter 3
Canada's Foreign Policy and Human Rights

I. Human Rights: International Standards and Definitions

Since World War II the international community has developed a set of standards which has become essentially international common law. They represent the concerted efforts of the member states of the United Nations to develop a system of universal values to which all states, regardless of ideological bent or political doctrine, should be expected to adhere in their treatment of their citizens.

In effect, these collected human rights instruments represent an obligation on the part of all states participating in the international system to promote not only the interest of their own citizens, but also the interests of the citizens of every state. In our view, signing the universal human rights declarations and codes obliges each state to restrain other states and their agents from violating the rights of their citizens.

Over the past twenty years, the inter-governmental human rights movement has been joined by the non-governmental human rights movement, which has sprung up all over the world to ensure that states comply with the standards to which they have agreed. However, in the last decade, both these movements have been seriously threatened by the growing number of states that have flouted world opinion. They are also endangered by the stalemate by the east, west, and third world over which rights ought to have priority. Furthermore, a certain fatigue has set in since the 1970s, and consequently some countries now argue that human rights are not really of such great consequence.

As churches engaged in mission and development in many parts of the world, we have observed firsthand the most shameless violations of peoples' fundamental rights. In the worst situations, members of our partner churches overseas have themselves become part of the flood of refugees from their homelands, seeking asylum in Canada.

Stemming the flow of political and economic refugees is an increasingly urgent issue. The churches believe that the only real solution lies in tackling the root causes — the factors that deny so many of the world's citizens their basic human rights and needs.

The churches assume that all people everywhere, regardless of their ideological, cultural, or political system, wish to be free from disappearance, from arbitrary arrest and detention, torture, and extra-judicial execution and from systematic state-sponsored racial discrimination. We consider these basic rights. We also consider basic needs — for food, water, shelter — to be inviolable rights, without which it is impossible for human beings to sustain life. The churches regard these basic rights and basic needs as an immovable floor, below which no citizen or state can be allowed to fall without threatening the basic ground rules of the international order on which all states rely for their own security and for the security of their citizens.

The churches ask for a commitment by the Canadian government that it will place priority on the pursuit of a basic rights and basic needs floor, both in its multilateral relations and in its bilateral relations with other governments. In addition, we would urge the government to pursue the implementation of human rights coming above the basic rights and basic needs floor. Those rights constitute "a movable ceiling," a goal towards which states should progress steadily on schedules that reflect their cultural, historical, and economic differences.

The seriousness with which the Canadian government has taken its own obligations under the international agreements, its practice of reporting on its implementation in UN arenas, and its development of open and frequent consultation with the non-governmental human rights movement within Canada and abroad are much admired by our colleagues in countries whose governments have not been open to the role of citizens in the pursuit of human rights.

In unequivocally guaranteeing the human rights of Canadians by the "Charter of Rights and Freedoms," the Canadian government has made a public declaration that such rights are part of Canada's value system. By ratifying the "International Covenant on Civil and Political Rights," Canada has extended that value system to its position in the international arena.

Canadian churches support the government in these declarations and put forward recommendations which in our judgement would most effectively apply them to all areas of our country's foreign policy. We would urge the government to build on the impetus created by its own efforts in the past and pursue with greater vigour its obligations to those peoples in other countries who are subject to disappearance, arbitrary arrest and torture, detention, and execution.

II. Developing a Human Rights Policy: Monitoring Its Application

The Canadian government claims that the promotion and protection of international standards of basic human rights are an integral part of its foreign policy objectives. Nevertheless, it appears that at present it does not yet have a coherent human rights policy to shape its external affairs decisions.

The churches therefore recommend that:

26. Canada should begin at once to develop a human rights policy which will detail the criteria by which the human rights situation in a country can be assessed....

27. An annual public review of the observance of human rights in countries of particular interest to Canada should be conducted by a mandated parliamentary committee....

28. The Canadian government should place before the public the sources and data it uses when judgements are made concerning infractions of internationally-accepted human rights....

29. Although the churches would prefer a policy of full disclosure on commercial transactions, at the very least, Canada should require disclosure of the nature of transactions between Canadian companies and governments which are known to be guilty of gross and systematic violations of basic human rights....

III. The Specific Applications of Applying Human Rights Standards to Canada's Foreign Policy

A. Human Rights, Refugees, and Canada's Immigration Policies

. . . .

The churches recommend that:

30. Canada should promote the international elimination of refugee reception and determination policies and practices which deny persons the right to flee and have access to refuge, such as indiscriminate tourist visa requirements and such as detention and other deterrence measures....

31. Canada should remove the tourist visa requirements for countries where the human rights situation is severe, and where Canada is a logical and accessible place of refuge, for example, Guatemala.

B. Human Rights and the Policies of Government Agencies Promoting Exports

. . . .

The churches recommend that:

32. The Export Development Act should be amended to require the Export Development Corporation to assess all available information about a country's observance of and respect for basic human rights, before it agrees to extending financial support facilities for

exports there. The EDC should also report on facilities granted and
its rationale for these decisions....

33. The EDC should withhold financial support facilities for trade to
countries that engage in a consistent pattern of gross violations of
human rights until such time as internationally recognized human
rights organizations such as Amnesty International, the International Commission of Jurists and the UN Commission on Human
Rights have reported the cessation of gross and systematic violations of human rights.

34. One director of the EDC should be appointed with a specific
responsibility to present such human rights concerns....

35. In deciding when to extend PEMD grants (Program for Export
Marketing Development) to specific countries, therefore, the
government should consider the recipient country's record on
human rights.

C. Human Rights and Private Sector Exports and Investments

. . . .

The churches recommend that:

36. Export permits should not be issued for military and strategic
goods and technology destined to countries with a record of gross
and systematic violations of human rights; and that COCOM's [Co-
ordinating Committee of NATO member states and Japan] performance characteristics be the common criteria for all such
Canadian exports.

37. Parliament, through the Standing Committee on External Affairs
and National Defence, or a sub-committee thereof, should annually
review Canadian exports of military and strategic goods and technology in the context of Canada's protection of internationally accepted human rights standards....

38. Parliament should act to prohibit exports of military and strategic
goods and technology to regimes engaging in a consistent pattern
of gross violations of internationally recognized human rights
standards....

39. Provisions should be made to require public disclosure of outstanding loans to foreign governments or their agencies of amounts
totalling more than $1 million incurred by Canadian private banks
or other Canadian financial institutions directly or through consortia with other international lenders.

40. In the interest of public accountability, Canadian banks and other financial institutions should be required to disclose the amount and the dates of such loans and publish them as a matter of record.

41. In order to preserve the principle of client/banker confidentiality and in order to safeguard the principle of competition, financial institutions should not be required to make such disclosures prior to 30 days following the signing of such agreements.

D. Human Rights and Canada's Role in Multilateral Financial Institutions

. . . .

The churches recommend that:

42. The Canadian government should establish basic human rights criteria as a co-determinant of Canada's voting decisions in the International Monetary Fund (IMF)....

43. The Canadian government and parliament should enact legislation that would require:
a) a careful scrutiny of a country's human rights record before credit decisions are made at international financial institutions in which Canada has membership;
b) opposition to applications for credits from any government that is engaged in or that condones consistent and gross violations of internationally accepted basic human rights.

44. Funding to assist the basic needs of the poor in countries with repressive regimes should be channelled through non-governmental organizations with the competence necessary to deliver the aid to those for whom it was intended.

Chapter 4
Canada and the Pursuit of Collective Security

An enduring principle of Canadian foreign policy is that Canada's national security cannot be assured in isolation, but that it must be part of a collective, international enterprise. Inasmuch as this is a recognition that the security of nations, no less than of persons, is indivisible and is most readily assured when the security of one's neighbours is also a central objective, it is a welcome principle. Within the evolution of Canadian foreign policy, however, the principle of "collective security" has taken on other, less desirable elements.

For a middle power that shares a continent with a superpower, collective (for continental) undertakings frequently become, not so much joint enterprises as occasions for the former to demonstrate support for the initiatives of the latter. Here, again, inasmuch as Canadians honour the traditions of liberty and political participation that are entrenched in the United States, and inasmuch as Canadians wish to participate in preserving and extending those traditions, expressions of solidarity with US initiatives true to those traditions are a welcome element of Canadian foreign policy. But within the evolution of "collective security" practices, Canada has frequently failed to make critical distinctions between those initiatives which honour supportable traditions and those which derive from the less honourable dimensions of a superpower's pursuit of global influence.

In Canada, the principle of "collective security" has become infused with the assumption that the fate of Canada as a prosperous, secure nation is directly tied to the fate of the United States. This, in turn, has come to be understood as a requirement that, at the core of Canadian security policy, solidarity with the United States is fundamental, and that it must even take precedence over independent Canadian assessments of the requirements for international peace and security.

The current debate over Canadian participation in the US Strategic Defence Initiative (SDI) is in many instances a debate over whether Canada can afford to jeopardize its relationship with the United States by not participating in SDI, whatever the intrinsic merits, or lack of them, of SDI itself. Similarly, the debate over the testing of cruise missiles in Canadian territory was frequented by interventions from government representatives claiming that Canada had what amounted to a moral obligation to support its allies, without second-guessing alliance decisions.

This particular interpretation of "collective security" — i.e. the close identification of Canada's fate with the fate of the United States as a superpower — is central to Canada's official assessments of the chief threats to Canadian security. These threats are taken to be two-fold:

1. The most immediate threat, with the most devastating potential consequences, is the threat that conflict between the United States and the Soviet Union will escalate and lead to nuclear war;
2. The second threat, a prominent focus of the foreign policy Green Paper, is that the North American economy will become increasingly vulnerable to external developments that will gradually erode our competitiveness and will therefore lead to deteriorating economic standing for Canada and the United States within the international economic order (a secondary element of this economic threat is that Canada, if it does not remain supportive and co-operative, will lose standing within the US sphere).

Certain military requirements are seen to flow from these two threats.

In the first instance, the threat of nuclear war must be reduced through deterrence, preferably at lower levels of armaments. Canada has assumed that deterrence is enhanced in two ways — first, by supporting the United States in the deployment of its nuclear forces; second, by encouraging more effective arms control.

In the second instance, the military response to the threat of declining competitiveness is through support of the global military strength of the United States (with a sustained alliance under US leadership in western

Europe being a central element of reliable US military strength globally). US military strength is, in fact, seen to be the final guarantor of the global strategic interests of the west....

Even though security for even the wealthier countries, as reflected in the Green Paper, has become an economic preoccupation, military force is still central to its pursuit. The protection of world markets, of access to raw materials and fuels, and of access to cheap labour and secure investments for surplus capital, are prominent responsibilities assigned to modern military forces. To meet these responsibilities, world military forces, led by but not confined to the superpowers, have perfected means of direct intervention, of the provision of arms to proxy or surrogate forces, and of intimidation by means of brandishing conventional and nuclear forces....

Canada is not a primary actor in this activity. Under the policy of "collective security," the primary miliary role is performed by the leadership of this collectivity, the United States, while Canada plays a supporting role. Canada's primary function within the collectivity is not military; instead it is to confer legitimacy on the alliance leadership and on the methods it employs. Hence, Canada has the important job of providing political support to the United States in its appointed task by declaring solidarity with, and support for, the military policies of the United States (e.g. by declaring its support for US "star wars" research). In certain circumstances, Canada expands this function to include symbolic military support to the US and the alliance (e.g. by stationing Canadian forces in Europe or by permitting cruise missile testing in Canada). And, in some circumstances, support is extended to the supply of essential military support (e.g. by making available Canada's northern territory for air surveillance and, if the advocates of strategic defence prevail, for air combat in the event of a Soviet/American war).

To its credit, Canada has also regularly taken advantage of its position as a supporting player to press the leadership to modify its policies (e.g. in pursuing certain arms control policies and in occasionally urging the US to adopt more moderate policies).

We fear that the foreign policy Green Paper ... is designed to generate public discussion about how Canada can perform its assigned roles more effectively, and that it is explicitly not intended to foster discussion of the appropriateness of the roles themselves. The government has already indicated, for example, that the principle of "collective security" is not negotiable. It is our intention, however, to challenge the principle of "collective security," as it has evolved in practice, and to put forth an alternative principle of "common security."

I. From Collective Security to Common Security

A. Security as Idolatry

The legitimate human longing for security can be approached in two basic, but opposite, ways. The first is to identify security as the primary objective and then to set about advancing and protecting that security with whatever means are available and within whatever conditions prevail. The second is to assume security to be a consequence or product of a social/political/spiritual environment and thus to set as the objective the promotion of social conditions based on norms related to love and justice, which serve the welfare and security of persons.

The tradition out of which we speak counsels the latter approach. Jesus told his followers that if they were to seek first the righteousness of God (justice), those other things for which they longed — peace, contentment, security — would come to them. We believe this to be so also for nations. The true security of individuals and nations must ultimately be seen as the consequence or product of global justice.

Indeed, the acute insecurity which Canadians and people the world over now experience is in no small measure the consequence of the unrestrained pursuit of security. The pursuit of absolute security, as a primary objective calling forth primary human loyalties, is, in the language of our faith, idolatrous. National military policies too often are a reflection of a national obeisance to the idol of security, with devastating consequences for national security. Weapons research is driven by the pursuit of a final, technological solution to the security problem. When Alfred Nobel invented dynamite and gun-powder, calling it "security powder," he declared that it was his objective "to discover a weapon so terrible that it would make war eternally impossible." While his inventions permitted the development of genuinely terrible weapons, they turned out not to be so terrible as to make war impossible. Untold millions have been killed by the weapon that was to make war impossible, and now, of course, we have another version of such a weapon. Nuclear weapons were to make war, by virtue of their terror, obsolete; but once again the pursuit of technologically-induced national security has driven military planners to re-design and re-deploy nuclear weapons in ways which will make them suitable for war-fighting.

National policy must be redirected — away from the pursuit of a technologically-imposed security and toward the fostering of social conditions conducive to the security of all.

B. Security as the National Interest

Nationally, security is now taken, within northern industrialized societies in particular, to be synonymous with the national interest. The contemporary use of military force by the major powers, therefore, has come to focus, not so much on the defence of national territory and those national institutions that facilitate political participation and the mediation of justice, as on the protection of what is defined as the national interest — i.e. national economic and political status within a hierarchical international economic order. For the states near the top of the hierarchy, the primary objective of what they call "security" policy is to maintain their predominance, if not domination, in the world order and to preserve the prerogatives of power.

Northern industrialized countries (east and west) have come to depend for their "way of life" (their place in the global hierarchy), on the consumption of an inordinate share of the earth's resources and upon systems of mass production that require markets around the globe for that production to be sustained. With this competition for resources and markets prominently cast into East-West ideological terms, the major powers seek to share global events in line with their particular interests — their interests being defined primarily as assured access to the raw materials, fuels, and markets upon which economic prosperity and political predominance are built.

C. The Militarization of the Pursuit of the National Interest

Military forces are thus deployed as the final guarantor of the national interest thus defined. Military forces of major powers function on a global scale as a means of intimidation and direct intervention, while the military forces of smaller powers in the third world use military hardware provided by their northern backers to exercise local control over social and political developments.

Power projection (or intervention) forces, weapons supplied to local "client" military forces (the arms trade), and nuclear weapons for purposes of intimidation, represent the three major thrusts of the military pursuit of the national interest....

The major powers have come to pay increasing attention to the development of the capacity to intervene militarily in the states and regions in which their interests are directly threatened. The United States and the Soviet Union are both in the process of expanding their capacity to project military power, by the development of long-range military transport capabilities, by the pre-positioning of military equipment at key locations, by the development of naval operations in seas adjacent to regions of interest, and by the arming of interventionist forces. The United States is building up a rapid deployment force for this purpose and it is worth noting that the largest single military export in Canadian history was to supply armoured vehicles (built under licence by General Motors of Canada) to the US rapid deployment force.

The Soviet Union's most prominent interventionist force is located on its western border, available to intervene in the affairs of its eastern Europe allies if it deems its interests to be directly threatened there. Other such forces are currently engaged in Afghanistan and the Soviet Union is also increasing its sea and air transport facilities as a means of extending its global reach.

Another means of influencing the course of events in states and regions where interests are threatened is through the supply of military equipment to sympathetic regimes. This supply of arms is now part of an international arms trade of $30-$40 billion annually. The arms trade not only distorts the economies of the importing states, but its more immediate effects are to exacerbate local political conflicts, by making military solutions more readily available, by prolonging war when it does break out, and by making war more lethal through the introduction of more sophisticated weapons systems.

Nuclear weapons too are mobilized in the pursuit of strategic interests. Former President Richard Nixon, in an interview with *Time*, has indicated four occasions on which he contemplated the use of nuclear weapons. Prominent in each of the circumstances was the intent of the President to influence the behaviour of the Soviet Union in areas of the third world in which US strategic interests were deemed to be threatened. In other words, nuclear weapons are not deployed for the sole purpose of deterring nuclear attack on the territory of the state deploying them — they are deployed because they are believed to have utility in the pursuit of global influence....

These three military activities — intervention, arms transfers, and nuclear intimidation — are responses to what, in the 1980s, are considered the chief threats to political and economic security. The current acceleration of military research, deployments, and intervention are central to efforts of the economically powerful to reduce their economic vulnerability.

The result, of course, is that military forces are made central to national security policies. Parallel to this militarization of national territory and policies, we now witness also the militarization of extra-national territory, or the earth's commons — the ocean depths, the atmosphere and orbital space. Whatever security once was available to states behind the natural common barriers of distance and the oceans, is now lost through the militarization of the entire planet.

II. Building a Secure International Order

A. Common Security

These developments ... call for responses that do not necessarily conform to the politics of "realism" or self-interest. They call for a rejection of fortress security in favour of a security that flows out of conditions of global justice.

We suggest that a shift in emphasis in Canada's security policies from the former to the latter can be facilitated by two levels of response.

In the first instance, the character of contemporary insecurity requires a new understanding of the fundamental sources of security and a clarification of the social and political objectives that can help to create the conditions of enhanced security. The policies most relevant to the creation of a more secure international order are not related to military preparations. The policies advocated elsewhere in this brief, relating to trade, development assistance, human rights, etc., speak directly to the question of security inasmuch as they foster the welfare of persons and the conditions that contribute to social and political peace.

In the second instance, the magnitude of the threat posed by the militarization of the planet calls for urgent measures to reduce the likelihood of war and the unleashing of those weapons of mass, global destruction which represent the most immediate and total threat to global security. There are, therefore, changes in long-term military objectives, and in measures related to arms control policies that can also contribute to an international order that is based more on justice and equity than on the pursuit of self-interest bolstered by the threat of unrestrained violence.

The following sections suggest avenues for a "permanent Canadian peace initiative," focussed on efforts to reduce the threats of foreign military intervention, to control the international arms trade, and to control and eventually eliminate nuclear weapons.

B. Non-intervention

The assumption of Soviet expansionism, restrained only by the threat of western force, must itself be more closely examined. Third World nationalism and self-determination are positive elements that undermine the influence of both superpowers and, in the end are likely to be more effective means of containing expansionist states than is military competition between expansionist states....

The churches recommend that:

45. **Canada should bring before the United Nations a proposal for a non-intervention convention or treaty....**

46. **Peacekeeping should become a priority for the Canadian armed forces and Canadian defence procurement and training should reflect that priority....**

47. **Canada should continue to support the development of an independent means of monitoring arms control agreements and related activities on which all nuclear weapons states can rely — specifically the proposed international satellite monitoring agency....**

48. **Canada should take initiatives in support of the development of demilitarized zones in the common regions of the globe, including the oceans, Antarctica and outer space. This includes support for the movement for a nuclear-free Pacific and the establishment of the Indian Ocean as a zone of peace.**

C. Controlling the Arms Trade

International efforts to limit the global arms trade have come to a virtual halt. None of the various suggestions and initiatives of the past decade, including the proposals for an international arms trade register, has led to any action. The Stockholm International Peace Research Institute suggests, however, that more open reporting of arms transfers could still be an important confidence-building measure for efforts to control the arms trade. Inasmuch as secrecy promotes suspicion, more openness in arms transfers could help to alleviate the concerns of neighbouring states....

The churches recommend that:

50. **Canada should sponsor a United Nations General Assembly action, directing the Secretary General to study the feasibility of establishing an international arms trade register or some other means of**

effectively monitoring international arms transfers as a basis on which to introduce actual control measures.

51. Canada should provide full disclosure of its own arms sales so that they can be subjected to public scrutiny to ensure that the government's own guidelines are being honoured and to identify ways in which those guidelines may need to be strengthened....

52. Canada should prohibit the export from Canada of weapons systems designed and/or destined for interventionary armed forces, as part of our support for a non-intervention convention.

53. Canada should prohibit the export from Canada of components for nuclear weapons or their delivery systems, or for weapons and communications systems which are designed to facilitate the use of nuclear weapons.

54. Canada should require a regular parliamentary review, perhaps by the Standing Committee on External Affairs and National Defense, of military exports.

55. Canada should prohibit the sale of military equipment or other forms of "security" assistance to regimes with a pattern of gross violations of internationally recognized human rights.

D. Controlling Nuclear Weapons

We express our regard for the security of the earth from the perspective of stewards, rather than rulers, of God's creation. And because we have regard for the security of the earth for not only this, but also succeeding generations, we cannot accept as "defence" any measures which threaten the planet itself.

This has particular implications for our attitude towards nuclear weapons, and we must say without reservation that nuclear weapons are ultimately unacceptable as agents of national security. We can conceive of no circumstances under which the use of nuclear weapons could be justified and consistent with the will of God, and we must therefore conclude that nuclear weapons must also be rejected as means of threat or deterrence.

We acknowledge, however, that nuclear weapons have nevertheless become central to the national security systems of the major powers, including those states which Canada describes as allies. The common and uncompromised objective of all states must be the elimination of nuclear weapons from national security systems, but we also acknowledge that the process of disarming can itself be destabilizing and fraught with danger. We therefore reiterate our support for a carefully-planned, multilateral process for the reduction (and eventual elimination) of nuclear weapons....

The arms race, the competition for weapons systems that will produce advantages for their deployers, is out of control. We urge Canadian policy to recognize the urgent need to establish control over nuclear weapons, and the following recommendations suggest some policy options for Canada....

56. Canada should re-affirm its proposals to suffocate the arms race by seeking limits on the testing of new weapons systems. This should include measures to prohibit the testing of nuclear warheads, including an immediate moratorium pending agreement on a long-term comprehensive test-ban, measures to prohibit the testing of nuclear weapons delivery vehicles, including the cruise missile, and measures to prohibit the testing of elements of strategic defence systems, as called for in the ABM Treaty....

57. Canada should clarify its operational definition of deterrence and identify the types of weapons systems appropriate to that understanding of deterrence and that Canada vigorously oppose the deployment of weapons systems designed for first-strike and war-fighting purposes.

58. Canada should support measures to prevent the further deployment of destabilizing weapons systems, namely by supporting the nuclear freeze, and that Canada call for a change in NATO's nuclear doctrine to provide for a declaration of no-first-use of nuclear weapons....

59. Canada should reject strategic defence in principle, including research (in the US, the Strategic Defence Initiative).

60. Canada should declare that Canadian territory will not be available for the deployment of elements of strategic defence forces.

61. Canada should, consistent with the rejection of strategic defence, take appropriate measures to ensure that there is no Canadian participation, through public or private institutions, in the US Strategic Defence Initiative....

62. The Canadian government should not fund research into strategic defence and should prohibit Canadian research institutions and commercial firms from participating in SDI research....

Appendix 2

Brief to the Minister for External Affairs
Re: Policy in Southern Africa

Canadian Council of Churches
July 1987

(Editor's Note: In the summer of 1987, Canada was preparing to give leadership within the Commonwealth on the matter of apartheid and comprehensive sanctions against South Africa. The Canadian Council of Churches forwarded to the minister for external affairs a statement summarizing the positions advanced by the churches in over fifteen years of discussions with government. Excerpts from the brief, including its key recommendations, appear below.)

I. Proposals for Further Immediate Canadian Sanctions Against South Africa

A. Withdrawal of Canadian Investment from South Africa

The Canadian government should legislate the immediate withdrawal of Canadian investment from South African enterprises which supply, directly or indirectly, the South African military, police, or nuclear sectors, or which play a strategic role in the maintenance of apartheid.

This withdrawal of investment should include the termination of franchise, licensing or management agreements with or for any entity in South Africa.

The Canadian government has previously stated that it does not promote disinvestment for Canadian companies operating in South Africa. Rather, the Government urges Canadian companies that have chosen to stay in South Africa to implement the principles of the Canadian Code of Conduct. Compliance with the Code is voluntary.

The churches believe, however, that employment practices that are perhaps only marginally better than those of South African companies, and affecting only a fraction of the black workforce nationwide, cannot be used as justification for investments which are helping South Africa become strategically self-sufficient and able to resist external pressures in support of internal pressure for the dismantling of apartheid....

B. Withdrawal of Canadian Investment from Namibia

The Canadian government should legislate the immediate withdrawal of Canadian investment from Namibia. The major Canadian investor in Namibia is Rio Algom, with a 10% interest in Rossing Mine, a uranium mine. The Canadian churches support the position of the Council of Churches of Namibia, which represents more than 75% of the population. They believe that sanctions, including the withdrawal of investment from Namibia, should be imposed in order to increase the pressure on South Africa to end its illegal occupation.

The Canadian government has already recognized the immorality of taking resources out of Namibia while it is under South African occupation. In 1985, it announced that the Canadian crown corporation, Eldorado Nuclear Ltd., would enter no new contracts for the processing of uranium from Namibia. It is equally wrong for a Canadian company, through its investment directly in Namibia, to assist in the depletion of non-renewable resources and to lend legitimacy and support to the illegal regime. Short of legislating disinvestment, at the very least the Canadian government should refuse to allow Rio Algom to receive tax credits for taxes paid to the illegal South African regime. It should also include Canadian companies operating in Namibia within the purview of the Canadian Code of Conduct.

The churches have made these proposals in previous correspondence with the Canadian government. The response has been inadequate. The Government states that it will not legislate disinvestment in Namibia, as this would run contrary to its position on extraterritoriality. Yet in the case of Namibia, it is difficult to understand how arguments about extraterritoriality can be applied. Canada does not recognize South Africa's claim to administer Namibia and any decision to withdraw Canadian investment from Namibia would support the position of the United Nations Council for Namibia, established by the UN General Assembly in 1967 to administer the territory until independence....

C. Code of Conduct for Companies Remaining in South Africa

The Code of Conduct would continue to apply to companies not required by the Canadian government to leave South Africa and choosing to remain there. The Code should be strengthened, broadened to include Namibia, and made mandatory. The churches have serious reservations about the usefulness of any Code in the present situation as a tool for forcing fundamental change in South Africa. The current Code merely provides, for a company adhering to its very weak requirements, a Government-approved excuse for remaining in South Africa.

The Code should be strengthened to require active opposition to apartheid laws; inclusion of elected representatives of black workers in the monitoring and signing of compliance reports; and disclosure of sales, so that those of possible strategic support to the South African regime are revealed....

Finally, information on each company's compliance with the Code should be publicly available....

D. Legislating an End to Exports from Canada to South Africa of Military or Strategic Goods or Technology

The Canadian government should legislate an end to all exports to any purchaser in South Africa of military or strategic goods or technology.

In a document accompanying new Canadian government guidelines for military exports, 10 September 1986, the following policy on military exports to South Africa was stated:

> We in Canada have agreed to limit exports of all military goods to military end-users in accordance with the UN Security Council Resolution 418 (1977), and more recently, we decided to refuse to export strategic and military goods to all RSA departments and agencies.

The 1977 mandatory arms embargo requires that "all States cease forthwith any provision to South Africa of arms and related material of all types...." It does not suggest that the restriction applies only to "military end-users" in South Africa, recognizing the likelihood that any military exports would be diverted to military end-users....

The 10 September 1986 statement also establishes that the Canadian government will continue to prohibit the sale of strategic goods, such as computers, only to the South African government and its agencies. In October 1985, the Nassau Commonwealth Accord called for a ban on the sale and export of computer equipment capable of use by the South African police, military or security forces. Canadian churches hoped that as a result the Canadian government would adopt a policy to ban the sale of all strategic and dual-purpose goods to any purchaser in South Africa. However, Canadian policy continues to permit the sale of such equipment to the South African private sector ... and it is clear that the equipment could be easily diverted to military or police uses.

E. Imposing Bans on Imports from South Africa

At the London Commonwealth Summit meeting, the Canadian government agreed to a ban on imports of uranium, coal, iron and steel from South Africa. It had already requested a voluntary ban on the import of Krugerrands, the South African gold coin. The impact of these measures would be strengthened by the following actions:

—The Government should interpret this ban to include an immediate end to the import of Namibian uranium for processing by Eldorado Nuclear, a Canadian crown corporation.

—South Africa pays for imported goods and technology which are essential to its domestic armaments industry and other sectors of its economy through payments received for South African exports, as well as through other forms of foreign capital transfers (foreign investment and foreign loans). While the current ban on imports of agricultural products, uranium, coal, iron and steel covers the bulk of imports to Canada, the Government should consider a ban on all remaining imports from South Africa.

F. Voluntary Bans Should Be Made Mandatory

Voluntary bans presently in effect — the ban on loans to South African public and private sector; on the import of Krugerrands; on the sale and export of oil to South Africa; on the promotion of tourism to South Africa; and on new investment or reinvestment of profits — should be implemented on a legislated basis.

While present circumstances in South Africa make it unlikely, for economic reasons, that companies will violate certain voluntary bans — for example, the ban on loans — other bans, such as the oil embargo, may be violated by companies seeking an opportunity to make money through sanctions-busting. Furthermore, in the absence of adequate laws in Canada for disclosure of information about loans, investment and trade, the public has no means of monitoring the implementation of a voluntary "ban."

II. Proposals for Initiatives to Strengthen the Frontline States

A. Increased Aid for Countries under Heavy Pressure

It is important to respond to requests of the Frontline States for financial assistance so that they can keep their economies relatively stable and maintain a minimal level of services to their people despite the ongoing emergency. We urge you to provide financial aid at this time, beyond the usual development assistance to the Frontline States in recognition of the increased pressures they are suffering.

It has become necessary to build security provisions into all aid projects in the region so what Canada gives is not taken away by South African subversion or direct attack. The Beira corridor is a possible region of concentration....

B. Creating an Independent Infrastructure in the Frontline States

We appreciate what Canada has already done through SADCC and through bilateral aid projects to support transport, power and communications alternatives in the Frontline States, so that their dependence on the Republic of South Africa could be diminished, and indeed ended as soon as possible. We urge you to increase, intensify and to speed up these programmes....

C. Supporting the Former Portuguese Territories in the Region

Canada's close relationships with the Commonwealth countries in Southern Africa were greatly enhanced by the Prime Minister's visit; we also urge that positive support be increased for the former Portuguese territories, which are also very much on the "front line."

We cannot forget that a decade ago, the Canadian government supported the Portuguese colonial administration and did nothing to support the liberation movements although we in the churches pleaded for such initiatives. These two countries came into independence in an unprepared and disorganized state; they now occupy key positions in the struggle for the liberation and peaceful development of Southern Africa....

We strongly urge CIDA to raise Mozambique from a Category 3 to a Category 2 country.... We also urge you to consider establishing some direct diplomatic presence in Maputo and Luanda....

D. Limiting the Forces of Destabilization

The Canadian government should ensure that there will not be Canadian support of any kind for the forces of UNITA in Angola and the MNR in Mozambique, both of which are used by the South African government to subvert the recognized governments in these countries.... The Canadian government should use any influence it has on the governments of Malawi and Zaire to eliminate their support for South African destabilization policies ... Canada could urge them not to allow their countries to be used as bases for training, for attack, or as channels for passage of supplies and personnel to these movements.

III. Namibia

A. We strongly urge the government to withdraw from the Contact Group and to refer the issue of implementation of Resolution 435 for the Independence of Namibia back to the United Nations.

B. We urge that Canada support the implementation of Decree No. 1 of the United Nations Council for Namibia which prohibits the exploitation of Namibian resources as long as Namibia remains illegally occupied by the South African government.

C. The situation of near-war which has existed throughout the border regions of Namibia and Angola for many years, makes worse an already complex tragic situation. Together with other countries, Canada should explore every alternative to easing this situation, not excluding the establishment of a UN observer team or peace-keeping force in this area.

Appendix 3

The International Debt Crisis: Discussion Paper for the Canadian Churches, July 1989

Introduction

> The government keeps telling us that we must work harder, to produce more, and, at the same time, consume less, in order to have more to export, and with these exports to pay — not the debt! — only the interest on the debt.... This year alone ... we must export 650,000 tons of meat! Not to mention soybeans, corn and other food exports. We in the Third World are exporting food while we are dying of hunger.

> *(Father Jose Alamiro, a Franciscan priest in Brazil)*

> We will not tolerate economic formula, will not apply economic indices ... which fail to assert the primacy of the human condition.... Nutrition imbalances are as crucial as trade imbalances. High infant mortality requires just as immediate and as serious attention as high rates of inflation or huge budget deficits.... Therefore, a basic test for all stabilization, adjustment and development programs is whether they will improve the human condition from their inception, or, on the contrary, worsen it.

> *(from the Khartoum Declaration, a statement of a conference of African governments held in Khartoum, Sudan, March 1988, under the auspices of the United Nations Economic Commission for Africa)*

The poor in our world have become poorer. In the past ten years, despite massive development assistance, the gulf which divides the world's people into rich and poor, into powerful and powerless, has grown wider.

There are several reasons for this deterioration, but one stands out from the others, both because of its significance and its complexity. Many developing countries are deeply in debt to the governments and banks of Europe, North America and Japan. Despite their efforts to meet interest payments, many countries are in such economic distress that they can only make partial payments, or none at all. Unpaid interest is added to the principal, and the mountain of debt continues to grow.

Banks and governments in the creditor nations now realize that the loans made to many of these countries can never be repaid under current conditions. Yet they cannot agree on an alternative way of resolving the crisis.

Meanwhile, debtor nations continue to be pressed to pay as much as they can. Conditions imposed by the international financial institutions force them to impose stringent "austerity measures" on their people, many of whom are already among the poorest on earth.

Our church partners in these debtor countries are keenly aware of this crisis and the hardships it has caused. People's organizations and the governments of these countries have wrestled with the problem and have put forward their own proposals, which merit careful consideration by the creditors.

As the people of the world call on the international community to redress the injustices caused by the debt crisis, so we as Christians and Canadians call on our government and banks to accept their social responsibility to work towards a resolution of the problems.

The solutions which must be found will require complex political and economic negotiations, but the determination needed to carry them through must grow from a passion for justice and fair dealing. As Christians, we must raise our voice in unison with the victims of this crisis; we are calling for justice, not charity....

Recommendations to the Canadian Government and Banks
I. Recommendations Addressed to Government

1. The present crisis: addressing the problems caused by structural adjustment programs.

Since long before the debt crisis was widely recognized, a country experiencing problems servicing its external debt has had to apply to the International Monetary Fund (IMF). This body, usually working with the World Bank, carries out an analysis of the country's situation; if the country enters into an agreement with the IMF, it agrees to institute changes in its economic policies which are termed "structural adjustments" as well as introducing austerity measures. These changes must be carried out if the country's debt is to be rescheduled, and if it is to be declared eligible for any new resources, from either the multilateral bodies (IMF, the World Bank, and the regional development banks) or from the individual countries which make up these organizations and have their own bilateral aid programmes.

These changes, although "voluntarily" adopted by the country, reflect the analysis which was carried out by the international financial institutions, and their prescriptions for changes to the economy.

The record of past years has shown that very often debtor countries find these conditions impossible to fulfill within the short time line laid down in the agreement they have made with the IMF. Those who do manage to fulfill the requirements have found them destructive to the well-being of the majority of their people, at least in the short term. In addition, in the case of a number of countries, development goals which had been established previously for the country have had to be abandoned or severely modified.

The economic philosophy underlying IMF policies (on which its rec-ommendations for structural adjustments are made) is very clearly ar-ticulated. This is the belief that an open economy, one which participates without reservation in the international trading system, is the economic model best suited to all countries. In order to move a country towards this open economy, the following measures are usually called for:
— reduction in government expenditure and the size of the public sector
— rationalization, and often privatization, of public enterprises
— removal of subsidies and price controls
— higher interest rates to encourage investment
— removal of trade and exchange controls in order to promote an ex-port-oriented trade policy
— higher prices for agricultural producers, especially producers of ex-port crops.

As can be seen, these policies reflect the prevailing business and political philosophies of many Western countries.

The churches, however, have serious reservations about the benefits of "opening up" the economy of a small country so that its resources can be developed on a large scale by international companies, if the main purpose of such development is to generate exports to earn the exchange needed to service external debts.

On the one hand, we recognize the importance of bringing the deb-tors' balance of payments problems under control, and so we acknow-ledge the importance of increasing export earnings to provide exchange for some level of debt servicing. Increased export earnings are also necessary in order to purchase the essential imports for its development. Offsetting these requirements, however, the churches would place equal, if not greater, emphasis on the obligation of the debtor govern-ment to provide its citizens with their essential requirements — food, shelter and a minimal level of health care, education and basic infra-structure. If the two obligations are in conflict, the churches would place a higher priority on the debtor government's responsibility to its people than on its obligation to service its debt in full.

The churches also have concerns about the IMF model of develop-ment because it increases developing countries' dependence on overseas markets, and their vulnerability to manipulation by powerful trans-national corporations. Complete isolation for a country is neither possible nor desirable. On the other hand, forcing small weak economies to participate in the international trading community as it is presently structured makes them vulnerable to domination by external economic powers. Some of those who had tried to protect themselves from such domination by planning more self-reliant economic strategies are now no longer able to do so. In that they are no longer able to shape their own economic priorities, they have already lost their sovereignty.

In the view of our partners in the debtor countries, who have ex-perienced IMF-backed conditions at first hand, they are excessively harsh and inflexible. We strongly regret the fact that the Canadian government, like other creditor governments, links its debt relief to African countries to their acceptance of these conditions.

The churches acknowledge that any solution to the debt crisis requires that the problems of economic mismanagement in the debtor countries be addressed. However, we believe that in most cases there are other problems which must be tackled if these countries are to be able to provide a better life for all their people. In addition to changes in economic policies which would encourage local initiative and eliminate waste and corruption, the churches would welcome conditions on new loans relating to the protection of human rights, the provision of basic needs, and the ability of a country's leadership to establish a free, just, and sustainable society.

> **The churches recommend that the Canadian government, as a member of the International Monetary Fund, urge that the policy conditions which the Fund attaches to the credits which it extends to debtor countries (which are also widely treated as prerequisites for assistance from other donors) be changed.** *New conditions should ensure that basic human rights are respected, that the already poor in these countries are not further deprived, and that their governments are not so constrained as to be unable to promote further development along lines which they deem appropriate;* **further, the churches recommend that the Canadian government also promote adherence to these policy prescriptions at the World Bank and the international regional development banks, of which Canada is a member.**
>
> (Recommendation #1)

Various measures have been suggested which would "cushion the impact" of IMF-backed austerity measures on the most vulnerable sectors of society. As we have stated, our preference would be for the adoption of entirely new forms of conditionality. Nevertheless, for humanitarian reasons we must support the call for remedial measures, and urge that the IMF, as a minimum response to the present situation, give immediate attention to the social effect of its present conditions.

The United Nations' children's fund — UNICEF — has prepared a report on the impact of the adjustment policies which many developing countries have had to adopt during the 1980's at the insistence of the IMF, the World Bank, and the regional development banks.... These statistics show the impact of these policies on the most vulnerable segment of society — its children.

UNICEF makes a number of specific recommendations for short-term modifications to the process of structural adjustment which we would support.

In particular, we commend the recommendation that when the IMF instructs a government to reduce its overall spending, those parts of public spending which directly affect the health and well-being of the poor, and particularly the children of the poor, be exempted. We also welcome their suggestion that debtor countries should involve government officials responsible for health, education and agriculture in debt negotiations.

The churches commend the recommendations found in the UNI-CEF study, and urge the Canadian government to use its influence to have them widely applied to all IMF debt negotiations.

(Recommendation #2)

2. Moving to a resolution of the debt crisis.

The essential first step towards resolving the debt crisis is for all parties to agree that it must be resolved. The agreement reached by the Group of Seven Economic Summit in June 1988 to facilitate debt relief to the sub-Saharan African countries, limited though it was, shows that progress is possible if governments find the requisite will. Further progress is being made, albeit slowly, through the proposal put forward by U.S. Treasury Secretary Nicholas Brady.

Nevertheless, we are gravely disturbed at the slowness with which the whole debt problem has been addressed, and echo the many appeals from our partners that the nations of the world, together with the financial institutions, make the resolution of this question a matter of the highest priority.

We realize that all parties to the debt crisis operate under constraints which are often defined by law. Nevertheless, these laws are themselves the product of political negotiations, and can be altered, given the willingness to do so. For, unless new solutions are found, the burden will continue to fall on the debtor countries, pressing most heavily on the classes within those countries least responsible for incurring the debt, and least capable of further sacrifice to pay it. Therefore:

The churches urge the Canadian government to take a stronger lead, in cooperation with other concerned countries, both creditors and debtors, and the commercial lenders, in finding ways of resolving the debt crisis.

(Recommendation #3)

Canada's traditional role in international affairs is to work with others through multilateral channels, a method which is particularly appropriate in the present crisis. The following recommendations point to several initiatives we urge the government to undertake.

a) A new framework for international trade

The debt crisis is only one of many symptoms of disorder in the international financial system. The agreements signed at Bretton Woods four decades ago no longer adequately guide international commerce and finance.

The churches urge the government of Canada to advocate and actively promote the calling of a new round of multilateral negotiations on the creation of a new framework for international trade and finance which would provide greater stability and a more equitable basis for economic relationships. Such a framework should respect the rights and advance the development efforts of Third World countries, enhance their ability to pursue self-reliant development, make provision for an increased flow of development assistance (as well as for adequate bridging assistance for countries facing serious foreign exchange crises) and promote more responsible stewardship of the earth's resources and environment.

(Recommendation #4)

b) An international conference on North-South issues

In the past few years, strong requests have come from debtor countries, notably those in Africa and Latin America, for a global conference which would include both creditors and debtors. This call was supported by many Canadian individuals and groups who submitted briefs to the Special Joint Parliamentary Committee on Canada's International Relations, and appears as one of that Committee's recommendations to government.

More recently, in July 1989, the leaders of Third World countries who were present at the Group of Seven Summit in Paris issued a pressing call for a "North-South" conference which would address the debt crisis and other outstanding economic issues between the developed and developing countries. This could be seen as an initial step in the more comprehensive negotiations which could lead to a "new Bretton Woods."

The churches request the Canadian government to consider sympathetically the call of many of the debtor countries for an international conference on the debt crisis and other outstanding economic issues. This conference would be concerned with establishing criteria for the progressive reduction of insupportable debt, and with determining ways of moving towards more equitable terms of trade. It should be preceded by preparatory negotiations in which Canada and other middle powers from both North and South could play a creative role.

(Recommendation #5)

c) Expansion of the Group of Seven

In recent years, the Group of Seven, the self-appointed management committee of the international economic system, has managed the world's economic affairs through ongoing consultation and its annual "Economic Summit." Its membership, the United States, Britain, France, West Germany, Japan, Italy, and Canada represents exclusively the viewpoints of the developed world. If access to the Group of Seven is based on economic size, Brazil has arguably a better claim to membership than does Canada.

If such an ad hoc mechanism for managing the world's economy is to continue, the churches recommend that its size be expanded to include two major Third World governments, one of whom should be Brazil, and the Soviet Union. Such a grouping would be far more representative of the world's peoples, all of whom are affected by decisions taken in this forum. Therefore,

The churches recommend that Canada propose that the Group of Seven be expanded to include Brazil, one other major developing country, and the Soviet Union.

(Recommendation #6)

3. Addressing the debt crisis

While the churches have expressed strong concern over the worsening situation within many debtor countries where the weight of austerity cutbacks falls heavily on the most vulnerable sections of society, they are also gravely concerned by the scandal which has developed over the past few years as resources are drained from the developing countries to the wealthy countries of the industrialized world.

In the judgment of the churches, *the goal should be to end the "debt crisis" by reducing each country's debt to the point where there is no longer a net outflow of capital, and the country has sufficient resources left after servicing its reduced debt to maintain its responsibilities to its people, and invest in its own development.* Countries should not be required to divert their economies from development models designed to improve the quality of life for all their citizens to models dictated principally by the need to earn foreign exchange to service their debt.

Recent developments, particularly the introduction of the Brady Proposal with the backing of the U.S. government, indicate that there is some recognition of the seriousness of the situation. The recent rescheduling of Mexico's debt shows that at last there is general acceptance of the principle that there must be some measure of debt reduction.

However, it has been widely predicted that Mexico's economic problems could not really be addressed without a reduction of at least 50%, and it remains to be seen if the reduction, although an important breakthrough, will be adequate. Moreover, other countries which are not as strategic to American interests fear that they will not be given as preferential treatment.

The churches support the principle of reducing the debt of the heavily indebted countries of Latin America, Africa, Asia and the Caribbean, through whatever mechanisms can be mutually agreed upon with the lending institutions; in addition, the churches support the principle of eliminating the debt owed by the poorest countries, specifically those in sub-Saharan Africa, to the governments of the industrialized countries. These initiatives should be combined with a requirement that governments give greater attention to the maintenance of basic human rights.

(Recommendation #7)

a) Assessment of country situations

The "country by country" approach is valid in that each country's situation is different. However, we would maintain that the goal as stated above is the same in each case. The first step in each debt settlement negotiation would be to establish a mutually agreed-upon assessment of the country's situation. This would require the participation of all its major creditors and their governments, and a general willingness to accept a reduction in the size of the debts outstanding.

We can suggest several guides as indicators of the level to which a country's debt should be reduced.

One approach frequently suggested is to write the debt down to the level it would have been if the historic level of real interest rates had been in place throughout the past decade. It is generally recognized that a major contributing factor to the growth in the Third World debt was the period (early 1980s) of interest rates nearing 20%. It is not generally known that the real interest rates being paid on Third World debt remained above 10% until 1986. Historically, real interest rates have averaged around 1.0% to 1.5%, a much more achievable level. (Real interest rates are not to be confused with minimal interest rates.)

Recalculating interest payments to reflect the real rates prevailing prior to 1981 has been proposed by a number of analysts of the debt crisis. In effect, a negotiated settlement would retroactively write off excessive interest payments.

Another method of calculating the level of debt reduction required is to follow the criteria suggested in the second paragraph of this section. Given a realistic estimate of the level of export earnings, how much will the country require to ensure that its people's basic needs are met, while retaining a domestic surplus which can be invested in its own growth and development?

Our judgement is that these two goals will require very substantial reductions in debt servicing, as well as substantial new resources. As we have already seen, many Latin American countries estimate that only a debt reduction of 50% would make any real difference to their ability to achieve economic stability, let alone their chances of achieving the two goals we have suggested.

Assessment of the level of debt which a country can service should include the total amount of capital borrowed and repaid, the total amount of interest paid, the rates of interest, and the change in terms of trade over the period of indebtedness. Of vital importance would be an evaluation of the impact of present debt servicing on the poorest sectors of the population, as well as the impact on development and human rights.

It is vital that a country's "ability to service its debt" be judged not only in relation to its export earnings, or to the price of commodities, but also in the context of its need to promote a policy of autonomous, self-reliant development, bearing in mind specific "quality of life" indices, which would gauge the impact of the debt servicing.

b) Settlement

The next step following a negotiated assessment of each country's situation would be a settlement of its external debt in the form of a broad agreement which would include partial debt reduction, rescheduling of the balance on manageable terms, and new resources, both aid and investment. Therefore,

> **The churches strongly urge the Canadian government together with Canadian banks to take the lead with other governments and banks in advocating negotiations with countries experiencing difficulty in meeting the interest and debt-repayment obligations of their international debt.**

> **The goal of such negotiations would be to eliminate, or reverse, the net outflow of capital from the country concerned, and to reduce the debt to a level which is humanly possible for these countries to carry, and which will leave within the countries sufficient capital to promote their own development. This should be achieved through an agreement which would normally include significant debt reduction, a rescheduling of the balance on manageable terms, and a renewed flow of development assistance and foreign investment. Canada should take the lead in the Group of Seven in advocating that the level of Third World debt be recalculated using real interest rates of 1.0-1.5% retroactively applied, the resulting calculation to be used as the basis for debt reduction in negotiated settlements.**

(Recommendation #8)

The remaining eight recommendations provide specific examples of actions following from this central recommendation....

> **The churches urge the government to instruct the Export Development Corporation (EDC) to write down the debt of the sub-Saharan African countries, or at the very least reschedule it for long periods of time at minimal interest rates; other developing countries should be offered the most concessionary possible terms.**

(Recommendation #9)

. . . .

The churches recommend that negotiations with debtor countries include the elimination of some debts as being illegitimate and therefore not morally binding within the context of a negotiated settlement.

(Recommendation #10)

. . . .

The churches urge the Canadian government to study the implications of requiring the full disclosure of large-scale foreign assets held in Canada, and Canadian assets abroad, and to investigate ways and means by which flight capital could be encouraged to return to developing countries.

(Recommendation #11)

. . . .

The churches urge the Canadian government to facilitate the investment of Canadian business in so-called "problem debtor countries," provided that its effect on the country will be positive in social as well as economic terms, that it will not hinder the ability of the government concerned to pursue independent, self-reliant development, and that its operations will be ecologically sustainable.

(Recommendation #12)

. . . .

The churches urge the government of Canada to provide increased aid to developing countries struggling with a debt burden, and increased access to Canadian markets.

(Recommendation #13)

. . . .

The churches recommend that all potential buyers of Third World debt, whether commercial buyers, non-profit organizations, or church development agencies, should examine proposals to exchange debt for equity on a case by case basis, assessing each carefully for its potential impact on the country concerned, and examining them in the light of the criteria outlined in section II of this paper.

(Recommendation #14)

. . . .

The churches urge the banks not to withdraw from lending to the less developed countries (LDC's), but to maintain their banking relationship with them, offering as generous and flexible terms as possible, and continuing to make a constructive contribution to their economies.

(Recommendation #15)

. . . .

The churches recommend to the Canadian government that a) tax deferrals on loan loss provisions be discontinued unless the benefits therefrom are shared in an equitable manner with the debtor countries, or b) tax credits be provided only when debt is actually written off and deducted in the accounts of the bank.

(Recommendation #16)

Notes

Chapter 3

1   Cranford Pratt, Gregory Baum, et al. *Peace, Justice and Reconciliation in the Arab-Israeli Conflict* (New York: Friendship Press, 1979), p.3.
2   David Bercuson, *Canada and the Birth of Israel: A Study in Canadian Foreign Policy* (Toronto: University of Toronto Press, 1985), p. 232.
3   Ibid., p. 26.
4   Ibid., p.8.

Chapter 5

1   Canadian Council of Churches, *Canada's International Relations: An Alternate View: An Enhanced World Role for Canada*, Brief submitted by the CCC to the Special Joint Committee on Canada's International Relations, November 1985, pp. 1-2.
2   Cranford Pratt, ed., *Internationalism under Strain* (Toronto: University of Toronto Press, 1989), p. 37.
3   Ian Stuchberry, *We Are the Branches: Primate's World Relief and Development Fund: The First 25 Years* (Toronto: PWRDF, 1985), pp. 13-14.
4   Canadian Catholic Organization for Development and Peace, *Principles and Policies* (Toronto: CCODP, 1983), p. 2.
5   Sithembiso Nyoni, speaker at WCC Resource Sharing Consultation, El Escorial, Spain, 1987.
6   Stuchberry, *We Are the Branches*, p. 13.
7   Ibid., p. 46.
8   Mission Statement, Presbyterian World Service (PWS), Don Mills, 1988, p. 1.
9   PWS Project Criteria, PWS Committee document, 1988, p. 6.
10 Taskforce on the Churches and Corporate Responsibility (TCCR), *Working Paper for the Canadian Churches on the International Debt Crisis* (Toronto, September, 1988).
11 We seldom remember that the very first of the ecumenical justice coalitions was the Interchurch Campaign Committee that brought the development agencies together to produce common fund-raising materials; most of the Protestant churches were represented by staff of their stewardship departments. When it became evident that no education as opposed to promotion would be done by this committee, Ten Days was formed. The Campaign Committee continues to function in much the same way as it did in the beginning.
12 CIDA, *Sharing Our Future: Canadian International Development Assistance* (Hull, Quebec, 1987), p. 43.

13 CCC, *The Churches' Perspective on Canada's Official Development Assistance*, Brief to the Standing Committee on External Affairs and International Trade, Toronto, 1986.

14 The official name of the committee was the Standing Committee on External Affairs and International Trade (SCEAIT), and its report on Canada's Official Development Assistance policies and programs was called *For Whose Benefit?* (Ottawa, May 1987).

15 SCEAIT, *For Whose Benefit?*, Appendix D, pp. 147-62.

16 CCC, *Canada's International Relations*, p. 13.

17 Official Development Assistance from all countries to the Third World amounted to "...about one-third the amount the Third World paid to service its US$1 trillion debt." (CIDA, *Sharing Our Future*, p. 20).

18 TCCR, *The International Debt Crisis: A Discussion Paper Prepared for the Canadian Churches* (Toronto, August 1989). This was a revision of the earlier *Working Paper for the Canadian Churches on the International Debt Crisis*. The 1989 version represented the consensus reached during the course of church discussions to that point.

19 Ibid., p. 21.

20 CIDA, *Sharing Our Future: Canadian International Development Assistance* (Hull, Quebec, 1987), p. 43.

21 Ibid., p. 23.

22 Partnership Africa Canada, "Gender and Development," ed. Yolanda Mennie, Brochure (Ottawa, 1989), p. 2.

23 In 1876, a year after the formation of the Presbyterian Church in Canada, the Foreign Missionary Committee suggested to the women that a Women's Foreign Missionary Society (WFMS) be formed. Similar initiatives took place in the Methodist, Congregational, and Anglican churches, while communities of Catholic sisters also took up service overseas. Jean Campbell, ed., *A Lively Story, Historical Sketches of the Women's Missionary Society (Western Division) of the Presbyterian Church in Canada 1864-1989* (Toronto, 1989), p. 2.

24 Oral history, Canadian Presbyterian missionaries in Calabar, Nigeria, recorded by Marjorie Ross, 1964.

Chapter 6

1 The original membership of TCCR has grown since its inception in 1975, when it comprised the Anglican, Lutheran, Presbyterian, and United churches and the Baptist Federation of Canada, as well as four religious orders. By 1988 the original church membership had remained the same but for the loss of support of the Baptists. It has gained that of the Mennonite Central Committee, while the membership of religious orders has increased to nine. The Canadian University Service Overseas (CUSO) and the Na-

tional Board of the Young Women's Christian Association have joined as consultative members.

2 As this volume is dedicated to foreign policy-related activities of the Canadian churches, this chapter excludes a review of significant TCCR activity related to domestic issues. However, the point just made on our initiatives involving Canadian government departments on foreign policy issues can also be made about domestic concerns, which most frequently involve environmental issues and those related to the rights of Canadian native peoples. In such cases as well, we approach the companies concerned and the relevant government departments.

3 *Vancouver Sun*, 5 May 1988.

4 "Canadian Policy towards Southern Africa," Brief presented by the TCCR to the Hon. Mark MacGuigan, secretary of state for external affairs, and the Hon. Herb Gray, minister of industry, trade and commerce, 5 May 1981, and the government's reply to the members of the TCCR, 15 June 1982.

5 The only change that we could register, after years of arguing with the government about the immorality if not illegality of importing Namibian uranium, refers to a report in 1985 that the import permits that used to list "Namibia" as the "country of origin" would now require the name of the "country of export," which was "South Africa." This change was intended to blur the fact that the imported uranium originated in Namibia.

6 TCCR, *Annual Report 1983-1984*, p. 58. Sources: *Chile Economic News, Wall Street Journal, Financial Times of Canada, Financial Times* (London), *Journal of Commerce, Latin American Survey, Euromoney, EDC News*.

7 Ibid., p. 35.

8 Brief submitted to the House of Commons Standing Committee on Finance, Trade and Economic Affairs by the Taskforce on the Churches and Corporate Responsibility, 6 November 1978.

9 It is estimated that in 1988 Canadian banks had about $23 billion in outstanding debts owed by "problem debtor" countries, i.e., those governments unable to service their debts. See TCCR, *Working Paper for the Canadian Churches on the International Debt Crisis* (Toronto, September 1988), prepared by the Taskforce, pp. 20, 25.

Chapter 9

1 Jose Zalaquett, "The Human Rights Issue and the Human Rights Movement," *Background Information*, United Church of Canada 1981, no. 3 (World Council of Churches), p. 44; United Church of Canada, *Report of the Committee on the Church and International Affairs*, September 1962.

2 Bonnie Greene, United Church of Canada, Memorandum to the author, 15 April 1981.

3   Department of External Affairs, *Foreign Policy for Canadians* (Ottawa, 1970).

4   Garth Legge et al., "The Black Paper: An Alternative Policy for Canada Towards Southern Africa," *Behind the Headlines* 30 (September 1970).

5   John W. Foster, *A Report by the Canadian Church Observer on the United Nations Commission on Human Rights*, April 1982, p. 8. See also Bill Fairbairn, *The United Nations Commission on Human Rights, 42nd Session, A Report by the Canadian Church Observer*, June 1986, p. 2.

6   I have relied heavily here on a memorandum prepared by Bonnie Greene for the Working Unit on Social Issues and Justice of the United Church, entitled "Human Rights and Social Justice: Recent Action of the Canadian Churches" (April 1982).

7   Harry Carter, "Responding to Domestic Groups Regarding Canadian Policy towards Southern Africa," in Don Munton, ed., *Groups and Government in Canadian Foreign Policy: Proceedings of a Conference, Ottawa, Canada, 9-11 June 1982* (Toronto: Canadian Institute of International Affairs, 1985), pp. 78-81.

8   This conclusion has been expressed by the churches on many occasions. It is supported as well by a number of independent studies, in particular, T.A. Keenleyside, "Canada-South Africa Commercial Relations 1977-1982: Business as Usual," *Canadian Journal of African Studies* 17, no. 3 (1983): 465.

9   There is a striking similarity between TCCR's brief to Joe Clark (16 May 1985) and the government's policy initiatives of July and September 1985. For such a comparison, see TCCR, *Annual Review, 1984-85*, pp. 24-27.

10 See TCCR, *Widening, Tightening and Intensifying Economic and Other Sanctions against South Africa*, Brief presented to Joe Clark, 20 July 1988.

11 The Honourable Allan MacEachen, "Human Rights and Canadian Foreign Policy," *Statements and Speeches*, 83/6 (Ottawa, 1983), p. 4.

12 For a full discussion of the link Canada has made between its development assistance program and its promotion of human rights, see T.A. Keenleyside, "Development Assistance," in Robert O. Matthews and Cranford Pratt, eds., *Human Rights in Canadian Foreign Policy* (Montreal: McGill-Queen's University Press, 1988).

13 *Globe and Mail*, 12 June 1985.

14 ICCHRLA, *Submission to the Canadian Ambassador to the 40th Session of the United Nations Commission on Human Rights*, p. 90. See also ICCHRLA, *Canada in the Americas: Advocate of Peace* (Toronto 1985); and ICCHRLA, *1986 Annual Report, General Concerns and Brief Country Reports* (Toronto, 1987).

15 TCCR, *Proposal to Establish a Parliamentary Mechanism for Review of the Interrelationship between Canadian Foreign Policy and International*

Human Rights Observance, Brief submitted to the Parliamentary Task Force on Reform of the House of Commons, May 1985.

[16] CIDA, *To Benefit a Better World* (Ottawa 1987), pp. 52-54; Cranford Pratt, "Ethics and Foreign Policy: Canada's Development Assistance Programme," *International Journal* 44, no. 2 (Spring 1988).

[17] MacEachen, "Human Rights," p. 2.

[18] Stanley Hoffman, "The Hell of Good Intentions," *Foreign Policy,* no. 29 (Winter 1977-78), pp. 3-4.

[19] Cranford Pratt, "Dominant Class Theory and Canadian Foreign Policy: The Case of Counter-Consensus," *International Journal* 39, no. 1 (Winter 1983-84): 127-29.

[20] Blair Dimock, "Interest Groups in the Canadian Foreign Policy Process: A Conceptual Overview," in Munton, *Groups and Government,* pp. 23-25.

[21] Dimock, "Interest Groups," p. 5.

[22] Ibid.

[23] Cranford Pratt, "Dominant Class Theory," and "Canadian Foreign Policy, Bias to Business," *International Perspectives,* November/December 1982, pp. 3-6.

[24] Pratt, "Dominant Class Theory," pp. 4, 127.

[25] From a World Council of Churches document, quoted in Zalaquett, "The Human Rights Issue," p. 45.

[26] Pratt, "Dominant Class Theory," p. 119.

Index

242.